Internet and Intranet

INTERNET AND INTRANET

Rajeev Ranjan

CENTRUM PRESS
NEW DELHI-110002 (INDIA)

CENTRUM PRESS
H.O.: 4360/4, Ansari Road, Daryaganj,
New Delhi-110002 (India)
Tel: 23278000, 23261597, 23255577, 23286875
B.O.: No. 1015, Ist Main Road, BSK IIIrd Stage,
IIIrd Phase, IIIrd Block, Bangalore-560085 (INDIA)
Tel: 080-41723429
Email: centrumpress@gmail.com
Visit us at: www.centrumpress.com

Internet and Intranet

First Edition, 2011

PRINTED IN INDIA

Printed at Tarun Offset Printers, Delhi-110053

Contents

Preface

Intranets have changed the way organizations around the world communicate. Many business people are intimidated by this technological revolution but they need not be The Human Side of Intranets guides you through the daunting task of transforming communication within your business. Intranet provides details on critical elements such as network hardware, databases and data conversion, and Web page design. Internet explains how to choose intranet development tools, server software, browsers, editors, viewers, plug-ins and "bundled" versus "unbundled" solutions.

Author

1

Internet Technology

INTERNET

The arrival of the Internet made communication between machines much easier and a number of open protocols and applications were developed to make use of this. Of these, E-mail was the forerunner and there can be few academics and students that do not have access to this now. E-mail has its limitations and it was the World Wide Web that really brought the world of networked computers to the general public.

The open standards of many of the technologies and the ease with which anyone could publish information encouraged participation by all and we need to remember what is about these technologies that makes them attractive when we try to deploy them for education. However, initially, a relatively small number of University lecturers adopted it for a range of teaching purposes but even fewer did more than post information about their courses or actual lecture notes - usually not modified in any way to take advantage of the strengths of the media such as hypertext.

One of the strengths and principle attractions of the Web is that it can provide authoring access to anybody and this is quite different from the one-way nature of education through CAL or any other media that predated it. The fact that the technology facilitates this does not of course mean that it will take place but then this is true of any educational forum.

While far from needing programming skills, it still takes a certain amount of technophilia to publish a Web page.

Creating them is trivial but actually publishing them can be tedious if the institution has not provided a simple means to do so. This is all about information rather than teaching and learning and it soon becomes obvious to any treading this path that you cannot take the people out of the learning equation entirely. Learning is about interaction and interaction with information alone is not enough.

HISTORY

The original concept for the Internet was developed in 1962 by Paul Baran of the RAND Corporation. RAND in the 1960s was a Cold War military think tank. RAND was commissioned by the US military to find a way to maintain military communication in the event of a nuclear attack.

The idea was to create a network that has no central control that could be targeted in an attack. Baran laid out a plan using packet switching technology to maintain communications through a network of multiple communications paths. The idea for multiple paths allowed communications to continue in the even that any one or more sections of the network were neutralized due to a nuclear blast.

In 1968, a contract was awarded by ARPA (Advanced Research Projects Agency) to a company called BNN to build the first network model, which was then called ARPANET. The original ARPANET used a Honeywell computer to handle the network switching. The original network linked four nodes: the University of California in Santa Barbara, the University of California in Los Angeles, the University of Utah and SRI in Stanford.

A major event in the history of the Internet occurred in 1972 when Ray Tomlinson of BNN developed the first e-mail programme. Also in 1972, ARPA changed its name to DARPA (Defence Advanced Research Projects Agency). DARPA and Stanford were collaborating on the development of TCP/IP, which became the main communications protocol for the Internet. TCP/IP was a huge breakthrough because it allowed different types of computers on different networks to communicate with one another. Prior to this breakthrough, computers could only communicate with other computers on the same type of network. The name "Internet" was first used in the development of TCP

In 1976, Dr. Robert Metcalfe of Xerox's Palo Alto Research Facility developed Ethernet, which allowed data to be moved extremely fast. This breakthrough allowed local area networks (LANs) to become practical. Actually, in 1976, extremely fast meant a 56Kbps connection, which is the same speed that most narrowband dial-up connections still operate on due to the limitation of telephone wiring.

In 1983, every computer connected to ARPANET was required to use TCP/IP, which became the core Internet communications protocol. Also in 1983, the University of Wisconsin developed the Domain Name System (DNS), which allowed TCP/IP packs to be delivered to a server representing a domain name. Because the Internet actually operates on IP addresses, domain names must be translated into IP addresses by Domain Name Servers. This made it much easier to remember addresses for different nodes on the Internet.

1984 saw the Internet split into two entities. MIL NET became focused on the needs of the military and military development projects. ARPANET became focused on advanced research. The US Department of Defence continued to fund and support both networks. Also in 1994, the first high-speed Internet backbones were installed by MCI. The new network was called NSFNET (National Science Foundation Network)

In 1985, the first.com domain name was registered by Symbolics, who still uses it today. In 1985, the Internet was strictly a text-based system. There were no images or web sites as we see today. Internet sites consisted of pages of text messages.

In 1990, the US Department of Defence replaced the old ARPANET infrastructure with the the new, high-speed NSFNET backbone. Also in 1990, Tim Berne's-Lee of CERN began working with a hypertext system that would eventually lead to the creation of the World Wide Web, for which he is best known. Tim Berners-Lee is frequently called the father of the world wide web due to his work in developing the concepts In 1992, the World Wide Web was introduced by CERN. The World Wide Web incorporated hypertext linking capabilities, a standardized HTML scripting language, standardized resource identifiers (URIs/URLs) and utilized a client-server model for requesting web pages and objects using a hypertext transport protocol (HTTP) model.

In 1993, the National Science Foundation created interNIC, which leads to the implementation of several Internet services, including formalized domain registration services by Network Solutions. Marc Andersen and the University of Illinois introduced Mosaic, the first graphical user interface for the World Wide Web. Andreessen would go on to start Netscape in order to further develop and commercialize the use of browsers. Compuserve and other subscription information services began offering businesses and home users access to the Internet through their information networks.

By 1995, large numbers of users were were joining the Internet community and business began thinking of ways to use the Internet to sell products and services. Since then, the evolution and growth of the Internet has been rapid.

It is important to note that the Internet and the World Wide Web are not really one and the same. The Internet refers to the massive network of networks, which is basically the hardware infrastructure. The World Wide Web is a combination of methods and protocols for accessing the information over the Internet.

SIZE

No one knows for certain because it is growing so rapidly. Estimates range from 12 billion web documents to over 20 billion. It could actually be much larger than that.

INTERNET FOR MILITARY

The original concept developed by RAND was for a military communications network. It evolved into more of an academic study involving better ways to communicate information. For many years the Internet was only available to universities and research facilities. There was military funding and research from DARPA, which kept the project alive, so there was a strong military interest as the project evolved through the 1960s, 1970s and early 1980s.

There are people who played important roles in the history of the Internet project who say it was not a military project, but that is a bit of a denial regarding where the concept originated and where much of the funding came from. It is safe to say that by the time the concept of the World Wide Web started to emerge, the Internet was no longer a military project.

FireFTP is a FireFox-only add-on, which means that it will not work with Internet Explorer. Installation is simple. Just go to the FireFTP download page and click on the Download button. Make sure you are using FireFox when you visit the page. The browser add-on will automatically install in a few seconds.

After installation, you can find the FTP utility in the FireFox Tools menu. Click on it and it will open in a browser window. Just like FileZilla, FireFTP allows you to set up and save FTP connection accounts and allows quick connects for occasional FTP connections that you do not want to store. The only difference is that an Account is saved, while a QuickConnect is not.

When you start up FireFTP, you will see multiple panes. The panes on the left side represent the local directories on your PC. The panes on the right display remote directories on your web site after you have connected to your server. To set up an account, click on the Create an account... selection from the drop-down menu in the top left-hand corner. The Account Manager dialog box will display. From there you can enter the FTP information for your web site.

The Account Name will be displayed on the drop-down menu. The account information can be obtained from your hosting company. The Category is optional and can be used if you have a lot of FTP accounts that you want to set up in logical group sonthe menu. The Host is typically your domain name, *i.e.,* tech-evangelist.com. If you are using a dedicated IP address, you can use the IP address.

Some hosting companies require the use of special Host addresses:

- The Login is your username for the FTP account.
- The Password is the password for the FTP account.

To set up an account, you only need to enter the Account Name. Any information that you enter will be stored when you same the account. If you are using a laptop that could be stolen, it is a good idea to leave the password blank. FireFTP will prompt you for missing information when you try to connect to your server.

The Account Manager also has a Connection tab where you can set up any special connection information, such as a non-standard port number. You can also designate default directories for both the Local (your PC) and the Remote (the server) sides of the connection. This feature saves a lot of time because you do not have to search for files on your PC if you store them in a special location.

FILES

Use the Browse button to the right of the path displayed just above the Local pane. You can select any location that you have access to on your network. Make sure that the proper directories are selected in both the left-hand pane (Local) and the right-hand-pane (Remote). Highlight the files your wish to transfer in the left window and click the right arrow in the center bar. You can also transfer files from the server to your PC. It is important to make sure that you have the proper directories selected.

To disconnect from your server, use the Disconnect button to the right of the drop-down menu. Once a connection is made, the Connect button turns into the Disconnect button. This is easy to set up, although the location for the change is not very intuitive. On the top right-hand side of the FireFTP window there is a Tools selection. Select Tools > Options. Check the box named Show Hidden Files. This is found in the Connection tab in the Account Manager dialog box. The easiest way to set this up is to make the connection to your server, select the proper directories for both the left-hand and right-hand panes, then select the Edit button next to the drop-down menu. Select the Connection tab. You should see both the Local and Remote directory paths displayed. Click on the Use Current button next to each, and then click OK. The next time you connect to your server, the default directories will be used. If you need a real nice, lightweight and simple FTP utility, it is worthwhile to take a look at FireFTP. I was pleasantly surprised with this one.

WEB SERVER

A web proxy server, sometimes called a web proxy, can serve a variety of purposes. Many of the purposes for using a proxy server are legitimate, but others are suspicious and sometimes malicious. Using a simple definition, a proxy is basically a server that sits between a user and the destination server that the user is accessing. It is an intermediary or go-between that requests resources from the destination server on the user's behalf. On of the most common uses of a proxy server is for anonymous web surfing. When a user is connected through a proxy server, the IP address of the web proxy is used to communicate with the destination server and thus the IP address of the user is hidden. This can be used to allow a user access to systems where their access might normally be blocked, or because an IP address identifies a user's geographic location, it can be used to disguise the country where a user is located.

There are thousands of free proxy servers set up in countries around the world, and lists of these servers can easily be found on the web. When a user visits one of these sites, they enter the web address of the site they wish to visit. From that point on, the true IP address of the user is protected and the destination server only sees the IP address of the proxy server.

Students use web proxies to allow them to access web sites whose IP addresses are blocked by their school's server.

For example, if a school has blocked all the known IP addresses for porn sites, students might still be able to access these sites through a proxy. Because of uses intended to circumvent normal security, lists of the IP addresses of known proxy servers are available, which can also be blocked by a company or school network. If you are concerned about protecting your identity while on the web, a proxy server can help with anonymity. But be aware that these servers can have a malicious intent and can be used to cache information that passes through them, which means that you never want to use one of these intermediaries to log into your bank account or any web site where exposing user IDs and passwords can be detrimental. This can be a path to identity theft.

There are other malicious uses for these servers. Many e-commerce sites capture the IP addresses of customers who purchase products. They are used to identify the geographic location of a customer to help prevent fraud. If a customer's street address is in Boston, but their IP address identifies their geographic location as Nigeria or China, the chances are more than good that a stolen credit card is being used. Many sophisticated online thieves use domestic drop points or freight forwarding companies where products are shipped and later forwarded to the thief. They have also learned to use web proxy servers to hide their location, or make it appear that they are located in a country not known for credit card fraud.

There are many legitimate uses for proxy servers. AOL has traditionally cached commonly visited web pages and altered JPG images by compressing them to speed up web access for their users. They can also be used by schools and companies to filter content, and by ISPs that restrict access to family friendly content. If you are going to use a proxy server, try to identify those that are legitimate. Many are, but some are not. As a general rule, never access sensitive sites that require a user ID and password. This includes your e-mail accounts.

USING PHP

A shopping cart is an essential component of every e-commerce site. Although there are literally hundreds of shopping carts to choose from, only a few stand out. PHP is the preferred shopping cart language because it is the most popular web development language on the Internet. When combined with the MySQL database, PHP is unbeatable for cost effectiveness.

The selection of the best shopping cart for your web site is an issue that should not be taken lightly. The user-friendliness built into your shopping cart can be a major factor when it comes to retaining visitors and converting them into customers. Numerous studies have shown that the checkout process associated with a poorly designed cart can be a major factor affecting shopping cart abandonment during the checkout process.

The following is brief list of the most popular shopping carts that utilize both PHP and MySQL. Both PHP and MySQL are free (no licensing issues) and are offered with almost all non-Microsoft web site hosting. This gives this combination a low-cost advantage, both for the cost of obtaining, modifying and maintaining your shopping cart system. Indeed, many of the most popular shopping carts using PHP and MySQL are free and most have a wide range of support available through numerous forums.

All of these shopping cart options are complete e-commerce storefronts, complete with category pages, product pages, checkout processes and much more. All have a wide range of mods available that add functionality to the e-commerce sites.

OS COMMERCE

First and foremost is os Commerce, the biggest player in open source shopping carts. osCommerce has been around for more than six years and includes a large community of users and supporters. osCommerce is a complete e-commerce storefront. The basic osCommerce download is very functional and there is a wide selection of plugin mods that add functionality and features. More than 100 templates are available that change the look and feel of a storefront.

When considering shopping carts, CRE Loaded has been referred to as osCommerce on steroids. CRE Loaded is built on osCommerce. Different versions include large collections of already-installed mods so that you have a highly functional and heavily equipped version of of osCommerce as soon as it is installed. There are small one-time fees associated with purchasing a copy of CRE Loaded, but the costs are minimal.

Zen Cart is a derivative of osCommerce. The group that focuses on this cart started with a version of osCommerce a few years ago and used it as a basis for building their own open source shopping cart. it is therefore similar to osCommerce in some ways, but has its own user and developer community. Support is provided through a very active forum where members help each other to solve issues related to e-commerce and the use of Zen Cart. The best part is that it is a very stable cart with loads of built-in functionality and it is free.

This is another contender when it comes to popular and very functional shopping carts. Cube Cart has both a free and low-cost version available. They are both the same, but it will cost you $89.95 if you wish to remove the Cube Cart copyright notice and link from the page footers. Sometimes this makes sense if you are in a competitive market and you do not want your competitors to know which shopping cart you are using.

OBSERVATIONS

Any of the choices listed above are good choices for an e-commerce web site. One thing to note is that most of the systems have all of the functionality turned on when you install the cart. This tends to degrade speed performance due to numerous unnecessary database lookups. After installing one of these shopping cart systems, you need to become familiar with the administration area and then should turn off every feature that you really do not need.

Most of these systems have manuals available, either in hardcopy or downloadable format. Your learning curve will likely be shortened if obtain the manual and go through it in great detail. Which one did we like best? We decided to go with Zen Cart due to the very active user forum and the superior support we see from the development staff. You should, of course, make your own decision. You cannot go wrong with any of these PHP shopping cart choices.

TROUBLESHOOTING

Outbound e-mail uses a process called SMTP (simple mail transport protocol). SMTP is the standard for e-mail transmissions across the Internet. SMTP is generally used to send messages from a mail client (Thunderbird) to a mail server. The e-mail is stored on the server until retrieved by another e-mail client using a PC P3 or IMAP retrieval protocol. Outbound e-mail problems can be frustrating to deal with because you rarely see an indicator as to what might be causing the problem. However, there are fewer factors involved when setting up the SMTP section in Thunderbird, so isolating the problem can be much simpler. Unlike setting up an e-mail retrieval for inbound e-mail, with SMTP, a single SMTP setup can be used to cover all of your e-mail addresses, regardless of how many different ISPs are involved.

Most SMTP mail servers are set up to allow e-mail accounts from other ISPs to be run through them. Thunderbird identifies the first SMTP account that you set up as being the default account. That is because in most cases it can be shared by all of your e-mail accounts.

Most of the configuration issues with sending e-mail can be resolved in the Server Settings section in Thunderbird.

- Select Account Settings from the Tools menu.
- Scroll down to the bottom of the list if e-mail accounts.
- Select Outgoing Server (SMTP).

When you are sure that this information is correct, click the OK button, shut down Thunderbird and then start it up again to make sure that any new settings are loaded. If you have multiple e-mail accounts and you know that inbound e-mail is working, try sending a test message to another of your e-mail addresses. If it still does not work or you see an error, make sure that you Internet access is active. If you can access the Internet using your browser, you should be able to send e-mail messages once the SMTP information is correct. If you are still having trouble connecting to the SMTP server, Thunderbird will usually display a message, but depending on the type of error, sometimes it does not. Most of the time the User Name is just the account name, but some configurations may require a complete e-mail address. If one way does not work, try the other.

If your SMTP server requires a secure connection, you may have to check the SSL box. I sometimes use the SMTP server at my AT&T account. AT&T connections usually require that you check the SSL box. If you are having connections problems, post your issues in the Comments below. Try to give us as much information as you can and we will see if we can help you to get connected.

INCOMING E-MAILS

Most e-mail addresses today use the POP3 (Post Office Protocol 3) Internet protocol for receiving e-mail. With POP3 your e-mail is held on a mail server. You can download your mail to an e-mail client. Typically, the e-mail is deleted from the server when it is downloaded, but it can be set up to retain the e-mail messages.

An alternative Internet mail protocol is IMAP (Internet Message Access Protocol). IMAP provides some enhanced capabilities and is useful for dealing with large volumes of mail that may need to be organized. Most hosing companies today use POP3. If you are not sure about your situation, ask the ISP or hosting company. The e-mail documentation they provide will usually tell you which protocol you are working with.

Most of the configuration issues with receiving e-mail can be resolved in the Server Settings section for each e-mail address in Thunderbird.

Each e-mail address is configured separately:

- Select Account Settings from the Tools menu.
- Select Server Settings under the e-mail address you wish to troubleshoot.

The first thing to check is the Server Name. This identifies your mail server. You will need to get this information from your hosting company or ISP. Most mail servers are identified by using a subdomain preceding the domain name, such as mail.tech-evangelist.com. Some use other subdomain names, such as ipostoffice.tech-evangelist.com. Once again, the only way to know is to find out how your mail server is configured.

Next, check the User Name. Sometimes this is the entire e-mail address and sometimes is is just the account name, which is the portion of the e-mail address to the left of the @ sign. The third item to test is the Security Settings. Most mail servers do not use a secure connection, so Never would be checked. I've seen a few that use TLS (Transport Layer Security), which is a type of secure connection. If Never didn't work, try TLS, if available.

There are also a few e-mail servers that use SSL (Secure Sockets Layer) for secure connections. Secure connections encypt the messages as they are downloaded, which prevents others from intercepting your messages. I have an AT&T e-mail account that requires SSL. When you click the SSL radio button, the port number will change. You can also try checking the Use Secure Authentication box, but thus far I have never had to do that when setting up an e-mail account.

There is a very small possibility that your ISP or hosting company is using a non-standard port. Thunderbird does allow you to change the port, but you should never do that unless instructed to do so by your ISP or hosting company. If the port is wrong, you will not make the proper server connection. If none of this works, make sure that you do indeed have an active Internet connection. If your browser can access the Internet, you should be able to retrieve your e-mail.

By now your problems receiving e-mail should have been resolved. Most of the time when I've run into issues setting up new e-mail accounts in Thunderbird, the issue was an incorrect User Name or Security Setting. Remember to save the settings each time you make a change by clicking the OK button. It is also best if you shut down and restart

Thunderbird to make sure that your changes are reloaded. After that, test it again.

CREATING E-MAIL SIGNATURE

A signature in an e-mail is kind of like a footer on a web page. It is generally used to convey contact information, legal notices and other repetitive information. This is something that you may not want to re-type every time you send an e-mail message. Thunderbird allows you to create as many signatures as you wish. You can assign a different signature to each individual e-mail address.

The first thing you need to know is that you must create the signature file in a pure text editor, such as Microsoft's Notepad. Do not use Word or any type of text editor that may embed codes in the text. You can save these files anywhere on your PC, but it makes sense to store them somewhere where they will not get separated from the rest of your Thunderbird files. In a previous tutorial, I changed the file location for the Thunderbird files in order to make it easier to back up these files.

I simply created a new folder called "signatures" in the folder with the rest of the Thunderbird files. Like I said, you can store them anywhere, but when you do it this easy, the signatures stay with your Thunderbird files if you need to move them to another PC or if you have to restore a PC from your backup files.

Next, you will need to assign a signature to each e-mail address. From the Tools menu, select Account Settings... Highlight an e-mail address on the left-hand column. On the right, check the box that says "Attach this signature:" and then click the Choose button to navigate to your signatures folder. Select the file that you want to attach. Click the OK button to save your settings. You will need to repeat this process for each e-mail address where you wish to add a signature. If you add a URL to the signature file, most e-mail clients will turn it into a hyperlink. But if you need to spruce it up of if you wish to use HTML in a signature instead of plain text, here is what you need to do. Create a text file in the same manner as described above. When you save the file, save it with a.html extension, rather than a.txt extension. Thunderbird will then recognize it as an HTML file. You can then use coloured fonts, hyperlinks or just about any type of CSS, as long as you use inline CSS styles.

When you are using CSS in e-mail messages, make sure that you fully specify the URLs to images and store the images on your server. Don't try to embed images or send them with the message.

It won't work well with many browsers.One more thing that has to be mentioned about HTML in signatures is that the message must be sent in HTML mode for the HTML and CSS to work. When you send any message that contains HTML, Thunderbird will ask you if you want to send it in in Plain Text. You do have to click on the Send in HTML Only or Send in Plain Text and HTML for the HTML and CSS to render properly.

SPAM AND JUNK MAIL

No one want to receive spam, but today it is almost inevitable that most e-mail addresses will eventually end up on spam lists. I have always protected my e-mail addresses, but recently ended up receiving more than 100 spam messages per day on my most important e-mail address used only by my business clients.

It turns out that a client thought she was doing me a favour when she posted it on a forum, along with a recommendation. As part of my battle to eliminate spam, I found that Thunderbird contains some amazingly powerful spam and junk mail controls that are very effective at filtering unwanted e-mail. This tutorial shows you how to turn these filters on and configure them to meet your needs.

There are actually several methods for filtering out spam using Thunderbird's tools. I used all of them in conjunction and found that Thunderbird effectively filtered out almost every undesirable message. It is also amazingly accurate and only very rarely grabs a legitimate message and identifies it as spam.

PRE-FILTERING SPAM MESSAGES

The first level for setting up spam filtering is to do it at the server level or on your personal computer. If you have a web site, your hosting company might already offer spam filtering software, such as Spam Assassin or Spam Pal. This step is not absolutely necessary, but it does make the process of identifying and fiitering spam more effective.

SpamAssassin is commonly found on Linux or Unix Apache servers. SpamAssassin checks messages coming through a hosting service's e-mail system. It does not actually filter the spam out, but rather uses heuristic algorithms that analyse a message. It then assigns a spam score. Thunderbird can use this score to determine if a message is likely to be spam. If your web site runs on Unix or Linux and uses a control panel such as Pleske or cPanel, check to see if SpamAssassin is included. You will find it under Mail, SpamAssassin. If the message near the top indicates that SpamAssassin is disabled, click the box labeled Enable SpamAssassin. Do not click the box labeled Enable Spam Box.

SpamPal is a different type of filtering system that installs on your PC. SpamPal uses spam block lists (lists of IP addresses used by spammers) to identify spam messages. I have not tried it, but if your hosting company does not use SpamAssassin, or if you do not have a web site (and therefore do not use a hosting company), you might want to try installing it. You will find it atspampal.org.

CONFIGURING JUNK MAIL

The first step is to configure Junk Settings:

- Select Account Settings from the Tools menu. Thunderbird allows you to configure each e-mail address separately.
- Select Junk Settings under one of your e-mail addresses.
- Check all of the boxes in the Junk Settings display. If you don't use SpamAssassin or SpamPal, skip that checkbox. If you do use one of these tools, make sure the box is checked and the proper filter selected.

- Checking "Move new junk messages to Junk folder" will create a Junk folder under the selected e-mail address. You can set the nuber of days before spam is deleted from the junk folder. It is a good idea to move the messages to this folder so that you can periodically review it for messages that may not be spam.

CONFIGURING PRIVACY SETTINGS

- Select Tools, Options.
- Select the Privacy button.
- Select the Junk tab.
- Choose how you want spam to be handled when you manually select it when reviewing your e-mails. When you are viewing messages and you identify a spam message, you can click on the column to the left of the date to send the message to the Junk folder. This also helps the system identify spam messages.

CONFIGURING MESSAGE FILTERS

When all else fails to identify spam, this is the way to do it. Message filters will search new messages for any keywords you designate. This section is pretty easy to figure out. Once again, you have to set up individual message filters for each e-mail address.

- Highlight an e-mail address in the main screen.
- Select Tools, Message Filters from the top menu.
- Click on the New button.
- Name your message filter at the top.
- Select the e-mail element that you wish to filter. Most spam keywords are going to be found in the Subject or Body.
- Select Contains.
- Enter the keyword or phrase you wish to use as a filter.
- Near the bottom of the displayed dialogue box, select the location to move any identified spam messages. The Junk folder for the current e-mail address is the

most logical place for these messages so that you can review them.

- Click OK.

That's about all there is to configuring Thunderbird to filter out spam messages. Although the configuration sections are a bit scattered throughout Thunderbird, once you know where to find them they are easy to use.

VIEW SOURCE

If you are an avid Internet user and use Internet Explorer as your browser, you have probably noticed that there are times when the View Source function in Internet Explorer occasionally stops working. For a Web developer or designer who likes to view the HTML code for a Web site, this can be frustrating. Fortunately, both the explanation to the problem and the solution are usually simple.

The root of the problem is that the browser cache has filled because of all the Web page code and images stored by the browser. The solution is to clear these temporary files and start out with a fresh cache. To do this,

- Select Tools on the top menu in Internet Explorer
- Select Internet Options...
- Click Delete Files in the Temporary Internet Files section

It may take several minutes to delete all the files in the cache, so don't panic if it appears like your PC has locked up. As soon as the hour glass once again turns into a mouse pointer, you can shut down Internet Explorer and start it up again. The View Source feature should now work once again.

If this does not fix the problem, you may have a more serious issue, such as a corrupted or deleted Notepad.exe programme file or problems related to the temporary files directory in Windows. Those problems are beyond the scope of this article. Other issues that have been reported that sometimes disable View Source include having a shortcut to Notepad on your desktop or having a shortcut named Notepad on your desktop. Renaming the shortcut should resolve those issues.

Most of the time, the problem tends to be related to the cache, so if you spend a lot of time on the Internet, it might be a good idea to clear the cache once a week.

MOZILLA THUNDERBIRD TIPS AND FAQS

Mozilla Thunderbird is, in my opinion, the absolute best free e-mail programme available. It doesn't have the vulnerabilities found with Outlook, primarily due to the fact that it is not an "attack target" like Microsoft products. Even when vulnerabilities are found, they are quickly patched by the community of developers that support Thunderbird. We've put together a list of tips to make your use of the Thunderbird e-mail application more enjoyable.

If you have a specific question regarding how to do something with Thunderbird, post a comment below and if we have a solution we will include the answer on either this tips page or in a separate tutorial.

Where do I Find the Download for Thunderbird

You can find the most current version at the Mozilla Thunderbird download page. Installation is pretty simple. If you are using Outlook, Eudora or another e-mail client, you can easily import your address book and messages during the installation.

Including Previous Message Text

We found this to be one of the annoying default features with Thunderbird. Unless you change the settings, when you forward a message with Thunderbird it will include the forwarded message as an attachment. I personally prefer that the forwarded text be included in the body of the message that I send.

This is easy to change:

- Click on the Tools menu
- Select Options
- Select Composition
- Select the General tab
- *At the top change Forward messages*: "As Attachment" to "Inline"
- Click OK

Your forwarded messages should now include the text of the forwarded message in the body of the e-mail just below any message text that you add. If you selected the default settings during the installation, Thunderbird will automatically download updates and let you know when they are ready for installation. You will find the settings for this under Tools, Options, Advanced and then select the Update tab. Check out our tutorial about setting up Thunderbird mailing lists.

This is really simple to do, but like many things with open source software, the solution is not always intuitive. This is an area where Thunderbird excels. We did a separate post on that called Thunderbird spam and junk mail filters. We tried several different methods to eliminate spam and this was the only system that eliminated it almost completely and at zero cost. We were very impressed.

String E-mail messages

They are hidden, but you can find them using the tips we offer in Thunderbird file location. This is very useful information if you wish to move the location to a Windows folder that can be easily backed up.

Changing Passwords

Ah-h-h, grasshopper. Passwords used to access your e-mail accounts are easy to change if you follow the instructions we offer in Changing Thunderbird .Passwords

Making Mozilla Thunderbird

When you set up Thunderbird as the default e-mail client, it will automatically open whenever you click on an e-mail address on a web page that uses the HTML mailto: protocol. To configure Thunderbird as the default e-mail client, simply Open the Tools menu, select Options and click on the General icon. Under system Defaults, check the box that says, "Always check to see if Thunderbird is the default e-mail client on startup." Click OK to save the setting. From now on, whenever the PC is booted it will check to see if Thunderbird is the default e-mail client. If one of the Windows programmes tries to change the setting to Outlook or if another programme changes it to something else, a message will be displayed that will allow you to change it back.

Most people are not aware of this, but when you delete an e-mail message with most e-mail clients, you do not actually delete the message. The message is simple flagged so that it does not appear in the e-mail list. Thunderbird never actually deletes a message unless you take some extra steps. First, select File, Empty Trash. Second, select File, Compact Folders. This deletes all of the flagged messages in the data files. This issue keeps coming up. It looks like you can use Thunderbird with a Yahoo account if you subscribe to Yahoo Mail Plus. The standard freebie Yahoo account does not offer POP3 access. See the following articles. You will find all of the proper configuration information posted there.

- Can I use Thunderbird to read and send my Yahoo! Mail?
- Can I POP my mail into a different e-mail client (like Thunderbird)?
- Yahoo outgoing e-mail problems with Thunderbird.

Preventing Thunderbird

This was a feature that was turned on by default in older versions of Mozilla Thunderbird. I think the default is turned off in newer versions. It is something that is not only annoying, but also presents security issues.

Turning the embedding feature off is easy. Just select the View menu. Make sure that Display Attachments Inline is unchecked. Changing Thunderbird's behaviour with outgoing e-mail attachments is easy to do, but is buried in the Config Editor. Make sure that you are using a current version of Thunderbird.

The location of the Config Editor has changed several times with different versions. Select the Tools menu, then Options, select the Advanced button, then the General tab and click on the Config Editor button. Scroll down until you find mail. content_disposition_type. If the value is not set to

1, double-click on that line and an Enter Integer Value dialog box will pop up. Change the value to 1 and click OK. Shut down Thunderbird and restart it for the change to take effect.

PROGRAMMER

When a non-technically inclined web site owner speaks with an experienced programmer, technical jargon frequently enters the conversation. Some programmers do that intentionally, just to show off their expertise. For others, it is just the way they talk because they are immersed in a technical working environment. If you get confused talking with IT people, you may find this jargon guide to be handy.

The technical language of programmers can sometimes be very difficult to understand. It is loaded with shortcuts, euphemisms and analogies. Frequently, the full name or technical term for the many special symbols or characters used in programming is just too cumbersome or boring to use in everyday technical conversations. Unique names or monikers for programming symbols has evolved. Most are intended to be humorous and help to liven up the communications between programmers.

The following are a few of the most common jargon and techno-terms used by professional programmers in everyday conversations amongst themselves. Step outside of your box for a few moments and compare the special characters to the jargon terms and you can easily envision the evolution of the terms.

- . *(dot)*: A dot is just a period in a file name or domain name, as in google-dot-com.
- * *(star, splat or spider)*: An asterisk is a wild card symbol used with servers and computer programmes.
- # (hash, pound, crunch, sharp)–Most commonly referred to as a hash, this symbol is commonly used to designate comments in many programming languages.
- *! (bang, pling, shriek, not)*: The exclamation point serves different purposes in different programming

languages, but it is most commonly used to reverse a Boolean evaluation. In other words, if a statement is true, it reverses it to false.

- *#! (hash-bang or sh-bang)*: When used as the first two characters on the first line of a programming script, a hash-bang causes Unix and Linux operating systems to execute that script using the interpreter specified by the rest of that line.
- *' (tick)*: This is a single quote commonly used to surround a string of characters.
- *" (snakebite, rabbit ears)*: A standard double quote. This jargon goes way back to the 1980s, so if you hear this, you are talking to an old-timer.
- *$ (buck, bling, cash)*: Used to designate a string variable in many programming languages.
- *() (left paren, right paren, open, close)*: Commonly used to group portions of algorithms or comparison statements. Algorithms and evaluations of statements always start with the inner-most set of parens in all programming languages.
- */ (wack, slash, stroke)*: A common slash character, most commonly used in directory paths on servers or to define a mathematical division.
- \ *(backslash, backwack, hack)*: A common blackslash used in some networking paths and also as a common designation for a escape character, which means that the next character in line should be taken literally and not executed.
- *{ } (left curly, right curly, hitchcocks*: Think Alfred Hitchcock silhouette, left banana, right banana)–Curly braces commonly used to group multiple programming statements.
- *~ (squiggle)*: A tilde character.
- *| (bar, pipe)*: A vertical bar character.
- *^ (hat)*: A caret character.
- *% (mod, grapes)*: Commonly used as a mathematical modulo character in programming languages.
- *& (amp, amper)*: An ampersand symbol.

W3C

You may find it interesting to learn how to eliminate every error message the W3C validator produces. It can be an educaticnal process even if you are a very experienced developer. Although you may think you know a lot about HTML or XHTML, you will likely find that you do not know as much as you thought you knew about the W3C's coding standards. Before you use the validator, a page needs to have a Doctype declaration.

The Doctype declaration, or DTD, needs to be the very first line of code on a Web page. The DTD sets the standard to be used in the validation. It also serves another purpose. Many modern browsers contain multiple rendering engines. If you do not set a standard to be used for rendering, the page may not look consistent across different browsers.

Note that all valid DTDs from HTML 4.01 on contain a link to a standards document. If your web page editor already adds a DTD with every Web page, it may not be valid if it does not contain a URL to the actual standards document.

Using the W3C validator is very easy. Just cut-and-paste or enter a complete URL to the Web page you wish to test. You may find some of the validation messages to be a bit cryptic, but the W3C provides links with most error messages that lead to additional information.

There are some common page elements that always produce errors or warnings, even though they do not negatively affect either browsers or search engine spiders. Microsoft-specific entity codes, such as copyright and other symbols may not be code compliant. The validator handles these errors well and typically offers the code compliant equivalent.

Body tag attributes such as leftmargin, right margin (Internet Explorer), marginheight, marginwidth (Netscape) are browser extensions that are not part of the official coding standards. These types of issues will not typically produce negative effects with either browsers or spiders, but do show up as errors because they do not comply with the standard. One type of nuisance error is a missing alt attribute in image tags. Current standards do require the use of the alt attribute in order to push designers and developers to use this attribute because it is beneficial for Internet users with vision impairments who utilize special browsers that describe images though the use of alt attributes. It may not make sense, however, to include text with every alt attribute. The code compliant workaround is to simply include an empty string value (alt="") for lines and other page elements that need no explanation.

It can sometimes be very beneficial to eliminate every error message displayed, and to assure complete and 100% compliance with the DTD standard you chose. Once a page has been validated as compliant, the W3C offers a cut-and-paste snippet of code that can be added to your Web pages as both a "gold star" certification of compliance and as a link to re-validate the code when you make changes.

AVOIDING SPAM

Despite anti-spam laws, the amount of spam e-mail messages I receive has grown enormously. You probably feel the same way. The problem with spam laws is that someone has to enforce them, but the e-mail spam problem is so enormous that only the largest and most aggressive USA spammers get prosecuted. Foreign spammers are not subject to USA laws and are much harder to identify. There are, however, some fundamental things that you can do to lessen the amount of spam that you receive, particularly if you have a business.

First and foremost, the best way to prevent your e-mail address from finding its way to a spam list is to never, under any circumstances, publish the e-mail address on a web page. Why? Because most e-mail ends up on spam lists because one of the hundreds of spam bots–also called e-mail harvesters–found it on a web site and automatically added it to a spam list. If you need to publish an e-mail address, create an image file for the e-mail address and display that. Spambots cannot read text in images, so they will not find the e-mail address if you display it in an image.

Second, never, ever click on a spam message or any links in a spam message. This includes links that assure that the message will be removed from the spammer's database. While this may work for legitimate sources of e-mail, I am willing to bet that few spammers really care about the laws, especially if they are in a foreign country. When you click on any link, you are very likely just verifying that your e-mail address is valid, which pretty much guarantees that it will be added to hundreds of spam lists.

Third, much of the spam that we receive comes from spammer programmes that randomly generate e-mail account names using the domain names of popular ISPs and then send an e-mail to that address. If it bounces back, they know the e-mail address is not valid. If it does not bounce back, it may be a valid e-mail address.

Many spammers use a library of account names that are attached to other libraries of domain names. The account name if the portion of the e-mail address found to the left of the @ symbol. The domain is the part to the right.

Due to the fact that we run several web-based businesses, we have noticed a pattern of account names that many spammers use to see if an e-mail address is valid. The account names are attached to lists of domain names that can easily be found on the web and are used to generate spam for commonly used e-mail addresses.

INTERNET TECHNOLOGY

The Internet has become critical to everyday life in domains as diverse as education, health, defence, commerce, travel and entertainment. The Internet was not designed for its current level of usage, and there is a need for simple constructs to allow the network to do better in terms of security, mobility and quality of service, among other things.

A number of global and local programmes of research (in the US, EU and further afield, eg Asia) are looking at future network architectures and building testbeds to evaluate new protocols and systems based on these new ideas. The most notable, in the US are the NSF Find programme and the GENI project to build infrastructure. In Europe we find a number of projects, with some interesting high-level thinking (eg the Eiffel project) and a set of testbed initiatives under the FIRE Programme.

While some researchers think there is a need for a'clean slate' design of the network of the future, much successful work is evolutionary rather than revolutionary, and this can be seen in the articles in this issue. Future core networks will leverage IP over simple, super-fast optical core networks. A major trend is that of virtualization, featuring the construction of optimized virtual networks that answer the needs of a collection of users or applications. A wide variety of wired and wireless access networks are available or being developed: FTTH/FTTO in the wired domain, and 3G/CDMA, LTE, WiFi, WiMax and Satellite in the wireless setting.

INTERNET MODELLING

It is quite important to comprehend how the complex systems that we build actually operate. This requires basic research on network modelling and simulation, eg, in order to derive the fundamental laws on network dynamics and control or to evaluate the ultimate capacity of self-organized wireless networks. It also requires advances in network measurements: traffic statistics, Internet probing and measurement, network inference and detection of anomalies and attacks.

INTERNET ALGORITHMS

The future of the Internet will require a wide range of computer science tools: verification; distributed algorithms (eg for consensus, and election and epidemic diffusion); resource management algorithms: resource allocation and scheduling; database algorithms: content storage, update and retrieval, content replication and consistency; search engines and the semantic Web.

A key cost in networking is the operations and management overheads. The scalability of the Internet is well known, but as distributed applications proliferate, a more autonomic approach is increasingly required. Spontaneous and self-organized networks emerge both in the wireless setting (eg with Wifi meshes or infrastructure-less wireless networks [MANETS]) and in the wired network setting (eg in peer to peer).

The Internet started by connecting computers and users to information, and then went on to connect users to each other with audio, video, games and social networking tools. Now the rapid evolution of pervasive, embedded networked devices means that we connect various types of devices to each other. There are far more computers in the world embedded in everyday objects (cars, domestic appliances etc) than there are on desktops.

The interconnection of the Internet with the physical world through sensors and agents and the tagging of industrial production by RFIDs will lead to new traffic and architecture challenges, with possibly hundreds of billions of new devices that will collect information and will have to be upgraded and managed remotely and conveniently. This will require new paradigms for routing, search, naming, maintenance, data survival etc.

The Internet of things extends to cars and other vehicles. Here the key potential is in safety: ABS in cars could communicate road surface conditions to following vehicles, setting speed and braking reactions sooner rather than too late. Traffic management and pollution sensing on cars can also make use of networking between cars, and from cars to roadside infrastructure. Tracking goods in transit on the road would allow logistics companies to optimize their freight operations, saving time and energy and perishable goods.

There is an important diversification of the nature of the content transported across the Internet: initially it was files, then real-time games, video, telephony and whiteboards, and now TV, video on demand etc. There has also been diversification of the localization of contents: with each user potentially a content producer (peer-to-peer applications). New interactions with data are appearing, as in Web 2.0 or the semantic Web, and applications continue to evolve and require new systems, measurements and management tools. Since its beginnings in 1992, the World-Wide Web has offered remote transactions for goods and services. Recently we have seen a rapid growth in the number of attacks on identity, since acquiring such information allows miscreants to commit fraud that is hard to detect.

Estimates vary, but the Internet and all its services consume something on the order of 4% of the energy in the developed world. Only simple measures are required to improve this by a factor of two. Furthermore, the Internet, as we have discussed above, can be used to monitor and control external devices (things, vehicles, services) and significantly reduce their unnecessary power consumption. Figures as high as 30% have been quoted for possible national savings of energy, if unused devices in all homes could be remotely turned off. The investment necessary to achieve this is relatively low, with what seems like a very big potential return.

THE INTERNET SERVICES

We are moving from a Web of documents to a Web of services and Web of knowledge. This has triggered an explosion of new applications such as SecondLife, FaceBook and LinkedIn. And there is more to come, with augmented reality, virtual worlds, real-time games and telepresence. New concepts such as service orchestrations are also emerging, and with them, new business models.

Setting The Context

- The invited article 'Starting the Debate: Agreeing on Disagreements' by Dirk Trossen, B.T., U.K., is a meta-discussion note, on how to trigger debate. As such, it is quite interesting as a methodology for encouraging architectural thinking in the long term.
- 'The Internet Engineering Task Force and The Future of Internet' by Emmanuel Baccelli, Thomas H. Clausen and Philippe Jacquet, INRIA Saclay, France, provides a useful reminder of the processes by which

standards are created, and an analysis of how future research might be delivered in the short to medium term.

Architecture

- 'Network Virtualization, a Perspective' by Anja Feldman, Mario Kind, Olaf Maennel, Georg Shaffrath and Christoph Werle: Virtualization, briefly defined above, can be seen as a way to overcome the ossification of the Internet, namely the general idea that one should not change a system or architecture that works well. The technical challenges and the business models associated with overlay networks and more generally with virtualization are thoroughly discussed in this invited paper.
- '*Y-COMM*: A New Architecture for Mobile Heterogeneous Communications' by Glenford Mapp suggests that the symmetric architecture we are used to in the Internet is perhaps not well adapted to wireless, and proposes an alternative, useful for promoting discussion (cf the EU ANA Project).

Modelling, Measurement and Management

- 'Epidemic Information Dissemination' by Laurent Massoulie (Invited paper): Epidemic algorithms became popular at the turn of the century with Peer-to-Peer applications. They are now being investigated by major companies designing efficient distributed live streaming mechanisms over the Internet. This beautiful line of research combines the design of innovative algorithms and the modelling of their execution over a large network, which allows one to prove their quasi-optimality.
- Understanding traffic entails delivering information efficiently to humans so that they can decide on actions to take. The article 'iMyNetScope- a Platform for Network Traffic Visualization and Analysis' by Pavel Minarik discusses one approach to this, and

presents one particularly interesting topic for today - the element of Cyber Defence.

- 'Unified Access to Internet Measurement Data' by Felix Strohmeier, Martin Nilsson and Demetres Antoniades: like the previous article, this touches on a timely topic - making sure we can all (as researchers or operations) access data easily (see also www.crawdad.org for an example of traffic archives in a standard form). Since the Internet is a federation of a vast number of networks (300 ISPs in the UK alone), we need clear and standard methods for exchanging data about operations. This applies equally to research networks such as those in FIRE.
- 'Privacy Aware Network Monitoring' by Peter Dorfinger, Carsten Schmoll and Felix Strohmeier describes a problem relevant to the research and operations community. Much work on the future Internet requires monitoring of research, but at the same time, real users require privacy. This article reminds us how important and difficult it is to reconcile these two aspects. Indeed, in gathering data about network use there are legal requirements relating to intercept laws and user privacy that must be met.
- 'Breaking the Weakest Link: Becoming a Trusted Authority on the Internet' by Marc Stevens is a reminder of the danger of security failures. The fact that even the basic technology of security is sometimes flawed is interesting. Systems are never perfect, and this is never more true than for security: we can never prove a system is secure, but only discover (eventually) when it no longer is!

Correctness and Robustness (and Self-Managed to Some Extent)

- '*ResiliNets*: Resilient and Survivable Networks' by David Hutchison and James P.G. Sterbenz: As discussed above, we need secure networks that are efficient and well managed. We also depend on these networks, and since individual components are never 100% immune from faults and failures, we need techniques to make the overall system more resilient than its components.

- 'Standardized Testware for Internet-Based Telecommunication Services' by Bostjan Pintar, Axel Rennoch, Peter Schmitting and Stephan Schulz: As Internet protocols grow in number and complexity each year, we need assurance that systems will behave correctly. This article outlines industrial solutions on the correct operation of the software systems (protocols) that make the Internet and its telecommunication infrastructure work.
- 'Network Description Tools and Standards' by Freek Dijkstra, Jeroen van der Ham and Ronald van der Pol: Setting up high-speed network connections - light paths - is still a manual effort taking two to three weeks. The network engineers need a clear picture of the network topology in order to plan and configure light paths. The Network Markup Language (NML) standardizes network topology and state information. The University of Amsterdam and SARA Computing and Networking Services in the Netherlands are contributing to this effort, with the ultimate goal being to automatically set up and manage light paths.

Novel Applications, Especially Multimedia

- 'Delay-Tolerant Bulk Internet Transfers' by Nikolaos Laoutaris and Pablo Rodriguez (invited paper): Using disruption-tolerant networking (DTN) techniques, but on the Internet rather than on challenged networks, produces very interesting results in terms of capacity. Throughput can be significantly increased for some applications, and there are some very well-motivated examples, such as backing up information between large data centres, using spare capacity in a smart and autonomic way.

- 'Resource Management for IPTV Distribution' by Henrik Abrahamsson and Per Kreuger: IPTV on AT&T and Telefonica's networks now has in excess of 12 million users, each with hundreds of channels of broadcast quality content. This makes for non-trivial deployments,– and the importance of resource management for the various different technologies is unquestionable.
- '*VISTO*: Visual Storyboard for Web Video Browsing, Searching, and Indexing' by Marco Pellegrini describes exciting work on future Internet killer applications.
- 'The New Role of Humans in the Future Internet' by Daniel Schall and Schahram Dustdar: Current service-oriented architectures typically orchestrate Web services. This article addresses architectures that combine Web and human services, where the latter are not limited to service consumption but may also undertake service production. The main emphasis is on the interfaces required in such architectures.

In The Home (Internet of Things, And Energy!)

- 'Orchestrating your Surroundings' by Pau Giner, Carlos Cetina, Joan Fons and Vicente Pelechano, UP Valencia, Spain, is an example of the 'Internet of Things' being at the centre of future Internet visions.
- 'An Autonomic Home Networking Infrastructure' by Thomas Luckenbach, Mario Schuster and Marc-Oliver Pahl: in line with the previous article but articulated with a vision of autonomic computing, this is on the important topic of home net automation. Home users are non-technical: they really do not want to become network managers, operators or system administrators. It is thus essential to make home networks 'plug and play'.
- 'Load-Balancing Energy-Usage of Household Appliances' by Lennart E. Fahlen: Energy is a highly relevant topic, as described above, and using the

Internet to control consumer electronics in the household is a promising way to reduce unnecessary consumption.

On the Road, Vehicular

- 'The Internet of Vehicles or The Second Generation of Telematic Services' by Markus Miche and Thomas Michael Bohnert: Like the Internet of Things, vehicular networking is just taking off. There are car-to-car and car-to-infrastructure communications standards as well as integration of satellite navigation, traffic monitoring, tracking, and cellular map systems.
- 'Web-Enabled Tracking Operations in Distributed Supply-Chains' by Zsolt Kemény and Elisabeth Ilie-Zudor: Using the Web to track logistical information about goods in the real world is already a huge business. This is a very useful article on the topic, which also relates to the previous article.

Awareness, Identity And Society

- 'Knowledge-Based Collaboration Patterns in Future Internet Enterprise Systems' by Gregoris Mentzas and Keith Popplewell is supporting virtual community patterns, a bit like eScience community work.
- 'Experiences from the Public Safety Arena for the Future Internet' by Socrates Varakliotis, Peter Kirstein and Steve Hailes: Since the Boxing Day tsunami and Hurricane Katrina, it has become clear that the Internet might be better used in support of communications during disasters. This is a useful note on work in the area.
- 'With Joint Forces - Establishing Situation Awareness for the Future Internet' by Tanja Zseby and Thomas Hirsch: Like Mentzas' article, we can build systems to track patterns of use. This can be used to support collaboration or to detect misbehaviour. Increasingly, though, agencies are beginning to monitor social networks for this purpose.

- 'Social Networking for a Pervasive Future Internet: the SOCIALNETS Project' by Stuart M. Allen, Marco Conti, Andrea Passarella and Roger M. Whitaker: A timely article on an increasingly important topic. This outlines several new aspects of social networking that our readership should know about.
- 'Owner-Centric Networking: A New Architecture for a Pollution-Free Internet' by Claude Castelluccia and Mohamed Ali Kaafar proposes a new Owner-Centric Networking architecture that provides individuals control over their contents. This architecture would considerably improve privacy on the Internet by limiting data pollution.
- 'Semantic Web for e-Commerce' by Bernd Gruber: The Web is the basis for most new applications (Web mail, photo sharing, social nets, maps) and is the basis for commerce, which drives real economies.

Wireless, Embedded

- 'Management of Future Mesh-Based Radio Access Networks' by Vangelis Angelakis, Vasilios Siris and Apostolos Traganitis: Community mesh wireless nets are becoming pretty widespread in some areas as an alternative to expensive cellular data services. Automating management is important; related work at Intel and Microsoft in the last couple of years has covered some aspects (AP selection) but the topic continues to be relevant.
- 'Testing Mobile Data Applications on Smartphoes with SymPA' by Almudena Díaz and Pedro Merino discusses further the shortcomings of operating system platforms for data networking on cell phones and related devices. This is important, since the largest growth in Internet-capable devices is currently in this area.

2

Internet Protocol

LAYERS

TCP/IP is a two-layer programme. The higher layer, Transmission Control Protocol, manages the assembling of a message or file into smaller packets that are transmitted over the Internet and received by a TCP layer that reassembles the packets into the original message.

The lower layer, Internet Protocol, handles the address part of each packet so that it gets to the right destination. Each gateway computer on the network checks this address to see where to forward the message. Even though some packets from the same message are routed differently than others, they'll be reassembled at the destination.

TCP/IP uses the client/server model of communication in which a computer user (a client) requests and is provided a service (such as sending a Web page) by another computer (a server) in the network. TCP/IP communication is primarily point-to-point, meaning each communication is from one point (or host computer) in the network to another point or host computer.

TCP/IP and the higher-level applications that use it are collectively said to be "stateless" because each client request is considered a new request unrelated to any previous one (unlike ordinary phone conversations that require a dedicated connection for the call duration). Being stateless frees network paths so that everyone can use them continuously. (Note that the TCP layer itself is not stateless as far as any one message is concerned. Its connection remains in place until all packets in a message have been received.) Many Internet users are familiar with the even higher layer application protocols that use TCP/IP to get to the Internet. These include the World Wide Web's Hypertext Transfer Protocol (HTTP), the File Transfer Protocol (FTP), Telnet (Telnet) which lets you logon to remote computers, and the Simple Mail Transfer Protocol (SMTP). These and other protocols are often packaged together with TCP/IP as a "suite."

Personal computer users with an analog phone modem connection to the Internet usually get to the Internet through the Serial Line Internet Protocol (SLIP) or the Point-to-Point Protocol (PPP). These protocols encapsulate the IP packets so that they can be sent over the dial-up phone connection to an access provider's modem.

USER DATAGRAM

Protocols related to TCP/IP include the User Datagram Protocol (UDP), which is used instead of TCP for special purposes. Other protocols are used by network host computers for exchanging router information. These include the Internet Control Message Protocol (ICMP), the Interior Gateway Protocol (IGP), the Exterior Gateway Protocol (EGP), and the Border Gateway Protocol (BGP).

An increasing number of people are using the Internet and, many for the first time, are using the tools and utilities that at one time were only available on a limited number of computer systems (and only for really intense users!). One sign of this growth in use has been the significant number of Transmission Control Protocol/Internet Protocol (TCP/IP) and Internet books, articles, courses, and even TV shows that have become available in the last several years; there are so many such books that publishers are reluctant to authorize more because bookstores have reached their limit of shelf space! This memo provides a broad overview of the Internet and TCP/IP, with an emphasis on history, terms, and concepts. It is meant as a brief guide and starting point, referring to many other sources for more detailed information. TCP and IP were developed by a Department of Defence (DOD) research project to connect a number different networks designed by different vendors into a network of networks (the "Internet"). It was initially successful because it delivered a few basic services that everyone needs (file transfer, electronic mail, remote logon) across a very large number of client and server systems.

NETWORK IN ARMY

The Army puts out a bid on a computer and DEC wins the bid. The Air Force puts out a bid and IBM wins. The Navy bid is won by Unisys. Then the President decides to invade Grenada and the armed forces discover that their computers cannot talk to each other. The DOD must build a "network" out of systems each of which, by law, was delivered by the lowest bidder on a single contract.

The Internet Protocol was developed to create a Network of Networks (the "Internet"). Individual machines are first connected to a LAN (Ethernet or Token Ring). TCP/IP shares the LAN with other uses (a Novell file server, Windows for Workgroups peer systems). One device provides the TCP/IP connection between the LAN and the rest of the world.

To insure that all types of systems from all vendors can communicate, TCP/IP is absolutely standardized on the LAN. However, larger networks based on long distances and phone lines are more volatile. In the US, many large corporations would wish to reuse large internal networks based on IBM's SNA. In Europe, the national phone companies traditionally standardize on X.25.

However, the sudden explosion of high speed microprocessors, fibre optics, and digital phone systems has created a burst of new options: ISDN, frame relay, FDDI, Asynchronous Transfer Mode (ATM). New technologies arise and become obsolete within a few years. With cable TV and phone companies competing to build the National Information Superhighway, no single standard can govern citywide, nationwide, or worldwide communications.

The original design of TCP/IP as a Network of Networks fits nicely within the current technological uncertainty. TCP/

IP data can be sent across a LAN, or it can be carried within an internal corporate SNA network, or it can piggyback on the cable TV service. Furthermore, machines connected to any of these networks can communicate to any other network through gateways supplied by the network vendor.

ADDRESSES

On top of these local or vendor specific network addresses, TCP/IP assigns a unique number to every workstation in the world. This "IP number" is a four byte value that, by convention, is expressed by converting each byte into a decimal number (0 to 255) and separating the bytes with a period. For example, the PC Lube and Tune server is 130.132.59.234.

An organization begins by sending electronic mail to Hostmaster@INTERNIC.NET requesting assignment of a network number. It is still possible for almost anyone to get assignment of a number for a small "Class C" network in which the first three bytes identify the network and the last byte identifies the individual computer.

The author followed this procedure and was assigned the numbers 192.35.91.* for a network of computers at his house. Larger organizations can get a "Class B" network where the first two bytes identify the network and the last two bytes identify each of up to 64 thousand individual workstations. Yale's Class B network is 130.132, so all computers with IP address 130.132.*.* are connected through Yale.

The organization then connects to the Internet through one of a dozen regional or specialized network suppliers. The network vendor is given the subscriber network number and adds it to the routing configuration in its own machines and those of the other major network suppliers.

There is no mathematical formula that translates the numbers 192.35.91 or 130.132 into "Yale University" or "New Haven, CT." The machines that manage large regional networks or the central Internet routers managed by the National Science Foundation can only locate these networks by looking each network number up in a table.

There are potentially thousands of Class B networks, and millions of Class C networks, but computer memory costs are low, so the tables are reasonable. Customers that connect to the Internet, even customers as large as IBM, do not need to maintain any information on other networks. They send all external data to the regional carrier to which they subscribe, and the regional carrier maintains the tables and does the appropriate routing.

New Haven is in a border state, split 50-50 between the Yankees and the Red Sox. In this spirit, Yale recently switched its connection from the Middle Atlantic regional network to the New England carrier. When the switch occurred, tables in the other regional areas and in the national spine had to be updated, so that traffic for 130.132 was routed through Boston instead of New Jersey. The large network carriers handle the paperwork and can perform such a switch given sufficient notice. During a conversion period, the university was connected to both networks so that messages could arrive through either path.

SUBNETS

Although the individual subscribers do not need to tabulate network numbers or provide explicit routing, it is convenient for most Class B networks to be internally managed as a much smaller and simpler version of the larger network organizations. It is common to subdivide the two bytes available for internal assignment into a one byte department number and a one byte workstation ID.

The enterprise network is built using commercially available TCP/IP router boxes. Each router has small tables with 255 entries to translate the one byte department number into selection of a destination Ethernet connected to one of the routers. Messages to the PC Lube and Tune server (130.132.59.234) are sent through the national and New England regional networks based on the 130.132 part of the number. Arriving at Yale, the 59 department ID selects an Ethernet connector in the C& IS building. The 234 selects a particular workstation on that LAN. The Yale network must be updated as new Ethernets and departments are added, but it is not effected by changes outside the university or the movement of machines within the department.

IP ROUTERS

There is concept of a session with a preselected path for all traffic. Consider a company with facilities in New York, Los Angeles, Chicago and Atlanta. It could build a network from four phone lines forming a loop (NY to Chicago to LA to Atlanta to NY). A message arriving at the NY router could go to LA via either Chicago or Atlanta. The reply could come back the other way.

There is no correct answer. Traffic could be routed by the "clockwise" algorithm (go NY to Atlanta, LA to Chicago). The routers could alternate, sending one message to Atlanta and the next to Chicago. More sophisticated routing measures traffic patterns and sends data through the least busy link.

If one phone line in this network breaks down, traffic can still reach its destination through a roundabout path. After losing the NY to Chicago line, data can be sent NY to Atlanta to LA to Chicago. This provides continued service though with degraded performance. This kind of recovery is the primary design feature of IP.

The loss of the line is immediately detected by the routers in NY and Chicago, but somehow this information must be sent to the other nodes. Otherwise, LA could continue to send NY messages through Chicago, where they arrive at a "dead end." Each network adopts some Router Protocol which periodically updates the routing tables throughout the network with information about changes in route status.

If the size of the network grows, then the complexity of the routing updates will increase as will the cost of transmitting them. Building a single network that covers the entire US would be unreasonably complicated. Fortunately, the Internet is designed as a Network of Networks. This means that loops and redundancy are built into each regional carrier. The regional network handles its own problems and reroutes messages internally. Its Router Protocol updates the tables in its own routers, but no routing updates need to propagate from a regional carrier to the NSF spine or to the other regions (unless, of course, a subscriber switches permanently from one region to another).

IBM DESIGN

IBM designs its SNA networks to be centrally managed. If any error occurs, it is reported to the network authorities. By design, any error is a problem that should be corrected or repaired. IP networks, however, were designed to be robust. In battlefield conditions, the loss of a node or line is a normal circumstance. Casualties can be sorted out later on, but the network must stay up. So IP networks are robust. They automatically (and silently) reconfigure themselves when something goes wrong. If there is enough redundancy built into the system, then communication is maintained.

In 1975 when SNA was designed, such redundancy would be prohibitively expensive, or it might have been argued that only the Defence Department could afford it. Today, however, simple routers cost no more than a PC. However, the TCP/IP design that, "Errors are normal and can be largely ignored," produces problems of its own.

Data traffic is frequently organized around "hubs," much like airline traffic. One could imagine an IP router in Atlanta routing messages for smaller cities throughout the Southeast. The problem is that data arrives without a reservation. Airline companies experience the problem around major events, like the Super Bowl. Just before the game, everyone wants to fly into the city. After the game, everyone wants to fly out. Imbalance occurs on the network when something new gets advertised. Adam Curry announced the server at "mtv.com" and his regional carrier was swamped with traffic the next day. The problem is that messages come in from the entire world over high speed lines, but they go out to mtv.com over what was then a slow speed phone line.

Occasionally a snow storm cancels flights and airports fill up with stranded passengers. Many go off to hotels in town. When data arrives at a congested router, there is no place to send the overflow. Excess packets are simply discarded. It becomes the responsibility of the sender to retry the data a few seconds later and to persist until it finally gets through. This recovery is provided by the TCP component of the Internet protocol.

TCP was designed to recover from node or line failures where the network propagates routing table changes to all router nodes. Since the update takes some time, TCP is slow to initiate recovery. The TCP algorithms are not tuned to optimally handle packet loss due to traffic congestion. Instead, the traditional Internet response to traffic problems has been to increase the speed of lines and equipment in order to say ahead of growth in demand.

TCP treats the data as a stream of bytes. It logically assigns a sequence number to each byte. The TCP packet has a header that says, in effect, "This packet starts with byte 379642 and contains 200 bytes of data." The receiver can detect missing or incorrectly sequenced packets. TCP acknowledges data that has been received and retransmits data that has been lost. The TCP design means that error recovery is done end-to-end between the Client and Server machine. There is no formal standard for tracking problems in the middle of the network, though each network has adopted some ad hoc tools.

TCP/IP AND INTERNET

For additional information and insight, readers are urged to read two excellent histories of the Internet: *Casting The Net: From ARPANET to INTERNET and beyond...* by Peter Salus and *Where Wizards Stay Up Late: The Origins of the Internet* by Katie Hafner and Mark Lyon.

EVOLUTION

While the Internet today is recognized as a network that is fundamentally changing social, political, and economic structures, and in many ways obviating geographic boundaries, this potential is merely the realization of predictions that go back nearly forty years. In a series of memos dating back to August 1962, J.C.R. Licklider of MIT discussed his "Galactic Network" and how social interactions could be enabled through networking. The Internet certainly provides such a national and global infrastructure and, in fact, interplanetary Internet communication has already been seriously discussed.

Prior to the 1960s, what little computer communication existed comprised simple text and binary data, carried by the most common telecommunications network technology of the day; namely, circuit switching, the technology of the telephone networks for nearly a hundred years. Because most data traffic is bursty in nature (*i.e.*, most of the transmissions occur during a very short period of time), circuit switching results in highly inefficient use of network resources.

The fundamental technology that makes the Internet work is called *packet switching*, a data network in which all components (*i.e.*, hosts and switches) operate independently, eliminating single point-of-failure problems. In addition, network communication resources appear to be dedicated to individual users but, in fact, statistical multiplexing and an upper limit on the size of a transmitted entity result in fast, economical networks.

In the 1960s, packet switching was ready to be discovered. In 1961, Leonard Kleinrock of MIT published the first paper on packet switching theory (and the first book on the subject in 1964). In 1962, Paul Baran of the Rand Corporation described a robust, efficient, store-and-forward data network in a report for the U.S. Air Force.

At about the same time, Donald Davies and Roger Scantlebury suggested a similar idea from work at the National Physical Laboratory (NPL) in the U.K. The research at MIT (1961-1967), RAND (1962-1965), and NPL (1964-1967) occurred independently and the principal researchers did not all meet together until the Association for Computing Machinery (ACM) meeting in 1967. The term *packet* was adopted from the work at NPL.

The modern Internet began as a U.S. Department of Defence (DoD) funded experiment to interconnect DoD-funded research sites in the U.S. The 1967 ACM meeting was also where the initial design for the so-called ARPANET — named for the DoD's Advanced Research Projects Agency (ARPA) — was first published by Larry Roberts. In December 1968, ARPA awarded a contract to Bolt Beranek and Newman (BBN) to design and deploy a packet switching network with a proposed line speed of 50 kbps. In September 1969, the first node of the ARPANET was installed at the University of California at Los Angeles (UCLA), followed monthly with nodes at Stanford Research Institute (SRI), the University of California at Santa Barbara (UCSB), and the University of Utah. With four nodes by the end of 1969, the ARPANET spanned the continental U.S. by 1971 and had connections to Europe by 1973.

The original ARPANET gave life to a number of protocols that were new to packet switching. One of the most lasting results of the ARPANET was the development of a user-network protocol that has become the standard interface between users and packet switched networks; namely, ITU-T (formerly CCITT) Recommendation X.25. This "standard" interface encouraged BBN to start Telenet, a commercial packet-switched data service, in 1974; after much renaming, Telenet became a part of Sprint's X.25 service.

The initial host-to-host communications protocol introduced in the ARPANET was called the Network Control Protocol (NCP). Over time, however, NCP proved to be incapable of keeping up with the growing network traffic load. In 1974, a new, more robust suite of communications protocols was proposed and implemented throughout the ARPANET, based upon the Transmission Control Protocol (TCP) for end-to-end network communication.

But it seemed like overkill for the intermediate gateways (what we would today call *routers*) to needlessly have to deal with an end-to-end protocol so in 1978 a new design split responsibilities between a pair of protocols; the new Internet Protocol (IP) for routing packets and device-to-device communication (*i.e.*, host-to-gateway or gateway-to-gateway) and TCP for reliable, end-to-end host communication. Since TCP and IP were originally envisioned functionally as a single protocol, the protocol suite, which actually refers to a large collection of protocols and applications, is usually referred to simply as *TCP/IP*.

TCP IP VERSIONS

The original versions of both TCP and IP that are in common use today were written in September 1981, although both have had several modifications applied to them (in addition, the IP version 6, or IPv6, specification was released in December 1995). In 1983, the DoD mandated that all of their computer systems would use the TCP/IP protocol suite for .long-haul communications, further enhancing the scope and importance of the ARPANET.

In 1983, the ARPANET was split into two components. One component, still called ARPANET, was used to interconnect research/development and academic sites; the other, called MILNET, was used to carry military traffic and became part of the Defence Data Network. That year also saw a huge boost in the popularity of TCP/IP with its inclusion in the communications kernel for the University of California s UNIX implementation, 4.2BSD (Berkeley Software Distribution) UNIX.

In 1986, the National Science Foundation (NSF) built a backbone network to interconnect four NSF-funded regional supercomputer centers and the National Center for Atmospheric Research (NCAR). This network, dubbed the NSFNET, was originally intended as a backbone for other networks, not as an interconnection mechanism for individual systems.

Furthermore, the "Appropriate Use Policy" defined by the NSF limited traffic to non-commercial use. The NSFNET continued to grow and provide connectivity between both NSF-funded and non-NSF regional networks, eventually becoming the backbone that we know today as the Internet. Although early NSFNET applications were largely multiprotocol in nature, TCP/IP was employed for interconnectivity (with the ultimate goal of migration to Open Systems Interconnection).

The NSFNET originally comprised 56-kbps links and was completely upgraded to T1 (1.544 Mbps) links in 1989. Migration to a "professionally-managed" network was supervised by a consortium comprising Merit (a Michigan state regional network headquartered at the University of Michigan), IBM, and MCI. Advanced Network and Services, Inc.

(ANS), a non-profit company formed by IBM and MCI, was responsible for managing the NSFNET and supervising the transition of the NSFNET backbone to T3 (44.736 Mbps) rates by the end of 1991. During this period of time, the NSF also funded a number of regional Internet service providers (ISPs) to provide local connection points for educational institutions and NSF-funded sites.

In 1993, the NSF decided that it did not want to be in the business of running and funding networks, but wanted instead to go back to the funding of research in the areas of supercomputing and high-speed communications. In addition, there was increased pressure to commercialize the Internet; in 1989, a trial gateway connected MCI, CompuServe, and Internet mail services, and commercial users were now finding out about all of the capabilities of the Internet that once belonged exclusively to academic and hard-core users! In 1991, the Commercial Internet Exchange (CIX) Association was formed by General Atomics, Performance Systems International (PSI), and UUNET Technologies to promote and provide a commercial Internet backbone service. Nevertheless, there remained intense pressure from non-NSF ISPs to open the network to all users.

It is worth saying a few words about the NAPs. The NSF provided major funding for the four NAPs mentioned above but they needed to have additional customers to remain economically viable. Some companies — such as then-Metropolitan Fibre Systems (MFS) — decided to build other NAP sites. One of MFS' first sites was MAE-East, where "MAE" stood for "Metropolitan Area Ethernet."

MAE-East was merely a point where ISPs could interconnect which they did by buying a router and placing it at the MAE-East facility. The original MAE-East provided a 10 Mbps Ethernet LAN to interconnect the ISPs' routers, hence the name. The Ethernet LAN was eventually replaced with a 100 Mbps FDDI ring and the "E" then became "Exchange." Over the years, MFS/MCI Worldcom has added sites in San Jose, CA (MAE-West), Los Angeles, Dallas, and Houston.

Other companies also operate their own NAPs. Savvis, for example, operates an international Internet service and has built more than a dozen private NAPs in North America. Many large service providers go around the NAPs entirely by creating bilateral agreement whereby the directly route traffic coming from one network and going to the other. Before their merger in 1998, for example, MCI and LDDS Worldcom had more than 10 DS-3 (44.736 Mbps) lines interconnecting the two networks.

The North American Network Operators Group (NANOG) provides a forum for the exchange of technical information and the discussion of implementation issues that require coordination among network service providers. Meeting three times a year, NANOG is an essential element in maintaining stable Internet services in North America. Initially funded by the NSF, NANOG currently receives funds from conference registration fees and vendor donations.

In 1988, meanwhile, the DoD and most of the U.S. Government chose to adopt OSI protocols. TCP/IP was now viewed as an interim, proprietary solution since it ran only on limited hardware platforms and OSI products were only a couple of years away. The DoD mandated that all computer communications products would have to use OSI protocols by August 1990 and use of TCP/IP would be phased out. Subsequently, the U.S. Government OSI Profile (GOSIP) defined the set of protocols that would have to be supported by products sold to the federal government and TCP/IP was not included.

Despite this mandate, development of TCP/IP continued during the late 1980s as the Internet grew. TCP/IP development had always been carried out in an open environment (although the size of this open community was small due to the small number of ARPA/NSF sites), based upon the creed "We reject kings, presidents, and voting. We believe in rough consensus and running code" [*Dave Clark, M.I.T.*]. OSI products were still a couple of years away while TCP/IP became, in the minds of many, the real open systems interconnection protocol suite.

It is not the purpose of this memo to take a position in the OSI vs. TCP/IP debate (although it is absolutely clear that TCP/IP offers the primary goals of OSI; namely, a universal, non-proprietary data communications protocol. In fact, TCP/IP does far more than was ever envisioned for OSI — or for TCP/IP itself, for that matter). But before TCP/IP prevailed and OSI sort of dwindled into nothingness, many efforts were made to bring the two communities together. The ISO Development Environment (ISODE) was developed in 1990, for example, to provide an approach for OSI migration for the DoD. ISODE software allows OSI applications to operate over TCP/IP. During this same period, the Internet and OSI communities started to work together to bring about the best of both worlds as many TCP and IP features started to migrate into OSI protocols, particularly the OSI Transport Protocol class 4 (TP4) and the Connectionless Network Layer Protocol (CLNP), respectively.

Finally, a report from the National Institute for Standards and Technology (NIST) in 1994 suggested that GOSIP should incorporate TCP/IP and drop the "OSI-only" requirement. [NOTE:Some industry observers have pointed out that OSI represents the ultimate example of a *sliding window*; OSI protocols have been "two years away" since about 1986.]

None of this is meant to suggest that the NSF isn't funding Internet-class research networks anymore. That is just the function of Internet2, a consortium of nearly 400 universities, corporations, and non-profit research oriented organizations working in partnership to develop and deploy advanced network applications and technologies for the next generation Internet. Goals of Internet2 are to create a leading edge network capability for the national research community, enable the development of new Internet-based applications, and to quickly move these new network services and applications to the commercial sector.

GROWTH

The ARPANET started with four nodes in 1969 and grew to just under 600 nodes before it was split in 1983. The NSFNET also started with a modest number of sites in 1986. After that, the network experienced literally exponential growth. Internet growth between 1981 and 1991 is documented in "Internet Growth (1981-1991)".

The Internet Software Consortium hosts the Internet Domain Survey (with technical support from Network Wizards, who originated the survey). According to their chart, the Internet had nearly 30 million reachable hosts by January 1998 and over 56 million by July 1999. Dedicated residential access methods, such as cable modem and asymmetrical digital subscriber line (ADSL) technologies, are undoubtedly the reason that this number has shot up to over 171 million by January 2003.

During the boom-1990s, the Internet was growing at a rate of about a new network attachment every half-hour, interconnecting hundreds of thousands of networks. It was estimated that the Internet was doubling in size every ten to twelve months and traffic was doubling every 100 days (for 1000% annual growth). For the last several year, the number of nodes has been growing at a rate of about 50% annually and traffic continues to keep pace with that growth.

And what of the original ARPANET? It grew smaller and smaller during the late 1980s as sites and traffic moved to the Internet, and was decommissioned in July 1990. Cerf and Kahn ("Selected ARPANET Maps," *Computer Communications Review*, October 1990) re-printed a number of network maps documenting the growth (and demise) of the ARPANET.

DOMAIN NAMES AND IP ADDRESSES

Although not directly related to the administration of the Internet for operational purposes, the assignment of Internet domain names (and IP addresses) is the subject of some controversy and a lot of current activity. Internet hosts use a hierarchical naming structure comprising a top-level domain (TLD), domain and subdomain (optional), and host name. The IP address space, and all TCP/IP-related numbers, have historically been managed by theInternet Assigned Numbers Authority (IANA).

Domain names are assigned by the TLD naming authority; until April 1998, the Internet Network Information Center (InterNIC) had overall authority of these names, with NICs around the world handling non-U.S. domains. The InterNIC was also responsible for the overall coordination and management of the Domain Name System (DNS), the distributed database that reconciles host names and IP addresses on the Internet.

The InterNIC is an interesting example of the recent changes in the Internet. Since early 1993, Network Solutions, Inc. (NSI) operated the registry tasks of the InterNIC on behalf of the NSF and had exclusive registration authority for the*.com.org.net,* and*.edu* domains. NSI's contract ran out in April 1998 and was extended several times because no other agency was in place to continue the registration for those domains. In October 1998, it was decided that NSI would remain the sole administrator for those domains but that a plan needed to be put into place so that users could register names in those domains with other firms.

In addition, NSI's contract was extended to September 2000, although the registration business was opened to competition in June 1999. Nevertheless, when NSI's original InterNIC contract expired, IP address assignments moved to a new entity called theAmerican Registry for Internet Numbers (ARIN). (And NSI itself was purchased by VeriSign in March 2000.)

The newest body to handle governance of global Top Level Domain (gTLD) registrations is the Internet Corporation for Assigned Names and Numbers (ICANN). Formed in October 1998, ICANN is the organization designated by the U.S. National Telecommunications and Information

Administration (NTIA) to administer the DNS. Although surrounded in some early controversy (which is well beyond the scope of this paper!), ICANN has received wide industry support. ICANN has created several Support Organizations (SOs) to create policy for the administration of its areas of responsibility, including domain names (DNSO), IP addresses (ASO), and protocol parameter assignments (PSO).

In April 1999, ICANN announced that five companies had been selected to be part of this new *competitive* Shared Registry System for the.com.net, and.org domains. The concept was that these five organizations could accept applications for names in these gTLD name spaces, with final approval by ICANN. By the end of 1999, ICANN had added an additional 29 registrars and there are several hundred registrars accredited by ICANN today. Definitive ICANN registrar accreditation information can be found at the ICANN-Accredited Registrars page.

Other top-level domain names use the two-letter country codes defined in ISO standard 3166; *munnari.oz.au*, for example, is the address of the 1990's Internet gateway to Australia and *myo.inst.keio.ac.jp* is a host at the Science and Technology Department of Keio University in Yokohama, Japan. Other ISO 3166-based domain country codes are *ca* (Canada), *de* (Germany), *es* (Spain), *fr* (France), *gb* (Great Britain) [NOTE: For some historical reasons, the TLD.*gb* is rarely used; the TLD.*uk* (United Kingdom) seems to be preferred although UK is not an official ISO 3166 country code.], *ie* (Ireland), *il* (Israel), *mx* (Mexico), and *us* (United States). It is important to note that there is not necessarily any correlation between a country code and where a host is actually physically located.

In addition, some countries allow their country codes to be used for other, commercial purposes. *E.g.*, the " Web site" domain.*ws* actually belongs to the country of Samoa and the tv.com domain belongs to the country of Tuvalu. One of the most authoritative and up-to-date listings can be found at the "Domain name registries around the world" page maintained by UNINETT Norid AS.

The host name *www.latimes.com,* for example, is assigned to a computer named *www* (probably, but not necessarily, a Web server) at the Los Angeles Times (*latimes*), within the commercial gTLD (*com*). The host name *mail.sover.net* refers to a host (*mail*) in the SoverNet domain (*sover*) within the network provider gTLD (*net*). Guidelines for selecting host names is the subject of RFC 1178.

There are several registries responsible for blocks of IP addresses and domain naming policies around the globe. The American Registry for Internet Numbers (ARIN), was originally responsible for the Americas (western hemisphere) and parts of Africa. In 2002, the Latin American and Caribbean Internet Addresses Registry (LACNIC) was officially recognized and now covers Central and South America, as well as some Caribbean nations. TheAfrican Regional Internet Registry (AfriNIC)has responsibility for sub-Sahara Africa. At this time, ARIN only covers North America. The European and Asia-Pacific naming registries are managed by Réseaux IP Européen (RIPE) and the Asia-Pacific NIC (APNIC), respectively.

These authorities, in turn, delegate most of the country TLDs to national registries (such as RNP in Brazil and NIC-Mexico), which have ultimate authority to assign local domain names. An excellent overview of the recent history and anticipated future of the registry system can be found in "Development of the Regional Internet Registry System" (D. Karrenberg et al.) in the *IP Journal,* Vol. 4, No. 4.

Different countries may organize the country-based subdomains in any way that they want. Many countries use a subdomain similar to the TLDs, so that*.com.mx* and*.edu.mx* are the suffixes for commercial and educational institutions in Mexico, and*.co.uk* and*.ac.uk* are the suffixes for commercial and educational institutions in the United Kingdom.

The *us* domain is largely organized on the basis of geography or function. Geographical names in the *us* name space use names of the form *entity-name.city-telegraph-code.state-postal-code*.us. The domain name *cnri.reston.va.us,* for example, refers to the Corporation for National Research

Initiatives in Reston, Virginia. Functional branches are also reserved within the name space for schools (K12), community colleges (CC), technical schools (TEC), state government agencies (STATE), councils of governments (COG), libraries (LIB), museums (MUS), and several other generic types of entities. Domain names in the state government name space usually take the form *department*.state.*state-postal-code*.us (*e.g.*, the domain name *dps.state.vt.us* points to the Vermont Department of Public Safety). The K12 name space can vary widely, usually using the form *school.school-district*.k12.*state-postal-code*.us (*e.g.*, the domain *ccs.cssd.k12.vt.us* refers to the Charlotte Central School in the Chittenden South School District which happens to be in Charlotte, Vermont.) More information about the *us* domain may be found in RFC 1480.

The biggest change to the TLD process was the introduction, in 2010, of TLDs that do not use Latin characters. These Internationalized Domain Names are described in detail at ICANN's Web site. More information about TLDs, the registration process, and new TLDs can be found at the ICANN New TLD Programme Web page.

Last but not least, there is the never-ending issue of who owns domain names and IP addresses. I will make no claim to provide an authoritative answer but... domain names are owned by whoever registers them. This alone is a potential problem. Some ISPs are obtaining names on behalf of their customers *and paying the annual fee.* The issue has already arisen, "Who owns the name? The registrar or the customer?" Most ISPs have stated that they believe that the customer owns the name, even if the ISP registers the name, because there would be no reason for them to keep the name. Consider, however, that *if* an ISP insisted that it owned a name, it essentially ties a customer to an ISP forever, destroying the concept of domain name portability.

There is also an issue of violation of trademark, service mark, or copyright in the choice and ownership of domain names. The Eagles Nest in Corfu, NY. I don't know anything about The Eagles Nest of Corfu, NY but it should not be mistaken for either Eagles Nest Enterprises of Grapevine, TX (the owner of *eaglesnest.com*) nor The Eagles Nest Internet Services of Newark, OH (owner of *theeaglesnest.com*).

In any case, suppose that Microsoft decided that someone using their service mark was not in their best interest and they pursued the issue; could they wrestle that domain name away from another registrant? Today's general rule of thumb is that if an organization believes that it's name or mark is being used in someone else's domain name in an unfair or misleading way, then they can take legal action against the name holder and the assignment of the name will be held up pending the outcome of the legal action. More information about this issue can be found at ICANN's Uniform Domain-Name Dispute-Resolution Policy Web page. By the way, this is, of course, the question behind the new industry of cybersquatting; someone registers a domain name hoping that someone else with buy it from them later on!

And what about IP addresses? Prior to the widespread use of CIDR, individual organizations were assigned an address (usually a Class C!) and domain name at the same time. In general, the holder of the domain name owned the IP address and if they changed ISP, routing tables throughout the Internet were updated.

After 1994, domain name and IP number ownership were separated. Today, ISPs are assigned addresses in blocks called *CIDR blocks*. A customer today, whether they already own a domain name or are obtaining a new one, will be assigned an IP address from the ISP's CIDR block. If the customer changes ISP, they have to relinquish the IP address.

A good overview of the naming and addressing procedures can be found in RFC 2901, titled "Guide to Administrative Procedures of the Internet Infrastructure."

TCP/IP PROTOCOL ARCHITECTURE

TCP/IP is most commonly associated with the Unix operating system. While developed separately, they have been historically tied, as mentioned above, since 4.2BSD Unix started bundling TCP/IP protocols with the operating system. Nevertheless, TCP/IP protocols are available for all widely-used operating systems today and native TCP/IP support is provided in OS/2, OS/400, all Windows versions since Windows 9x, and all Linux and Unix variants.

INTERFACE LAYER

The TCP/IP protocols have been designed to operate over nearly any underlying local or wide area network technology. Although certain accommodations may need to be made, IP messages can be transported over all of the technologies shown in the figure, as well as numerous others. It is beyond the scope of this paper to describe most of these underlying protocols and technologies.

Two of the underlying network interface protocols, however, are particularly relevant to TCP/IP. The Serial Line Internet Protocol (SLIP, RFC 1055) and Point-to-Point Protocol (PPP, RFC 1661), respectively, may be used to provide data link layer protocol services where no other underlying data link protocol may be in use, such as in leased line or dial-up environments. Most commercial TCP/IP software packages for PC-class systems include these two protocols. With SLIP or PPP, a remote computer can attach directly to a host server and, therefore, connect to the Internet using IP rather than being limited to an asynchronous connection.

PPP

It is worth spending a little bit of time discussing PPP because of its importance in Internet access today. As its name implies, PPP was designed to be used over point-to-point links. In fact, it is the prevalent IP encapsulation scheme for dedicated Internet access as well as dial-up access. One of the significant strengths of PPP is its ability to negotiate a number of things upon initial connection, including passwords, IP addresses, compression schemes, and encryption schemes. In addition, PPP provides support for simultaneous multiple protocols over a single connection, an important consideration in those environments where dial-up users can employ either IP or another network Layer protocol.

INTERNET LAYER

The Internet Protocol (RFC 791), provides services that are roughly equivalent to the OSI Network Layer. IP provides a datagram (connectionless) transport service across the network. This service is sometimes referred to as *unreliable* because the network does not guarantee delivery nor notify the end host system about packets lost due to errors or network congestion. IP datagrams contain a message, or one fragment of a message, that may be up to 65,535 bytes (octets) in length. IP does not provide a mechanism for flow control.

Domain Name System

While IP addresses are 32 bits in length, most users do not memorize the numeric addresses of the hosts to which they attach; instead, people are more comfortable with host names. Most IP hosts, then, have both a numeric IP address and a name. While this is convenient for people, however, the name must be translated back to a numeric address for routing purposes.

Earlier discussion in this paper described the domain naming structure of the Internet. In the early ARPANET, every host maintained a file calledhosts that contained a list of all hosts, which included the IP address, host name, and alias(es). This was an adequate measure while the ARPANET was small and had a slow rate of growth, but was not a scalable solution as the network grew.

[*Note*: A hosts file is still found on Unix systems although usually used to reconcile names of hosts on the local network to cut down on local DNS traffic; the file can usually be found in the/etc directory. On Microsoft Windows systems, the HOSTS file can typically be found in thec:\windows folder; in Windows NT, 2000, and later, it can be found in c:\winnt\system32\drivers\etc.]

To handle the fast rate of new names on the network, the Domain Name System (DNS) was created. The DNS is a distributed database containing host name and IP address information for all domains on the Internet. There is a single *authoritative name server* for every domain that contains all

DNS-related information about the domain; each domain also has at least one secondary name server that also contains a copy of this information. Thirteen *root servers* around the globe maintain a list of all of these authoritative name servers. Although most of the root servers have multiple instances around the globe to improve performance and minimize vulnerability to attack, most of the primary DNS root servers are in the U.S. with the remainder in Asia and Europe).

When a host on the Internet needs to obtain a host's IP address based upon the host's name, a DNS request is made by the initial host to a local name server. The local name server may be able to respond to the request with information that is either configured or cached at the name server; if necessary information is not available, the local name server forwards the request to one of the root servers. The root server, then, will determine an appropriate name server for the target host and the DNS request will be forwarded to the domain's name server.

ARP and Address Resolution

Early IP implementations ran on hosts commonly interconnected by Ethernet local area networks (LAN). Every transmission on the LAN contains the local network, or medium access control (MAC), address of the source and destination nodes. MAC addresses are 48-bits in length and are non-hierarchical, so routing cannot be performed using the MAC address. MAC addresses are never the same as IP addresses.

When a host needs to send a datagram to another host on the same network, the sending application must know both the IP and MAC addresses of the intended receiver; this is because the destination IP address is placed in the IP packet and the destination MAC address is placed in the LAN MAC protocol frame. (If the destination host is on another network, the sender will look instead for the MAC address of the default gateway, or router.)

Unfortunately, the sender's IP process may not know the MAC address of the intended receiver on the same network.

The Address Resolution Protocol (ARP), described in RFC 826, provides a mechanism so that a host can learn a receiver's MAC address when knowing only the IP address. The process is actually relatively simple: the host sends an ARP Request packet in a frame containing the MAC broadcast address; the ARP request advertises the destination IP address and asks for the associated MAC address. The station on the LAN that recognizes its own IP address will send an ARP Response with its own MAC address. As Figure 2 shows, ARP message are carried directly in the LAN frame and ARP is an independent protocol from IP. The IANA maintains a list of all ARP parameters.

IP Routing: OSPF, RIP, and BGP

As an OSI Network Layer protocol, IP has the responsibility to route packets. It performs this function by looking up a packet's destination IP NET_ID in a routing table and forwarding based on the information in the table. But it is *routing protocols,* and *not* IP, that populate the routing tables with routing information. There are three routing protocols commonly associated with IP and the Internet, namely, RIP, OSPF, and BGP.

OSPF and RIP are primarily used to provide routing within a particular domain, such as within a corporate network or within an ISP's network. Since the routing is *inside* of the domain, these protocols are generically referred to as *interior gateways protocols.*

The Routing Information Protocol version 2 (RIP-2), described in RFC 2453, describes how routers will exchange routing table information using a distance-vector algorithm. With RIP, neighboring routers periodically exchange their entire routing tables. RIP uses hop count as the metric of a path's cost, and a path is limited to 16 hops.

Unfortunately, RIP has become increasingly inefficient on the Internet as the network continues its fast rate of growth. Current routing protocols for many of today's LANs are based upon RIP, including those associated with NetWare, AppleTalk, VINES, and DECnet. The IANA maintains a list of RIP message types. The Open Shortest Path First (OSPF) protocol is a link state routing algorithm that is more robust than RIP, converges faster, requires less network bandwidth, and is better able to scale to larger networks. With OSPF, a router broadcasts only changes in its links' status rather than entire routing tables, making it more robust and scalable than RIP. OSPF Version 2 is described in RFC 1583.

The Border Gateway Protocol version 4 (BGP-4) is an *exterior gateway protocol* because it is used to provide routing information between Internet routing domains. BGP is a distance vector protocol, like RIP, but unlike almost all other distance vector protocols, BGP tables store the actual route to the destination network. BGP-4 also supports policy-based routing, which allows a network's administrator to create routing policies based on political, security, legal, or economic issues rather than technical ones. BGP-4 also supports CIDR. BGP-4 is described in RFC 1771, while RFC 1268describes use of BGP in the Internet. In addition, the IANA maintains a list of BGP parameters.

As an alternative to using a routing protocol, the routing table can be maintained using "static routing." One example of static routing is the configuration of a default gateway at a host system; if the host needs to send an IP packet off of the local LAN segment, it is just blindly forwarded to the default gateway (router). Edge router's, too, commonly use static routing; the single router connecting a site to an ISP, for example, will usually just have a static routing table entry indicating that all traffic leaving the local LAN be forwarded to the ISP's access router. Since there's only a single path into the ISP, a routing protocol is hardly necessary. All IP hosts and routers maintain a table that lists the most up-to-date routing information that that device knows. On a Windows system, you can examine the routing table by issuing a route print command; on Unix systems, use netstat -r.

IP Version 6

The official version of IP that has been in use since the early 1980s is *version 4*. Due to the tremendous growth of the

Internet and new emerging applications, it was recognized that a new version of IP was becoming necessary. In late 1995, IP version 6 (IPv6) was entered into the Internet Standards Track. The primary description of IPv6 is contained in RFC 1883 and a number of related specifications, including ICMPv6. The architecture and structure of IPv6 addresses is described in RFC 2373. In July 1999, the IANA delegated the initial IPv6 address space to the worldwide regional registries in order to begin immediate worldwide deployment of IPv6 addresses. More information can be found at APNIC, ARIN, and RIPE.

TRANSPORT LAYER PROTOCOLS

The TCP/IP protocol suite comprises two protocols that correspond roughly to the OSI Transport and Session Layers; these protocols are called the Transmission Control Protocol and the User Datagram Protocol (UDP).

Ports

Higher-layer applications are referred to by a port identifier in TCP/UDP messages. The port identifier and IP address together form a *socket*, and the end-to-end communication between two hosts is uniquely identified on the Internet by the four-tuple (source port, source address, destination port, destination address).

Port numbers are specified by a 16-bit number. Port numbers in the range 0-1023 are called *Well Known Ports*. These port numbers are assigned to the server side of an application and, on most systems, can only be used by processes with a high level of privilege (such as root or administrator).

Port numbers in the range 1024-49151 are called *Registered Ports*, and these are numbers that have been publicly defined as a convenience for the Internet community to avoid vendor conflicts. Server or client applications can use the port numbers in this range. The remaining port numbers, in the range 49152-65535, are called *Dynamic and/or Private Ports* and can be used freely by any client or server.

A complete list of port numbers that have been assigned can be found in the IANA's list of Port Numbers. An implementation-specific list of supported port numbers and services can be found in the services file, generally found in the/etc (Linux/Unix), c:\windows (Windows 9x, ME), orc:\$systemroot\system32\drivers\etc (Windows NT, 2000, et seq.) directory.

TCP

TCP, described in RFC 793, provides a virtual circuit (connection-oriented) communication service across the network. TCP includes rules for formatting messages, establishing and terminating virtual circuits, sequencing, flow control, and error correction. Most of the applications in the TCP/IP suite operate over the *reliable* transport service provided by TCP. The TCP data unit is called a segment; the name is due to the fact that TCP does not recognize messages, per se, but merely sends a block of bytes from the byte stream between sender and receiver.

The fields of the segment are:

- Source Port and Destination Port: Identify the source and destination ports to identify the end-to-end connection and higher-layer application.
- Sequence Number: Contains the sequence number of this segment's first data byte in the overall connection byte stream; since the sequence number refers to a byte count rather than a segment count, sequence numbers in contiguous TCP segments are not numbered sequentially.
- Acknowledgment Number: Used by the sender to acknowledge receipt of data; this field indicates the sequence number of the next byte expected from the receiver.
- Data Offset: Points to the first data byte in this segment; this field, then, indicates the segment header length.

UDP

UDP, described in RFC 768, provides an end-to-end

datagram (connectionless) service. Some applications, such as those that involve a simple query and response, are better suited to the datagram service of UDP because there is no time lost to virtual circuit establishment and termination. UDP's primary function is to add a port number to the IP address to provide a socket for the application.

ICMP

The Internet Control Message Protocol, described in RFC 792, is an adjunct to IP that notifies the sender of IP datagrams about abnormal events. This collateral protocol is particularly important in the connectionless environment of IP. ICMP is not a classic host-to-host protocols like TCP or UDP, but is host-to-host in the sense that one device (*e.g.*, a router or computer) is sending a message to another device (*e.g.*, another router or computer).

The commonly employed ICMP message types include:

- *Destination Unreachable*: Indicates that a packet cannot be delivered because the destination host cannot be reached. The reason for the non-delivery may be that the host or network is unreachable or unknown, the protocol or port is unknown or unusable, fragmentation is required but not allowed (DF-flag is set), or the network or host is unreachable for this type of service.
- *Echo and Echo Reply*: These two messages are used to check whether hosts are reachable on the network. One host sends an Echo message to the other, optionally containing some data, and the receiving host responds with an Echo Reply containing the same data. These messages are the basis for the Ping command.
- *Parameter Problem*: Indicates that a router or host encountered a problem with some aspect of the packet's Header.

TCP Logical Connections and ICMP

The server responds with a segment with the syn- and

ack-bits set, a Sequence Number of 1567, and an Acknowledgement Number of 801. The syn-bit and ISN of 1567 have the same meaning as above. The ack-bit indicates the value of the Acknowledgement Number field is valid and the ACK value of 801 is the way in which the server confirms the client's ISN. The final part of the three-way handshake is when the client sends a segment with just the ack-bit set. Note that the Acknowledgement Number field (1568) is one greater than the server's ISN.

This three-way handshake is sometimes referred to as an exchange of"syn, syn/ack, and ack" segments. It is important for a number of reasons. For individuals looking at packet traces, recognition of the three-way handshake is how to find the start of a connection. For firewalls, proxy severs, intrusion detectors, and other systems, it provides a way of knowing the direction of a TCP connection setup since rules may differ for outbound and inbound connections.

The second part of the TCP connection is data exchange. The information here is more or less made up for example purposes only; it shows a POP server sending a banner message to the client system, the user sending the"quit" command, and the server signing off. (Note that the"\n" indicates an"end-of-line" indicator.) These segments show the changing of, and relationship between, the client's and server's sequence and acknowledgement numbers.

The final phase is connection termination. Although TCP connections are full-duplex (even if a given application does not allow two-way simultaneous communication), the TCP protocol views the logical connection as a pair of simplex links. Therefore, connection termination requires four segments or, more properly, two pair of segments. In this case, the client sends the server a segment with the fin- and ack-bits set; the server responds with a segment with just the ack-bit set and the Acknowledgment Number is incremented. The server then sends a fin/ack segment to the client.

The paragraphs above describe a normal scenario setting up a TCP connection between a client and server. Two UDP hosts communicate in a similar fashion; one host sends a UDP datagram to the other which is presumably listening on the port indicated in the datagram.

TCP/IP APPLICATION LAYER

The TCP/IP Application Layer protocols support the applications and utilities that are the Internet. This section will list a number of these applications and show a sample packet decode of all protocol layers.

TCP and UDP Applications

Commonly used protocols (as shown in include:

- *Archie:* A utility that allows a user to search all registered anonymous FTP sites for files on a specified topic. Obsolete by the late-1990s, obviated by the World Wide Web.
- *BGP:* The Border Gateway Protocol version 4 (BGP-4) is a distance vector exterior gateway routing protocol, commonly used between two ISPs or between a customer site and ISP if there are multiple links. defines the structure of Internet names and their association with IP addresses, as well as the association of mail and name servers with domains.
- *Finger:* Used to determine the status of other hosts and/or users (RFC 1288).
- *FTP:* The File Transfer Protocol allows a user to transfer files between local and remote host computers (RFC 959).
- *Gopher:* A tool that allows users to search through data repositories using a menu-driven, hierarchical interface, with links to other sites. Obsolete today, obviated by the World Wide Web (RFC 1436).
- *HTTP:* The Hypertext Transfer Protocol is the basis for exchange of information over the World Wide Web (WWW). Various versions of HTTP are in use over the Internet, with HTTP version 1.1 (RFC 2616) being the most current. WWW pages are written in the Hypertext Markup Language (HTML), an ASCII-based, platform-independent formatting language (RFC 1866).

- *TACACS+:* The Terminal Access Controller Access Control System plus is a remote access protocol.
- *Telnet:* Short for Telecommunication Network, a virtual terminal protocol allowing a user logged on to one TCP/IP host to access other hosts on the network (RFC 854).
- *TFTP:* The Trivial File Transfer Protocol (TFTP) is used for some specialized simple file transfer applications.
- *Time/NTP:* Time and the Network Time Protocol (NTP) are used so that Internet hosts can synchronize their system time from well-known Internet time servers.

Protocol Analysis

Today's protocol analysers are usually software running on a computer or a specialized piece of hardware. In either case, the device's network interface card (NIC) operates in promiscuous mode so that the NIC captures every packet that flies by on the wire rather than only those packets addressed to this particular NIC. Most protocol analysers also provide a display with at least a partial interpretation of the packets.

After IP is the TCP information. Note that the destination port number is 110, the port associated with a POP3 server. Since the POP3 server port is the destination, it means that this packet contains a POP command to the server from the client (which we knew anyway by looking at the summary of frame 80 above).

Finally we see the POP3 command itself. When a POP3 client connects to the server, the first thing it does is send the username using the POP3 USERcommand. If the username is valid, the server asks for a password, which is sent from the client in a POP3 PASS command, which is shown here. The discussion here is only meant to readers a taste of one of the coolest tools that we get to play with in data communications; it is also an important tool for network managers and security administrators. There are a fair number of free or inexpensive software packet sniffers that one can acquire for Linux or Windows systems. One of the most popular istcpdump, which comes with many Linux distributions (*e.g.*, Red Hat 7.1). WinDump is a tcpdump implementation for Windows, and the same group distributes Analyser, a GUI packet sniffer. Ethereal is another GUI analyser, with version for both Windows and Linux. More information on these packages can be found at the author's Packet Sniffing and Protocol Analysis Software page.

COMMUNICATION PROTOCOL

TCP/IP is not merely a pair of communication protocols but is a suite of protocols, applications, and utilities. Increasingly, these protocols are referred to as the Internet Protocol Suite, but the older name will not disappear anytime soon. Applications and utilities reside in host, or end-communicating, systems. TCP provides a reliable, virtual circuit connection between the two hosts. (UDP, not shown, provides an end-to-end datagram connection at this layer.) IP provides a datagram (DG) transport service over any intervening subnetworks, including local and wide area networks. The underlying subnetwork may employ nearly any common local or wide area network technology.

Note that the term gateway is used for the device interconnecting the two subnets, a device usually called a router in LAN environments orintermediate system in OSI environments. In OSI terminology, a gateway is used to provide protocol conversion between two networks and/or applications. Internet specifications, standards, reports, humour, and tutorials are distributed as Request for Comments (RFC) documents. RFCs are all freely available on-line, and most are available in ASCII text format. Internet standards are documented in a subset of the RFCs, identified with an"STD" designation. RFC 2026 describes the Internet standards process and STD 1 always contains the official list of Internet standards.

PRACTICAL EXTRACTION AND REPORT LANGUAGE

Language historians will also note some vestiges of csh,

Pascal, and even BASIC-PLUS. Expression syntax corresponds quite closely to C expression syntax. Unlike most Unix utilities, perl does not arbitrarily limit the size of your data -- if you've got the memory, perl can slurp in your whole file as a single string. Recursion is of unlimited depth. And the hash tables used by associative arrays grow as necessary to prevent degraded performance.

Perl uses sophisticated pattern matching techniques to scan large amounts of data very quickly. Although optimized for scanning text, perl can also deal with binary data, and can make dbm files look like associative arrays (where dbm is available). Setuid perl scripts are safer than C programmes through a dataflow tracing mechanism which prevents many stupid security holes. If you have a problem that would ordinarily use sed or awk or sh, but it exceeds their capabilities or must run a little faster, and you don't want to write the silly thing in C, then perl may be for you. There are also translators to turn your sed and awk scripts into perl scripts. OK, enough hype.

STARTING PERL

Upon startup, perl looks for your script in one of the following places:

- Specified line by line via -e switches on the command line.
- Contained in the file specified by the first filename on the command line. (Note that systems supporting the #! notation invoke interpreters this way.)
- Passed in implicitly via standard input. This only works if there are no filename arguments -- to pass arguments to a stdin script you must explicitly specify a - for the script name.

DATA TYPES AND OBJECTS

Perl has three data types: scalars, arrays of scalars, and associative arrays of scalars. Normal arrays are indexed by number, and associative arrays by string. The interpretation of operations and values in perl sometimes depends on the requirements of the context around the operation or value. There are three major contexts: string, numeric and array. Certain operations return array values in contexts wanting an array, and scalar values otherwise.

(If this is true of an operation it will be mentioned in the documentation for that operation.) Operations which return scalars don't care whether the context is looking for a string or a number, but scalar variables and values are interpreted as strings or numbers as appropriate to the context. A scalar is interpreted as TRUE in the boolean sense if it is not the null string or 0. Booleans returned by operators are 1 for true and 0 or'' (the null string) for false.

There are actually two varieties of null string: defined and undefined. Undefined null strings are returned when there is no real value for something, such as when there was an error, or at end of file, or when you refer to an uninitialized variable or element of an array. An undefined null string may become defined the first time you access it, but prior to that you can use the defined() operator to determine whether the value is defined or not.

References to scalar variables always begin with'$', even when referring to a scalar that is part of an array. Thus:

```
$days          # a simple scalar variable
$days[28]      # 29th element of array @days
$days{'Feb'}# one value from an associative
                 array
$#days         # last index of array @days
but entire arrays or array slices are denoted
by'@':
@days              # ($days[0], $days[1],\|...
$days[n])
@days[3,4,5]       # same as @days[3.\|.5]
@days{'a','c'}  # same as ($days {'a'},
$days  {'c'})
and entire associative arrays are denoted by'%':
%days              # (key1, val1, key2, val2...)
```

Any of these eight constructs may serve as an lvalue, that is, may be assigned to. (It also turns out that an assignment is itself an lvalue in certain contexts--see examples under s, tr and chop.) Assignment to a scalar evaluates the righthand side in a scalar context, while assignment to an array or array slice evaluates the righthand side in an array context.

You may find the length of array @days by evaluating"$#days", as in csh. (Actually, it's not the length of the array, it's the subscript of the last element, since there is (ordinarily) a 0th element.) Assigning to $#days changes the length of the array. Shortening an array by this method does not actually destroy any values. Lengthening an array that was previously shortened recovers the values that were in those elements.

You can also gain some measure of efficiency by preextending an array that is going to get big. (You can also extend an array by assigning to an element that is off the end of the array. This differs from assigning to $#whatever in that intervening values are set to null rather than recovered.) You can truncate an array down to nothing by assigning the null list () to it. The following are exactly equivalent

```
@whatever = ();
$#whatever = $[- 1;
```

If you evaluate an array in a scalar context, it returns the length of the array. The following is always true:

```
scalar(@whatever) == $#whatever - $[+ 1;
```

If you evaluate an associative array in a scalar context, it returns a value which is true if and only if the array contains any elements. (If there are any elements, the value returned is a string consisting of the number of used buckets and the number of allocated buckets, separated by a slash.)

Multi-dimensional arrays are not directly supported, but see the discussion of the $; variable later for a means of emulating multiple subscripts with an associative array. You could also write a subroutine to turn multiple subscripts into a single subscript.

Every data type has its own namespace. You can, without fear of conflict, use the same name for a scalar variable, an array, an associative array, a filehandle, a subroutine name, and/or a label. Since variable and array references always start with'$','@', or'%', the"reserved" words aren't in fact reserved with respect to variable names. (They ARE reserved with respect to labels and filehandles, however, which don't have an initial special character.

Hint: you could sayopen(LOG,'logfile') rather than open(log,'logfile'). Using uppercase filehandles also improves readability and protects you from conflict with future reserved words.) Case IS significant--"FOO","Foo" and"foo" are all different names. Names which start with a letter may also contain digits and underscores. Names which do not start with a letter are limited to one character, *e.g.*"$%" or"$$". (Most of the one character names have a predefined significance to perl. More later.)

Numeric literals are specified in any of the usual floating point or integer formats:

```
12345
12345.67
.23E-10
0xffff       # hex
0377         # octal
4_294_967_296
```

String literals are delimited by either single or double quotes. They work much like shell quotes: double-quoted string literals are subject to backslash and variable substitution; single-quoted strings are not (except for \' and \e). The usual backslash rules apply for making characters such as newline, tab, etc., as well as some more exotic forms:

```
\t    tab
\n    newline
\r    return
\f    form feed
\b    backspace
\a    alarm (bell)
\e    escape
\033  octal char
\x1b  hex char
\c[   control char
\l    lowercase next char
```

```
\u    uppercase next char
\L    lowercase till \E
\U    uppercase till \E
\E    end case modification
```

You can also embed newlines directly in your strings, *i.e.* they can end on a different line than they begin. This is nice, but if you forget your trailing quote, the error will not be reported until perl finds another line containing the quote character, which may be much further on in the script.

Variable substitution inside strings is limited to scalar variables, normal array values, and array slices. (In other words, identifiers beginning with $ or @, followed by an optional bracketed expression as a subscript.) The following code segment prints out"The price is $100."

```
$Price ='$100';                    # not
                                   interpreted
print"The price is $Price.\n"; # interpreted
```

Note that you can put curly brackets around the identifier to delimit it from following alphanumerics. Also note that a single quoted string must be separated from a preceding word by a space, since single quote is a valid character in an identifier (see Packages).

Two special literals are __LINE__ and __FILE__, which represent the current line number and filename at that point in your programme. They may only be used as separate tokens; they will not be interpolated into strings. In addition, the token __END__ may be used to indicate the logical end of the script before the actual end of file.

Any following text is ignored, but may be read via the DATA filehandle. (The DATA filehandle may read data only from the main script, but not from any required file or evaluated string.) The two control characters ^D and ^Z are synonyms for __END__.

A word that doesn't have any other interpretation in the grammar will be treated as if it had single quotes around it. For this purpose, a word consists only of alphanumeric characters and underline, and must start with an alphabetic character. As with filehandles and labels, a bare word that consists entirely of lowercase letters risks conflict with future reserved words, and if you use the -w switch, Perl will warn you about any such words.

STATEMENTS

The only kind of simple statement is an expression evaluated for its side effects. Every simple statement must be terminated with a semicolon, unless it is the final statement in a block, in which case the semicolon is optional. (Semicolon is still encouraged there if the block takes up more than one line).

Any simple statement may optionally be followed by a single modifier, just before the terminating semicolon.

The possible modifiers are:

```
if EXPR
unless EXPR
while EXPR
until EXPR
```

The if and unless modifiers have the expected semantics. The while and until modifiers also have the expected semantics (conditional evaluated first), except when applied to a do-BLOCK or a do-SUBROUTINE command, in which case the block executes once before the conditional is evaluated.

This is so that you can write loops like:

```
do {
        $_ = <STDIN>;
  ...
} until $_ eq".\n";
```

EXPRESSIONS

This section has been split up into subsections based upon functionality, loosely based upon the Perl Reference Guide by Johan Vromans.

This is a departure from the original Perl manual, which should simplify on-line browsing. If you have problems with this organization, blame me (rgs@cs.cmu.edu) rather than Larry.

EXPRESSION TYPES

Flow Control Operations

do BLOCK

Returns the value of the last command in the sequence of commands indicated by BLOCK. When modified by a loop modifier, executes the BLOCK once before testing the loop condition. (On other statements the loop modifiers test the conditional first.)

do SUBROUTINE (LIST)

Executes a SUBROUTINE declared by a sub declaration, and returns the value of the last expression evaluated in SUBROUTINE. If there is no subroutine by that name, produces a fatal error. (You may use the"defined" operator to determine if a subroutine exists.) If you pass arrays as part of LIST you may wish to pass the length of the array in front of each array. (See the section on subroutines later on.) The parentheses are required to avoid confusion with the"do EXPR" form.

SUBROUTINE may also be a single scalar variable, in which case the name of the subroutine to execute is taken from the variable.

As an alternate (and preferred) form, you may call a subroutine by prefixing the name with an ampersand: &foo(@args). If you aren't passing any arguments, you don't have to use parentheses. If you omit the parentheses, no @_ array is passed to the subroutine.

The and form is also used to specify subroutines to the defined and undef operators:

```
 if (defined &$var) { &$var($parm); undef &$var;
}
```

do EXPR

Uses the value of EXPR as a filename and executes the contents of the file as a perl script. Its primary use is to include subroutines from a perl subroutine library.

```
 do'stat.pl';
is just like
```

```
eval \`cat stat.pl\`;
```

except that it's more efficient, more concise, keeps track of the current filename for error messages, and searches all the -I libraries if the file isn't in the current directory (see also the @INC array in Predefined Names). It's the same, however, in that it does reparse the file every time you call it, so if you are going to use the file inside a loop you might prefer to use -P and #include, at the expense of a little more startup time. (The main problem with #include is that cpp doesn't grok # comments--a workaround is to use";#" for standalone comments.)

Note that the following are NOT equivalent:

```
do $foo; # eval a file
do $foo(); # call a subroutine
```

Note that inclusion of library routines is better done with the"require" operator.

goto LABEL

Finds the statement labeled with LABEL and resumes execution there. Currently you may only go to statements in the main body of the programme that are not nested inside a do {} construct. This statement is not implemented very efficiently, and is here only to make the sed-to- perl translator easier. I may change its semantics at any time, consistent with support for translated sed scripts.

The concatenation assignment operator.

eq

String equality (== is numeric equality). For a mnemonic just think of"eq" as a string. (If you are used to the awk behaviour of using == for either string or numeric equality based on the current form of the comparands, beware! You must be explicit here.)

ne

String inequality (!= is numeric inequality).

lt

String less than.

gt

String greater than.

le

String less than or equal.

ge

String greater than or equal.

cmp

String comparison, returning -1, 0, or 1.

<=>

Numeric comparison, returning -1, 0, or 1.

=~

Certain operations search or modify the string"$_" by default. This operator makes that kind of operation work on some other string. The right argument is a search pattern, substitution, or translation. The left argument is what is supposed to be searched, substituted, or translated instead of the default"$_". The return value indicates the success of the operation.

(If the right argument is an expression other than a search pattern, substitution, or translation, it is interpreted as a search pattern at run time. This is less efficient than an explicit search, since the pattern must be compiled every time the expression is evaluated.) The precedence of this operator is lower than unary minus and autoincrement/decrement, but higher than everything else.

!~

Just like =~ except the return value is negated.

x

The repetition operator. Returns a string consisting of the left operand repeated the number of times specified by the right operand. In an array context, if the left operand is a list in parens, it repeats the list.

```
 print'-' x 80;  # print row of dashes
 print'-' x80;   # illegal, x80 is identifier
 print"\t" x ($tab/8),'' x.($tab%8);#   tab
over
 @ones = (1) x 80;       # an array of 80 1's
 @ones = (5) x @ones;   # set all elements to 5
```

x=

The repetition assignment operator. Only works on scalars.

The range operator, which is really two different operators depending on the context. In an array context, returns an array of values counting (by ones) from the left value to the right value. This is useful for writing"for (1..10)" loops and for doing slice operations on arrays.

In a scalar context.. returns a boolean value. The operator is bistable, like a flip-flop, and emulates the line-range (comma) operator of sed, awk, and various editors. Each.. operator maintains its own boolean state. It is false as long as its left operand is false. Once the left operand is true, the range operator stays true until the right operand is true, AFTER which the range operator becomes false again.

(It doesn't become false till the next time the range operator is evaluated. It can test the right operand and become false on the same evaluation it became true (as in awk), but it still returns true once. If you don't want it to test the right operand till the next evaluation (as in sed), use three dots (...) instead of two.) The right operand is not evaluated while the operator is in the"false" state, and the left operand is not evaluated while the operator is in the"true" state. The precedence is a little lower than || and &&.

The value returned is either the null string for false, or a sequence number (beginning with 1) for true. The sequence number is reset for each range encountered. The final sequence number in a range has the string'E0' appended to it, which doesn't affect its numeric value, but gives you something to search for if you want to exclude the endpoint. You can exclude the beginning point by waiting for the sequence number to be greater than 1. If either operand of scalar.. is static, that operand is implicitly compared to the $. variable, the current line number.

Examples:

As a scalar operator:

```
if (101.. 200) { print; } # print 2nd hundred
lines
next line if (1../^$/);    # skip header lines

s/^/>/ if (/^$/.. eof());   # quote body
```

```
As an array operator:
for (101.. 200) { print; }# print $_ 100 times
@foo = @foo[$[.. $#foo]; # an expensive no-op
@foo = @foo[$#foo-4.. $#foo]; # slice last 5
items
```

-x

A file test. This unary operator takes one argument, either a filename or a filehandle, and tests the associated file to see if something is true about it. If the argument is omitted, tests $_, except for -t, which tests STDIN. It returns 1 for true and'' for false, or the undefined value if the file doesn't exist. Precedence is higher than logical and relational operators, but lower than arithmetic operators.

The operator may be any of:

```
-r File is readable by effective uid/gid.
-w File is writable by effective uid/gid.
-x File is executable by effective uid/gid.
-o File is owned by effective uid.
-R File is readable by real uid/gid.
-W File is writable by real uid/gid.
-X File is executable by real uid/gid.
-O File is owned by real uid.
-e File exists.
-z File has zero size.
-s File has non-zero size (returns size).
-f File is a plain file.
-d File is a directory.
-l File is a symbolic link.
-p File is a named pipe (FIFO).
-S File is a socket.
-b File is a block special file.
-c File is a character special file.
-u File has setuid bit set.
-g File has setgid bit set.
-k File has sticky bit set.
-t Filehandle is opened to a tty.
-T File is a text file.
-B File is a binary file (opposite of -T).
```

```
-M Age of file in days when script started.
-A Same for access time.
-C Same for inode change time.
```

The interpretation of the file permission operators -r, -R, -w, -W, -x and -X is based solely on the mode of the file and the uids and gids of the user. There may be other reasons you can't actually read, write or execute the file. Also note that, for the superuser, -r, -R, -w and -W always return 1, and -x and -X return 1 if any execute bit is set in the mode. Scripts run by the superuser may thus need to do a stat() in order to determine the actual mode of the file, or temporarily set the uid to something else.

Example:

```
while (<>) {
        chop;
        next unless -f $_; # ignore specials
        ...
}
```

Note that -s/a/b/ does not do a negated substitution. Saying -exp($foo) still works as expected, however--only single letters following a minus are interpreted as file tests.

The -T and -B switches work as follows. The first block or so of the file is examined for odd characters such as strange control codes or metacharacters. If too many odd characters (>10%) are found, it's a -B file, otherwise it's a -T file. Also, any file containing null in the first block is considered a binary file. If -T or -B is used on a filehandle, the current stdio buffer is examined rather than the first block. Both -T and -B return TRUE on a null file, or a file at EOF when testing a filehandle.

If any of the file tests (or either stat operator) are given the special filehandle consisting of a solitary underline, then the stat structure of the previous file test (or stat operator) is used, saving a system call. (This doesn't work with -t, and you need to remember that lstat and -l will leave values in the stat structure for the symbolic link, not the real file.)

Example:

```
print"Can do.\n" if -r $a || -w _ || -x _;
stat($filename);
```

```
print"Readable\n" if -r _;
print"Writable\n" if -w _;
print"Executable\n" if -x _;
print"Setuid\n" if -u _;
print"Setgid\n" if -g _;
print"Sticky\n" if -k _;
print"Text\n" if -T _;
print"Binary\n" if -B _;
```

Here is what C has that perl doesn't:

unary &

Address-of operator.

unary *

Dereference-address operator.

(TYPE)

Type casting operator.

Like C, perl does a certain amount of expression evaluation at compile time, whenever it determines that all of the arguments to an operator are static and have no side effects. In particular, string concatenation happens at compile time between literals that don't do variable substitution. Backslash interpretation also happens at compile time. You can say

```
'Now is the time for all'."\n".
'good men to come to.'
```

and this all reduces to one string internally.

The autoincrement operator has a little extra built-in magic to it. If you increment a variable that is numeric, or that has ever been used in a numeric context, you get a normal increment.

If, however, the variable has only been used in string contexts since it was set, and has a value that is not null and matches the pattern/^[a-zA-Z]*[0-9]*$/, the increment is done as a string, preserving each character within its range, with carry:

```
print ++($foo ='99'); # prints'100'
print ++($foo ='a0'); # prints'a1'
print ++($foo ='Az'); # prints'Ba'
print ++($foo ='zz'); # prints'aaa'
```

The autodecrement is not magical. The range operator (in an array context) makes use of the magical autoincrement algorithm if the minimum and maximum are strings. You can say @alphabet = ('A'..'Z'); to get all the letters of the alphabet, or $hexdigit = (0.. 9,'a'..'f')[$num & 15]; to get a hexadecimal digit, or @z2 = ('01'..'31'); print @z2[$mday]; to get dates with leading zeros. (If the final value specified is not in the sequence that the magical increment would produce, the sequence goes until the next value would be longer than the final value specified.)

The || and && operators differ from C's in that, rather than returning 0 or 1, they return the last value evaluated. *Thus, a portable way to find out the home directory might be:*

```
$home = $ENV{'HOME'} || $ENV{'LOGDIR'} ||
    (getpwuid($<))[7] || die"You're
                          homeless!\n";
```

Along with the literals and variables mentioned earlier, the operations in the following section can serve as terms in an expression. Some of these operations take a LIST as an argument. Such a list can consist of any combination of scalar arguments or array values; the array values will be included in the list as if each individual element were interpolated at that point in the list, forming a longer single-dimensional array value.

Elements of the LIST should be separated by commas. If an operation is listed both with and without parentheses around its arguments, it means you can either use it as a unary operator or as a function call. To use it as a function call, the next token on the same line must be a left parenthesis.

(There may be intervening white space.) Such a function then has highest precedence, as you would expect from a function. If any token other than a left parenthesis follows, then it is a unary operator, with a precedence depending only on whether it is a LIST operator or not.

LIST operators have lowest precedence. All other unary operators have a precedence greater than relational operators but less than arithmetic operators. See the section on Precedence.

For operators that can be used in either a scalar or array context, failure is generally indicated in a scalar context by returning the undefined value, and in an array context by returning the null list. Remember though that there is no general rule for converting a list into a scalar.

Each operator decides which sort of scalar it would be most appropriate to return. Some operators return the length of the list that would have been returned in an array context. Some operators return the first value in the list. Some operators return the last value in the list. Some operators return a count of successful operations. In general, they do what you want, unless you want consistency.

Arithmetic Functions

atan2(Y,X)
Returns the arctangent of Y/X in the range -PI to PI.

cos(EXPR)
cos EXPR
Returns the cosine of EXPR (expressed in radians). If EXPR is omitted takes cosine of $_.

exp(EXPR)
exp EXPR
Returns e to the power of EXPR. If EXPR is omitted, gives exp($_).

int(EXPR)
int EXPR
Returns the integer portion of EXPR. If EXPR is omitted, uses $_.

log(EXPR)
log EXPR
Returns logarithm (base e) of EXPR. If EXPR is omitted, returns log of $_.

rand(EXPR)
rand EXPR
rand

Returns a random fractional number between 0 and the value of EXPR. (EXPR should be positive.) If EXPR is omitted, returns a value between 0 and 1. See also srand().

sin(EXPR)

sin EXPR

Returns the sine of EXPR (expressed in radians). If EXPR is omitted, returns sine of $_.

sqrt(EXPR)

sqrt EXPR

Return the square root of EXPR. If EXPR is omitted, returns square root of $_.

srand(EXPR)

srand EXPR

Sets the random number seed for the rand operator. If EXPR is omitted, does srand(time).

Conversion Functions

gmtime(EXPR)

gmtime EXPR

Converts a time as returned by the time function to a 9-element array with the time analysed for the Greenwich timezone. Typically used as follows:

```
($sec,$min,$hour,$mday,$mon,$year,$wday,$yday,$isdst)
=
                gmtime(time);
```

All array elements are numeric, and come straight out of a struct tm. In particular this means that $mon has the range 0..11 and $wday has the range 0..6. If EXPR is omitted, does gmtime(time).

hex(EXPR)

hex EXPR

Template is a sequence of characters that give the order and type of values, as follows:

A An ascii string, will be space padded.

a An ascii string, will be null padded.

c A signed char value.
C An unsigned char value.
s A signed short value.
S An unsigned short value.
i A signed integer value.
I An unsigned integer value.
l A signed long value.
L An unsigned long value.
n A short in"network" order.
N A long in"network" order.
f A single-precision float in the native format.
d A double-precision float in the native format.
p A pointer to a string.
v A short in"VAX" (little-endian) order.
V A long in"VAX" (little-endian) order.
x A null byte.
X Back up a byte.
@ Null fill to absolute position.
u A uuencoded string.
b A bit string (ascending bit order, like vec()).
B A bit string (descending bit order).
h A hex string (low nybble first).
H A hex string (high nybble first).

Each letter may optionally be followed by a number which gives a repeat count. With all types except"a","A","b","B","h" and"H", the pack function will gobble up that many values from the LIST. A * for the repeat count means to use however many items are left. The"a" and"A" types gobble just one value, but pack it as a string of length count, padding with nulls or spaces as necessary.

(When unpacking,"A" strips trailing spaces and nulls, but"a" does not.) Likewise, the"b" and"B" fields pack a string that many bits long. The"h" and"H" fields pack a string that many nybbles long. Real numbers (floats and doubles) are in the native machine format only; due to the multiplicity of floating formats around, and the lack of a standard"network" representation, no facility for interchange has been made.

This means that packed floating point data written on one machine may not be readable on another - even if both use IEEE floating point arithmetic (as the endian-ness of the memory representation is not part of the IEEE spec). Note that perl uses doubles internally for all numeric calculation, and converting from double -> float -> double will lose precision (*i.e.* unpack("f", pack("f", $foo)) will not in general equal $foo).

Examples:

```
$foo = pack("cccc",65,66,67,68);
# foo eq"ABCD"
$foo = pack("c4",65,66,67,68);
# same thing
$foo = pack("ccxxcc",65,66,67,68);
# foo eq"AB\0\0CD"
$foo = pack("s2",1,2);
#"\1\0\2\0" on little-endian
#"\0\1\0\2" on big-endian
$foo = pack("a4","abcd","x","y","z");
#"abcd"
$foo = pack("aaaa","abcd","x","y","z");
#"axyz"
$foo = pack("a14","abcdefg");
#"abcdefg\0\0\0\0\0\0\0"
$foo = pack("i9pl", gmtime);
# a real struct tm (on my system anyway)
sub bintodec {
 unpack("N", pack("B32", substr("0" x 32.
shift, -32)));
}
```

The same template may generally also be used in the unpack function.

unpack(TEMPLATE,EXPR)

Unpack does the reverse of pack: It takes a string representing a structure and expands it out into an array value, returning the array value. (In a scalar context, it merely returns the first value produced.) The TEMPLATE has the same format as in the pack function. Here's a subroutine that does substring:

```
sub substr {
  local($what,$where,$howmuch) = @_;
  unpack("x$where a$howmuch", $what);
}
and then there's
sub ord { unpack("c",$_[0]); }
```

In addition, you may prefix a field with a%<number> to indicate that you want a <number>-bit checksum of the items instead of the items themselves. Default is a 16-bit checksum.

For example, the following computes the same number as the System V sum programme:

```
while (<>) {
  $checksum += unpack("%16C*", $_);
}
$checksum%= 65536;
```

vec(EXPR,OFFSET,BITS)

Treats a string as a vector of unsigned integers, and returns the value of the bitfield specified. May also be assigned to. BITS must be a power of two from 1 to 32.

Vectors created with vec() can also be manipulated with the logical operators |, & and ^, which will assume a bit vector operation is desired when both operands are strings. This interpretation is not enabled unless there is at least one vec() in your programme, to protect older programmes.

To transform a bit vector into a string or array of 0's and 1's, use these:

```
$bits = unpack("b*", $vector);
@bits = split(//, unpack("b*", $vector));
```

If you know the exact length in bits, it can be used in place of the *.

String Functions

```
chop
chop(LIST)
chop(VARIABLE)
chop VARIABLE
```

chop

Chops off the last character of a string and returns the character chopped. It's used primarily to remove the newline from the end of an input record, but is much more efficient than s/\n// because it neither scans nor copies the string. If VARIABLE is omitted, chops $_.

Example:

```
while (<>) {
  chop; # avoid \n on last field
  @array = split(/:/);
  ...
}
```

You can actually chop anything that's an lvalue, including an assignment:

```
chop($cwd = \`pwd\`);
chop($answer = <STDIN>);
```

If you chop a list, each element is chopped. Only the value of the last chop is returned.

crypt(PLAINTEXT,SALT)

Encrypts a string exactly like the crypt() function in the C library. Useful for checking the password file for lousy passwords. Only the guys wearing white hats should do this.

eval(EXPR)

eval EXPR

eval BLOCK

EXPR is parsed and executed as if it were a little perl programme. It is executed in the context of the current perl programme, so that any variable settings, subroutine or format definitions remain afterwards. The value returned is the value of the last expression evaluated, just as with subroutines. If there is a syntax error or runtime error, or a die statement is executed, an undefined value is returned by eval, and $@ is set to the error message. If there was no error, $@ is guaranteed to be a null string. If EXPR is omitted, evaluates $_. The final semicolon, if any, may be omitted from the expression.

Note that, since eval traps otherwise-fatal errors, it is useful for determining whether a particular feature (such as dbmopen or symlink) is implemented. It is also Perl's exception trapping mechanism, where the die operator is used to raise exceptions.

If the code to be executed doesn't vary, you may use the eval-BLOCK form to trap run-time errors without incurring the penalty of recompiling each time. The error, if any, is still returned in $@. Evaluating a single-quoted string (as EXPR) has the same effect, except that the eval-EXPR form reports syntax errors at run time via $@, whereas the eval-BLOCK form reports syntax errors at compile time.

The eval-EXPR form is optimized to eval-BLOCK the first time it succeeds. (Since the replacement side of a substitution is considered a single-quoted string when you use the e modifier, the same optimization occurs there.) Examples:

```
# make divide-by-zero non-fatal
eval { $answer = $a/ $b; }; warn $@ if $@;
# optimized to same thing after first use
eval'$answer = $a/ $b'; warn $@ if $@;
# a compile-time error
eval { $answer = };
# a run-time error
eval'$answer ='; # sets $@
```

index(STR,SUBSTR,POSITION)

index(STR,SUBSTR)

Returns the position of the first occurrence of SUBSTR in STR at or after POSITION. If POSITION is omitted, starts searching from the beginning of the string. The return value is based at 0, or whatever you've set the $[variable to. If the substring is not found, returns one less than the base, ordinarily -1.

length(EXPR)

length EXPR

Returns the length in characters of the value of EXPR. If EXPR is omitted, returns length of $_.

q/STRING/

qq/STRING/

qx/STRING/

These are not really functions, but simply syntactic sugar

to let you avoid putting too many backslashes into quoted strings. The q operator is a generalized single quote, and the qq operator a generalized double quote. The qx operator is a generalized backquote. Any non-alphanumeric delimiter can be used in place of/, including newline. If the delimiter is an opening bracket or parenthesis, the final delimiter will be the corresponding closing bracket or parenthesis. (Embedded occurrences of the closing bracket need to be backslashed as usual.) *Examples*:

```
   $foo = q!I said,"You said,'She said it.'"!;
   $bar = q('This is it.');
   $today = qx{ date };
   $_.= qq
*** The previous line contains the naughty
word"$&".\n
              if/(ibm|apple|awk)/;  #:-)
```

rindex(STR,SUBSTR,POSITION)

rindex(STR,SUBSTR)

Works just like index except that it returns the position of the LAST occurrence of SUBSTR in STR. If POSITION is specified, returns the last occurrence at or before that position.

substr(EXPR,OFFSET,LEN)

substr(EXPR,OFFSET)

Extracts a substring out of EXPR and returns it. First character is at offset 0, or whatever you've set $[to. If OFFSET is negative, starts that far from the end of the string. If LEN is omitted, returns everything to the end of the string. You can use the substr() function as an lvalue, in which case EXPR must be an lvalue. If you assign something shorter than LEN, the string will shrink, and if you assign something longer than LEN, the string will grow to accommodate it. To keep the string the same length you may need to pad or chop your value using sprintf().

Array and List Functions

delete $ASSOC{KEY}

Deletes the specified value from the specified associative array. Returns the deleted value, or the undefined value if nothing was deleted. Deleting from $ENV{} modifies the environment. Deleting from an array bound to a dbm file deletes the entry from the dbm file.

The following deletes all the values of an associative array:

```
foreach $key (keys%ARRAY) {
  delete $ARRAY{$key};
}
```

(But it would be faster to use the reset command. Saying undef%ARRAY is faster yet.)

each(ASSOC_ARRAY)

each ASSOC_ARRAY

Returns a 2 element array consisting of the key and value for the next value of an associative array, so that you can iterate over it. Entries are returned in an apparently random order. When the array is entirely read, a null array is returned (which when assigned produces a FALSE (0) value). The next call to each() after that will start iterating again.

The iterator can be reset only by reading all the elements from the array. You must not modify the array while iterating over it. There is a single iterator for each associative array, shared by all each(), keys() and values() function calls in the programme. The following prints out your environment like the printenv programme, only in a different order:

```
while (($key,$value) = each%ENV) {
  print"$key=$value\n";
}
```

See also keys() and values().

grep(EXPR,LIST)

Evaluates EXPR for each element of LIST (locally setting $_ to each element) and returns the array value consisting of those elements for which the expression evaluated to true. In a scalar context, returns the number of times the expression was true.

```
@foo = grep(!/^#/, @bar); # weed out comments
```

Note that, since $_ is a reference into the array value, it can be used to modify the elements of the array. While this is useful and supported, it can cause bizarre results if the LIST is not a named array.

join(EXPR,LIST)
join(EXPR,ARRAY)

Joins the separate strings of LIST or ARRAY into a single string with fields separated by the value of EXPR, and returns the string. Example:

```
$_ = join(':',
$login,$passwd,$uid,$gid,$gcos,$home,$shell);
```

keys(ASSOC_ARRAY)
keys ASSOC_ARRAY

Returns a normal array consisting of all the keys of the named associative array. The keys are returned in an apparently random order, but it is the same order as either the values() or each() function produces (given that the associative array has not been modified). Here is yet another way to print your environment:

```
 @keys = keys%ENV;
 @values = values%ENV;
 while ($#keys >= 0) {
   print pop(@keys),'=', pop(@values),"\n";
 }
or how about sorted by key:

 foreach $key (sort(keys%ENV)) {
   print $key,'=', $ENV{$key},"\n";
 }
```

pop(ARRAY)
pop ARRAY

Pops and returns the last value of the array, shortening the array by 1. Has the same effect as

```
 $tmp = $ARRAY[$#ARRAY--];
```

If there are no elements in the array, returns the undefined value.

push(ARRAY,LIST)

Treats ARRAY (@ is optional) as a stack, and pushes the values of LIST onto the end of ARRAY. The length of ARRAY increases by the length of LIST. Has the same effect as

```
for $value (LIST) {
   $ARRAY[++$#ARRAY] = $value;
```

}

but is more efficient.

reverse(LIST)

reverse LIST

In an array context, returns an array value consisting of the elements of LIST in the opposite order. In a scalar context, returns a string value consisting of the bytes of the first element of LIST in the opposite order.

shift(ARRAY)

shift ARRAY

shift

Shifts the first value of the array off and returns it, shortening the array by 1 and moving everything down. If there are no elements in the array, returns th©e undefined value. If ARRAY is omitted, shifts the @ARGV array in the main programme, and the @_ array in subroutines. (This is determined lexically.) See also unshift(), push() and pop(). Shift() and unshift() do the same thing to the left end of an array that push() and pop() do to the right end.

sort(SUBROUTINE LIST)

sort(LIST)

sort SUBROUTINE LIST

sort BLOCK LIST

sort LIST

Sorts the LIST and returns the sorted array value. Nonexistent values of arrays are stripped out. If SUBROUTINE or BLOCK is omitted, sorts in standard string comparison order. If SUBROUTINE is specified, gives the name of a subroutine that returns an integer less than, equal to, or greater than 0, depending on how the elements of the array are to be ordered. (The <=> and cmp operators are extremely useful in such routines.) SUBROUTINE may be a scalar variable name, in which case the value provides the name of the subroutine to use. In place of a SUBROUTINE name, you can provide a BLOCK as an anonymous, in-line sort subroutine.

3

Role of Markup Language

HTML

HTML instructions divide the text of a document into blocks called elements. These can be divided into two broad categories -- those that define how the BODY of the document is to be displayed by the browser, and those that define information `about' the document, such as the title or relationships to other documents. The vocabulary of these elements and a description of the overall design of HTML documents is given in the rest of Section 2. The Last part of the section also describes standard naming schemes for HTML documents and related files.

The detailed rules for HTML (the names of the tags/ elements, how they can be used) are defined using another language known as the standard generalized markup language, or SGML. SGML is wickedly difficult, and was designed for massive document collections, such as repair manuals for F-16 fighters, or maintenance plans for nuclear submarines. Fortunately, HTML is much simpler!

However, SGML has useful features that HTML lacks. For this reason, markup language and software experts have developed a new language, called XML (the eXtensible markup language) which has most of the most useful features of HTML and SGML.

ELEMENTS

The HTML instructions, along with the text to which the instructions apply, are called HTML elements. The HTML instructions are themselves called tags, and look like <element_name> -- that is, they are simply the element name surrounded by left and right angle brackets.

Most elements mark blocks of the document for particular purpose or formatting: the above <element_name> tag marks the beginning of such as section. The end of this section is then marked by the ending tag </element_name> -- note the leading slash character"/" that appears in front of the element name in an end tag. End, or stop tags are always indicated by this leading slash character.

For example, the heading at the top of this page is an H2 element, (a level 2 heading) which is written as:

<H2> 2.1 Elements in HTML </H2>.

Empty Elements

Some elements are empty -- that is, they do not affect a block of the document in some way. These elements do not require an endingtag. An example is the <HR> element, which draws a horizontal line across the page. This element would simply be entered as

<HR>

Upper and Lower Case

Element names are case insensitive. Thus, the the horizontal rule element can be written as any of <hr>, <Hr> or <HR>.

Elements can have Attributes

Many elements can have arguments that pass parameters to the interpreter handling this element. These arguments are called attributesof the element. For example, consider the element A, which marks a region of text as the beginning (or end) of a hypertext link. This element can have several attributes. One of them, HREF, specifies the hypertext document to which the marked piece of text is linked.

To specify this in the tag for a you write:

```
<A HREF="http://www.somewhere.ca/file.html">
marked text </a>.
```

where the attribute HREF is assigned the indicated value. Note that the A element is not empty, and that it is closed by the tag </a>. Note also that end tags never take attributes -- the attributes to an element are always placed in the start tag.

HTML DOCUMENT STRUCTURE

HTML documents are structured into two parts, the HEAD, and the BODY. Both of these are contained within the HTML element -- this element simply denotes this as an HTML document.

The head contains information about the document that is not generally displayed with the document, such as its TITLE. The BODYcontains the body of the text, and is where you place the document material to be displayed. Elements allowed inside the HEAD, such as TITLE, are not allowed inside the BODY, and vice versa.

SCHEME FOR HTML DOCUMENTS

When your HTML browser (Netscape Navigator, Internet Explorer, Opera, lynx etc.....) retrieves a file, it must know what type of data it has received in order to know what to do with it. Hypertext (that is, HTTP) servers explicitly tell the browser the type of the data being sent. In other cases, such as when the browser is using FTP to access a remote file, or when the browser is reading a file from your local disk (such as when you are editing pages prior to publishing them to a Web server), the browsers"guesses" the data type from the filename extension -- that is the part after the dot in the filename. For example, HTML files are identified by names such as name.html, where the.html extension indicates an HTML document.

Four letter extensions are common. This is not a problem with UNIX computers or Macintoshes, since these machines place no restriction on the filename. DOS and Windows 3.1 machines are unfortunately restricted to a three letter extension. Generally the extension is truncated to three letters (*i.e.*.html becomes.htm).

Here are some of the standard extensions, and their meanings:

`.html (also.htm)`

HTML document, containing text and HTML mark-up instructions.

`.txt`

MIME Types and File Data Formats

The World Wide Web actually uses MIME types (Multipurpose Internet Mail Extension) to define the type of a particular piece of information being sent from a Web server to a browser. A browser in turn determines, from the MIME type, how the data should be treated.

Each browser has a configuration (menu or file) that maps the types of the data to particular functions. A browser can handle many types of data itself (*e.g.* HTML documents, GIF images) while other types are passed to auxiliary programmes, such as image viewers, movie or sound players, plugins, and so on.

HTTP servers send MIME contents-types header messages ahead of every file they deliver to a browser. This header explicitly tells the browser what type of data is being sent. Thus a server must have a way of telling the type of data it is sending. Usually the server has a configuration file that relates filename extensions to the appropriate MIME type.

For example, the MIME type for HTML documents istext/ html. Thus, if a browser reqests that a server send the file blobs.html, the server first looks up the MIME type corresponding to the.html extension. The server then sends a message to the browser saying that data of content-type text/ html is being sent, after which the server sends the actual data.

Other servers, such as FTP servers, do not send this MIME type information. In this case, the browser"guesses" the MIME type, based on the filename extension. Thus each browser must be configured with a list that relates typical extensions to the"most likely" type of data. This is also how a browser determines the type of files accessed locally of the computer.

More Information about MIME Types

For more information on MIME types see the Internet Draft document defining the MIME format: RFC 1341. I have also assembled a non-autoritative list of MIME types, which is useful for understanding the different types that are in current use.

VERSIONS OF HTML

HTML is an evolving language, and each new version is given a number. The first definitive version was HTML 2.0 -- this had most of the elements we know and love, but was missing some of the Netscape/Microsoft extensions, and did not support tables, or ALIGN attributes.

HTML 3 (late 1995) was an ambitious effort on the part of Dave Raggett to upgrade the features and utility of HTML. However, it was never completed or implemented, although many features were integrated in the next"official" version of HTML, known as HTML 3.2.

HTML 3.2 was the next official version, integrating support for TABLES, image, heading and other element ALIGN attributes, and a few other finicky details. HTML 3.2 is the current"universal" dialect -- essentially all browsers understand HTML 3.2. IT was, however, missing some of the Netscape/Microsoft extensions, such as FRAMEs, EMBED and APPLET. Support for these (after a fashion) came in HTML 4.0

HTML 4.01 is the current official standard. It includes support for most of the proprietary extensions, plus support for extra features (Internationalized documents, support for Cascading Style Sheets, extra TABLE, FORM, and JavaScript enhancements), that are not universally supported. Some of these enhancements are not discussed in these online notes. They are discussed in detail in The HTML 4.0 Sourcebook, available in most bookstores about the various versions of HTML, you are also referred to the bibliography, which contains references to the various specifications, and to my online resource that defines the structural rules of the different HTML variants, found at the URL However, the evolution of

HTML has now ceased -- HTML 4.01 is the last version of HTML. For the future, HTML is being replaced by a new language, called XHTML -- for the eXtensible HyperText Markup Language.

WHAT IS XHTML

The evolution of HTML has essentially stopped. Instead, HTML is being replaced by a new language, called XHTML. XHTML is in many ways similar to HTML, but is designed to work with the new eXtensible Markup Language, or XML, that will soon serve as the core language for designing all sorts of new Web applications, in which XHTML will be only one of many"languages." But, XHTML is designed to work with these other language, so that different documents, in different languages, can be easily mixed together.

For this to work, the rules for writing HTML documents had to change.

These rules are simple, and are as follows:

- All tag and attribute names must be in lowercase. Thus, you can't write

```
<A HREF="foo.html">...</A>
```

but must instead write this in lowercase, as:

```
<a href="foo.html">...</a>
```

- "Empty" tags must be written with an extra slash at the end. An empty tag is one like <br> or <img src="foo.html"> that doesn't have a </br> or <img> to end it. In XHTML, such tags must be written as: <br/ >, and <img src="foo.gif"/>.
- You can never omit an end tag. With HTML, you could sometimes leave off an end tag, as in

```
<p>..... paragraph text
<p>..... more paragraph text
```

With XHTML, you must always put in the end tag, so that the preceding must be written as:

```
<p>..... paragraph text </p>
<p>..... more paragraph text </p>
```

- Attributes must always have a value. In HTML you can sometimes omit atttibute values, as in

```
<hr size="2" noshade>
in XHTML, this would need to be written as:
<hr size="2" noshade="noshade"/>
```

- Attributes values must always be quoted.. In HTML you can sometimes omit the quotes,as in

```
<hr size=2>
```

in XHTML, this would need to be written as:

```
<hr size="2"/>
```

That's about it -- there are a few more subtle details, but essentially if you follow the above rules, then the documents you write are acceptable as XHTML. Thus it's easy to write up Web pages using the XHTML format -- they will work with today's HTML browsers, and are easily upward-compatible for the next-generation of Web browsers.

WHAT IS CSS

HTML or XHTML only divide a document up into paragraphs, lists, headings and so on, but does not really say how these things shouldlook. Rather, a browser generally makes some assumptions about how things should look -- and we're then stuck with those choices.

This could be changed given a way of controlling how different markup elements (like headings, paragraphs, etc) look. This is the role of CSS. Cascading Style Sheets, or CSS, is a language, separate from HTML or XHTML, designed for specifying the layout or formatting properties of the various HTML elements in a document. For example, a CSS statment like the following

```
body { font-family: Arial,helvetica,sans-serif;
colour: black;
background-colour: white;
}
```

means that, inside the BODY of a document, the desired font is Arial, the desired text colour is black, and the desired background colour for the page is white. More complicated rules let you control underlining of links, the placement of background images, the widths of margins, the colours of borders around paragraphs or headings, etc.

aAs an example, the page you are viewing has an"attached" style sheet to control how it looks. This stylesheet is includded into this document using a special link element of the form:

```
<link rel="stylesheet" href="stylesheet.css" >
```

where stylesheet.css contains the CSS document. You can click on the word stylesheet.css above to see this stylesheet document. CSS is a rich and complicated language -- in its own way just as complex as HTML. There is not much in this Website on CSS, although my book, The XHTML 1.0 Language and Design Sourcebook discusses CSS and XHTML in detail). The reference section of this Website, however, has a number of references to useful CSS information sites.

HEAD

The HEAD contains general information, or meta-information, about the document. It is the first thing in any document, lying above the BODY and just after the <HTML> tag starting the document.

The contents of the HEAD are not displayed as part of the document text: the displayed material is found within the BODY. Consequently, only certain mark-up elements can be placed within the HEAD.

These are:

- Base -- A record of the original URL of the document: This allows you to move the document to a new directory (or even a new site) and have relative URLs access the appropriate place with respect to the original URL.

Isindex -- Usually placed in the HEAD by the server or a server script/programme to indicate that a document is searchable.

- Link -- Defines the relationship(s) between this document and another or others. A document can have several LINK elements.
- Meta -- A container for document metainformation.
- Nextid -- A parameter used by automated HTML editors to create unique identifiers for the documents.

ISINDEX

This element tells the browser that the document is an index document. This causes the browser to create a user-input field into which the user can type words to be used in the index search. In a sense, this means that, in addition to being viewed and read, the"document" can in some way be examined or queried.

It is important to realise that this does not mean a simple text search through the document being viewed. When the user types in words and presses ENTER (or whatever key or button is appropriate) the search information is sent back to a server -- thus the server machine actually does the searching. In a sense, you can think of an ISINDEX document as being a front-end to a some kind of indexing or querying programme residing on the HTTP server.

Construction of ISINDEX Query

Keywords from ISINDEX queries are passed to the server by suffixing, to the URL from which the document originated, a question mark followed by a list of keywords, separated by plus signs. Thus if the URL for a document containing an ISINDEX element was

```
http://www.here.ca/cgi-bin/srch
```

then typing the word"instructional" into the ISINDEX query window and submitting the query would access the URL

```
http://www.here.ca/cgi-bin/srch?instructional
```

Appropriate Use of ISINDEX

The ISINDEX element is usually generated automatically by a server-side script, or gateway programme. You should not add this element by hand into a regular HTML document.

The use of ISINDEX to generate a server-side search is described. To some degree the use of ISINDEX has been supplanted by the more sophisticated FORMS interface.

Netscape Enhancements to ISINDEX

Netscape introduced two new attributes to the ISINDEX

element, which are commonly supported and with are included in the HTML 4.0 specification.

ENHANCEMENTS TO ISINDEX

HTML 4.0 introduces the additional attribute PROMPT, which allow the author to specify the prompt string for the ISINDEX query box. This is supported by most current browsers. Many also support an ACTION attribute, which lets an author specify the URL to which the query data should be sent. The general form is then:

```
<ISINDEX PROMPT="Enter Glossary Term"
ACTION="http://url_to_program/prog">
```

Both of these attributes are optional. The PROMPT attribute is not a problem, because if a browser does not understand PROMPT it will still present the query string. Note, also, that Netscape Navigator 2.0 uses HREF instead of ACTION.

LINK ELEMENT

The LINK element belongs within the HEAD element of an HTML document. It is to be used to indicate a relationship between the document and other documents or objects. Consequently a document may have any number of LINK elements, to indicate all the possible relationships between the document and other, related documents.

The LINK element is empty (i.e, there is no closing </ LINK>) but takes the same attributes as the Anchor (A) element. Typically, a LINK element would be used to indicate authorship, related indexes and glossaries, older or more recent versions, etc. Links can also indicate the tree structure in which the document was authored by pointing, for example, to the"parent","next" or"previous" documents.

LINK is currently used to referenced external cascading stylesheet files, using the format

```
<LINK HREF="url-to-stylesheet" REL="stylesheet">.
```

Examples of Link

```
<HEAD>
```

```
<LINK HREF="file2.html" REL="next">
<LINK HREF="/cgi-reg/gloss.pl" REL="glossary">
<LINK HREF="/cgi-bin/index.pl" REL="index">
<LINK HREF="toc.html" REL="contents">
<LINK HREF="file0.html" REL="previous">
</HEAD>
```

META

META is a general element for document meta-information -- that is, for information about the document that cannot be expressed by LINK, BASE or the other HEAD elements. There are two ways this can be expressed.

HTTP-Equivalent META Information

Sometimes you want a header to contain information that would ordinarily be returned by the server as a field in the HTTP headers. For example, you could use META to include an expiry date for files that are periodically updated. The META element would be:

```
<META HTTP-EQUIV="Expires" CONTENT="25-Dec-1995
12:00:00 GMT">
```

An alternative form is:

```
<META HTTP-EQUIV="Refresh" CONTENT="10">
```

in which case the browser would wait 10 seconds and then re-access the currently displayed document.

Arbitrary User-Specified META Information

A user might want to include information about the document, such as keywords for indexing, the name of the author, and so on.

This can be done with META elements such as the following:

```
<META NAME="author" CONTENT="Ian Graham">
<META NAME="keywords" CONTENT="html
documentation web url">
<META NAME="editor" CONTENT="HTML SuperPro">
```

The attribute NAME refers to arbitrary user-selected names, while HTTP-EQUIV means that the value has a real equivalent header in the HTTP protocol. Again this is only really useful given tools for processing these data. At present, there are very few tools that take advantage of META element content.

Commonly-Understood META Elements Formats

There are several other common META elements that are used to provide information to Web-indexing robots -- that is, the automated tools that retrieve Web pages and create searchable indexes, such as those found at Lycos, AltaVista, or Yahoo.

NEXTID

Note: At present, it is likely that NEXTID will be dropped from the HTML specification, since it is not terribly useful. You are therefore advised against wasting your time reading the rest of this page!

This tag has a single attribute, namely'the number of the next document-wide numeric identifier to be allocated of the form z123'. The NEXTID tag is designed for use by automatic hypertext editors, and is not intended for use by mere humans. People writing HTML should generally use mnemonic alphabetical identifiers.

Notes for Writers of HTML Editors

Old anchor ids should not be reused when modifying documents, as other documents may contain references that point to them.

Example of NEXTID

```
<HEAD>
<NEXTID N=z27>
.
.
</HEAD>
```

BODY

The BODY element contains all the content of a

document, as opposed to the HEAD, which contains information about the document. Various mark-up elements are allowed within the body to indicate headings, paragraphs, lists, hypertext links, images, and so on. These are described and illustrated in documents following this one.

The following shows typical use of HEAD and BODY elements, using this document as an example:

```
<HTML>
<HEAD>
<TITLE> BODY element in HTML </TITLE>
<BASE HREF="http://www.utoronto.ca/webdocs/
HTMLdocs/NewHTML/body.html">
</HEAD>
<BODY>
[<a href="htmlindex.html">ToC</a>]
[<a href="htmlindex.html">Up</a>]
<H1> BODY Element in HTML </H1>
<p> The BODY element contains all the content
of the document,
as opposed to the <a href="head.html">HEAD</
a>, which
contains information about the document. </
p>......
</BODY>
</HTML>
```

THE BACKGROUND ATTRIBUTE

In HTML 2.0, the BODY element had no attributes. Netscape 1.1 introduces the single attribute BACKGROUND. This allows you to specify an image file to use as a background (a bit like a watermark) behind the displayed text and graphics.

The following example (please read the following text and then follow the example link)

```
<BODY BACKGROUND="back/marble.gif">
<h1> Bla Bla Bla </h1>
<p> And still more text....
</BODY>
```

tiles the window background with the designated GIF image. Just click on the anchor to look at the example.

HTML 3.2 EXTENSIONS

Setting a background colour is not enough -- for example, if you set the background to black, you need to be able to change the colour of the text as well. Netscape introduced several new attributes for controlling the text colour. These are described below, and became, as of HTML 3.2, part of the HTML standard. There is also an example document illustrating these BODY attributes.

BGCOLOUR="#rrggbb"

Sets the background colour to the specified RGB colour value, where RR GG and BB are the hexadecimal colour codes for the Red, Green and Blue levels, ranging from 0 to 255 -- that is, 00 to FF. The colour"000000" is black, while"FFFFFF" is white. If there isalso a background image, the BGCOLOUR is used as the colour underneath the background image -- if the background image is transparent, this is the colour that shows through.

TEXT="#rrggbb"

Sets the default text colour to the specified RGB colour value.

LINK="#rrggbb"

Sets the default text colour of hypertext anchors to the specified RGB colour value.

VLINK="#rrggbb"

Sets the default text colour of visited hypertext links to the specified RGB colour value. Most browsers also support special colour names (white, blue, etc.).

NETSCAPE 4/INTERNET EXPLORER 4 EXTENSIONS

These browsers added attributes that set the padding around the text the page -- essentially setting the page margins. Of course, the two companies selected different names for these attributes. *These properties are*:

LEFTMARGIN="nn" (Navigator 4) and MARGINWIDTH="nn" (Internet Explorer 4/5)

Sets the page margin on the left (and right for Internet Explorer) of the page to be of size nn pixels.

TOPMARGIN="nn" (Naviagator 4) and MARGINHEIGHT="nn" (Internet Explorer 4/5)

Sets the page margin at the top of the page to be of size nn pixels.

ORGANIZATION OF ELEMENTS IN THE BODY

Text Block Elements

As mentioned on the previous page, the BODY element contains all the displayed content of a document. Structurally, the document content is organized into blocks of text, such as paragraphs, lists, headings, paragraphs, block quotations, and so on.

These are generically called block elements, since they"block" chunks of text together into logical units. Block elements can often contain other blocks -- for example, a list item can contain paragraphs or block quotations, so that these elements can often nest together.

The block-level elements are:

- Hn (Headings)
- P
- ADDRESS
- BLOCKQUOTE
- PRE
- HR
- FORM
- TABLE
- DIV (HTML 3.2 and up)

Text Emphasis Elements

At the next level down are text-level markup elements. These are elements that mark text for special meanings, for example, that a particular piece of text is emphasised (EM) or a citation (CITE), or that specify the desired physical formatting, such as boldface (B) or italics (I). These elements can usually appear anywhere inside a block element, with a few exceptions (you can't have images inside a PRE element).

Special Elements -- Hypertext Anchors

Analogous to the text-level markup is the anchor (A) element. This is the element that marks hypertext links. Obviously you want to know a lot about this one.

Character-Level Elements

Then are what I call character-level elements, namely line breaks (BR) and images (IMG). These are treated much like characters, and can appear wherever there is a character in a document.

Character References

Finally there are character or entity references. These are special HTML"escape" codes that can be used to enter special characters that are hard to type, such as accented or other non-ascii characters. You also need to use these to type angle brackets or ampersand characters -- as these are otherwise interpreted as HTML tags (<... >) or as the beginnings of character or entity references.

Section Headings

HTML allows for six levels of headings, marked by the element names H1, H2... H6. There is no forced hierarchy in these headings, but for consistency you should use the top level (H1) for main headings, and lower levels for progressively less important ones. In general hypertext documents should be broken up so that each page does not occupy much more than a single screen. In these cases you can use the H1 heading to mark the main document heading, and the others to mark subheadings.

HEADING ALIGNMENT: THE ALIGN ATTRIBUTE

HTML 3 proposed an ALIGN attribute to the heading element, which allows an author to"hint" at the desired alignment of the heading on the display.The possible values are ALIGN="left" (the default) to left-align the heading, ALIGN="center" to center the heading, and ALIGN="right" to right-align the heading. Several browsers understand left and center alignment, while very few understand right-alignment. Some examples are shown below.

Examples of Headings

The following examples show the HTML coding for the six heading types, along with the results (note that the results will vary from viewer to viewer)

```
<H1 align="left"> Heading type H1 </H1>
Heading type H1
<H2 align="center"> Heading type H2 </H2>
Heading type H2
<H3 align="right"> Heading type H3 </H3>
Heading type H3
<H4> Heading type H4 </H4>
Heading type H4
<H5> Heading type H5 </H5>
Heading type H5
<H6> Heading type H6 </H6>
Heading type H6
```

MARKING PARAGRAPHS

The P element marks a block of text as a paragraph -- the tag <P> marks the beginning of the paragraph, while the tag </P> marks the end of a paragraph. The end tag, however, is optional, as a paragraph is automatically ended when you start another paragraph, or when you start a heading, blockquote, list, table or form.

In general, a browser will add appropriate spacings and indents to indicate the paragraph. Note that the Netscape Navigator often adds extra vertical spacing after a paragraph if you end the paragraph with a </P> end tag.

This is a"bug" with Netscape, but can be used as a"feature" if you want to more finely control line spacings between a paragraph and a following element such as a table or a horizontal rule

Changes for HTML 3.2: Paragraph Alignment

HTML 3.2 introduced the ALIGN attribute to control the alignment of text, and also introduced ID to act as a location marker for the paragrah.

More specifically:

ALIGN ="left" |"center" |"right" |"justify"

ALIGN controls the alignment of text within the paragraph. Left and right alignment flush the text with the left and right margins, respectively, while center alignment centers the text. Justify should left and right justify the text.

Please select the"examples" anchor above to see examples of the different alignments.

ID ="name_token" (not widely supported)

Mark the paragraph for a possible reference via a URL. Thus, ID should act much like the NAME attribute of a hypertext anchor (A) element. However, this use for ID is currently only supported by the Internet Explrer 4. The value assigned to ID is a name token.

ADDRESS ELEMENT

The ADDRESS element is used for address information, signatures, statements of authorship, etc. It is often placed at the bottom (or top) of a document.

The rendering of the contents of the ADDRESS is left up to the browser -- most browsers render the ADDRESS in italics. It may also be right justified, or indented.

Examples of ADDRESS

```
<ADDRESS><A HREF="address.html">A.N.Other</A></
ADDRESS> </P>


<p><ADDRESS>
Newsletter  editor<br>
J.R.  Brown<br>
JimquickPost  News,  Jumquick,  CT  01234<br>
Tel  (123)  456  7890
</ADDRESS>  </p>
```

These are rendered as

R.N.Other

New Delhi

An address cannot contain P, BLOCKQUOTE, FORM or other block elements, but can contain text, text markup (emphasis, etc.), anchor elements or even images.

BLOCKQUOTE ELEMENT

The BLOCKQUOTE element defines a block quotation of text. A typical browser will render this in an appropriate way, for example by slightly indenting the text, or by italicizing it. BLOCKQUOTE also causes a paragraph break, and typically forces white space both before and after the quotation.

Attributes

In HTML 3.2 and up, BLOCKQUOTE can take the ALIGN attribute to specify how the text inside BLOCKQUOTE should be aligned.

The supported values are:

- Align="center" (center alignment)
- Align="left" (left alignment -- the default)
- Align="right" (right alignment)
- Align="justify" (left-right justification). Justify alignment is not widely supported.

DIV -- BLOCK DIVISIONS

HTML 3.2 introduced the element DIV, to allow you to block together other block body elements, and associate them together. This has practical purposes -- DIV can take the ALIGN attribute, and all blocks (P, BLOCKQUOTE, etc.) inside a DIV will inherit the text alignment specified by the outside DIV.

Structurally, DIV can also take the CLASS attribute, which is used to specify the semantic meaning of the block. For example <DIV CLASS="abstract">..... </DIV> could be used to mark out the block of text that is a document's abstract. This is very useful when organizing text, and is much desired by document authors. All modern browsers support the DIV element, but it is not supported by older browsers, such as Mosaic 2.0, Netscape Navigator 1.1 and Internet Explorer 2.0.

LISTS

HTML supports several elements for making lists. They can be divided into two types: glossary lists, and regular lists. Glossary Lists are denoted by the element <DL>, while regular lists are denoted by the elements <UL>, <OL>, <MENU> and <DIR>. Lists can be nested. Thus you can have a regular list within a regular list, a regular list within a glossary list, and so on. Some examples are shown below.

This document describes glossary lists. The following document ([Next] from the menu at the top of the page) explains the formatting of regular lists.

DL Element: Glossary Lists

This list type, also known as a definition list, is used to present a list of items along with descriptive paragraphs. This can be used for glossaries, but is also useful for presenting a named list of items and their meanings.

The items within the list are introduced by the two elements:

`<DT> -- The `Term' (a single line)`

`<DD> -- The `Definition' (may be multiple lines)`

DL can take a single attribute, COMPACT, to signify that the list is small (or large) and should be rendered in a physically compact way. This attribute is ignored by several browsers.

HTTP

Whenever your web browser fetches a file (a page, a picture, etc) from a web server, it does so usingHTTP - that's"Hypertext Transfer Protocol". HTTP is a request/ response protocol, which means your computer sends a request for some file (*e.g.*"Get me the file'home.html'"), and the web server sends back a response ("Here's the file", followed by the file itself).

That request which your computer sends to the web server contains all sorts of (potentially) interesting information. We'll now examine the HTTP request your computer just sent to this web server, see what it contains, and find out what it tells me about you.

ANALYSIS

Table. Source IP address, port and proxy

Source IP address:	122.162.191.159
Source port:	2834
Via:	not present
X-Forwarded-For:	not present

In order to send the appropriate response back to your computer, the web server necessarily knows your computer's IP address, and a port number to which to send the response. Your IP address seems to be 122.162.191.159, and the port number used was 2834.

On the other hand, there could be one or more proxy servers between your computer and the web server. If the HTTP request includes the header"Via", or"X-Forwarded-For", then that's a strong indication that there is at least one proxy server somewhere along the line.

If neither of those headers were present, that could mean that no proxy servers were involved, or it could mean that they just chose not to"reveal" themselves by adding those headers. In this case since there is neither a"Via" header nor a"X-Forwarded-For" header, there quite possibly isn't a proxy between your computer and the web server. However, this isn't definite - it might be that there is a proxy, but it just chose not to add the"Via"/"X-Forwarded-For" headers.

Your IP address

For now we'll assume your IP address is 122.162.191.159. Let's see what we know about that address.

IP address:	122.162.191.159
DNS name:	ABTS-North-Dynamic
159.191.162.122.airtelbroadband.in	

Lots more interesting information can be learned from your IP address. For example whereabouts you are on the Internet, (roughly) what city you're in, and who your ISP is.

Destination IP address, port, host and protocol

Destination IP address:	91.84.196.2
Destination port:	80
Host:	djce.org.uk
Protocol:	INCLUDED

These headers tell us which web server you were trying to contact. If that seems odd, bear in mind that many web sites can be"hosted" on a single server, so when the request is received it needs to know which web site you were attempting to access. The protocol used will almost always be either"HTTP/1.1" or"HTTP/1.0", and is a property of your computer's web browser and any proxies through which the request might have passed.

Requeste URI

`Requested URI: /dumprequest`

Together with the'Host' header and the destination port number (above), this specifies the document which should be retrieved.

Given all these values we can determine that the URL of the document which is being retrieved is:http://djce.org.uk/dumprequest

Request Method And Content

Request method:	GET
Data:	none

The request method is usually either"GET" or"POST". Basically if you fill in and submit a form on a web page it might generate a POST request (or it might be"GET"), whereas if you just click on a link, or activate one of your browser's"bookmarks" or"favourites", then the request method will always be"GET". Therefore, if it's"POST", we can tell that a form was definitely submitted. The contents of the form would appear here, and there would also be some"Content-" headers describing the data. Web browsers generate two kinds of"POST" data: either"multipart/form-data", which is used when uploading files to a web server, or the more common"application/x-www-form-urlencoded".

User Agent

User-Agent:	Mozilla/5.0 (Windows; U; Windows NT 5.1; en-US) AppleWebKit/534.10 (KHTML, like Gecko) Chrome/8.0.552.224 Safari/534.10
Accept:	application/xml, application/xhtml+xml, text/html;q=0.9, text/plain;q=0.8, image/png, */*;q=0.5
Accept-Charset:	ISO-8859-1,utf-8;q=0.7,*;q=0.3
Accept-Encoding:	gzip,deflate,sdch
Accept-Language:	en-US,en;q=0.8

The User-Agent header describes your web browser. Typically it contains the browser name and version (*e.g.* Firefox 1.0.7), your Operating System and version (*e.g.* Windows XP), and possibly additional information (such as which"service packs" you have installed).

The"Accept" headers describe what sort of things the web browser can handle, and what it would prefer to be given if there's a choice.

The"Accept" header itself describes which document types the web browser can handle, so for example we can tell whether your browser is capable of handling"image/png" graphics.

The"Accept-Charset" header describes what character sets are acceptable, so we can make some guesses as to what part of the world you might be in, and what language you might speak. For example, western European or north American users quite possibly only understand the"iso-8859-1","us-ascii" and"utf-8" character sets, whereas"big5" would suggest that you might be Chinese. "Accept-Encoding" describes the ability of your web browser to handle compressed transfer of documents. Nothing too interesting there, but it's another snippet of information about the browser you're using.

"Accept-Language" is more interesting though; it tells us what language(s) you prefer to receive your documents in - again, if the web server offers a choice. For example, if the header tells us that your preference is for"en-gb" followed by"en", that means you're probably an English-speaking Briton."pt-br" on the otherhand would suggest a Portuguese-speaking Brazilian.

Referring Page

`Referer: not present`

The"referer" header tells us which document referred you to us - in essence, if you followed a link to get to this page, it is the URL of the page you came from to get here.

If on the other hand you didn't follow a link - maybe you clicked on a browser"bookmark", or maybe you just typed the address of this page directly into your browser - then the"referer" will be missing. And yes, that isn't how it should be spelt.:-(

Cookies

`Cookie: not present`

Every time a web server provides you with a response (a page, a graphic, etc), it has the opportunity to send your browser a"cookie". These cookies are small pieces of information which your browser stores, and then sends back to that same web server whenever you subsequently request a document.

So there's two important points here:

1. Each cookie is only sent back to the same web site as it came from in the first place, and
2. The"contents" of the cookie (the data it contains) can only be made up of whatever information the web server already knew anyway.

For example, a web server can't just say"send me a cookie containing your e-mail address" unless that same web server had already sent you that information in the first place.

Connection control

`Connection:`	`keep-alive`
`Keep-Alive:`	`Not present`

These headers are used to fine-tune the network traffic between you and the web server. They don't tell us much, except a little about the capabilities of your web browser.

Cache control

Pragma:	not present
Cache-Control:	not present
If-Modified-Since:	not present

These headers control cacheing of the document. By examining them the we can detect if you used your browser's"refresh" button to force the page to reload.

For example, Mozilla (Netscape 6) sets"Cache-Control" to"max-age=0" when you use the"reload" button. MSIE 5.5 sets it to"no-cache" if you do a"hard" reload (while holding down the"control" key).

Authorisation

`Username: not present`

If you have"logged in" to a web site, your username appears here.

Note that this only applies to web sites which use proper HTTP authentication - typically, a"login" window pops up and you get three chances to enter your username and password, otherwise you see a page which says"Authentication Required" or similar. It doesn't apply to web sites where the"login" is a separate page.

It's also possible to supply the username and password in the URL you tell your browser to visit - for example, http://user:password@www.example.com/. In that case, the username would appear here too.

The *most interesting pieces of information contained in the request are:*

- The IP address of you and/or your HTTP proxy

- Which document you requested
- Which version of which browser you're using
- Which page you came from to get here (if you followed a link)
- Your preferred language(s)
- Cookies

The"odd one out" in that list is"cookies". That's because the cookies only send to the web server information which it had previously sent to you (and your browser accepted). However, the problem is in knowing what it means. The meaning of the cookie is only actually known to the web server.

If you can get your browser to show you your cookies, you might be able to make a good guess as to what it means - for example a cookie called"LastLoginName" with a value of"fred" probably means that when you last logged in on that site, you used the username"fred". However, a cookie called"TGIDX" with a value of"wl4o6ulhw48l w845yh68 hylohw45" is meaningless to everybody except the web server, so you really have no idea what information that cookie actually holds.

4

Web Organization

SECTION

MARKUP LANGUAGES SECTION

Includes all markup languages including HTML, XML, and SGML. Documentation in this section currently includes an HTML Guide, XML Guide, and a Document Type Definition (DTD) reading reference.

CGI SECTION

Includes four documents describing implementation of the client to server web interface. It includes information about the common gateway interface (CGI), server side includes (SSI), JavaScript, and writing perl script programmes

HTTP SECTION

Thic section currently includes an HTTP Reference which is based on RFC 2616. It has brief descriptions of the HTTP request and response headers and also lists the possible response headers such as 404 (not found). PHP - PHP is a scripting language that runs on the web server and the script code is embedded in the HTML document. It is easy to use with syntax similar to C which is why it is so popular.

PHP

JAVA

Documentation is beirg generated for this section. It currently contains some web links.

MIME SECTION

This section describes Multipurpose Internet Mail Extension along with its purpose and it also includes a few MIME related web links.

GRAPHICS

Gif files used to add graphics to web pages.

WORLD WIDE WEB

There are many types of technologies which are used to support the world wide web and more are being developed all the time. There are several groups involved in the development and coordination of these technologies.

IAB ·

Internet Architecture Board. Web site: IAB. The IAB websites states that"The IAB does not aim to produce polished technical proposals on such topics. Rather, the intention is to stimulate action by the IESG or within the IETF community that will lead to proposals that meet general consensus."

IANA

Internet Assigned Numbers Authority. Web site: IANA. They control the assignment of internet addresses and domain names.

IESG

The Internet Engineering Steering Group. Web site: IESG. According to RFC 2418, the IESG"has responsibility for developing and reviewing specifications intended as Internet Standards."

IETF

The Internet Engineering Task Force. Web site: IETF. Their web site says"The Internet Engineering Task Force (IETF) is a large open international community of network designers, operators, vendors, and researchers concerned with the evolution of the Internet architecture and the smooth operation of the Internet."

InterNIC

Internet Network Information Center, the authority for allocating internet addresses. Web site: InterNIC.

IRTF

Internet Research Task Force. Web site: IRTF. Their web site states their mission is"To promote research of importance to the evolution of the future Internet by creating focused, long-term and small Research Groups working on topics related to Internet protocols, applications, architecture and technology."

- *Isoc*: Internet Society, promotes internet policies. Web site:ISOC.
- *Istf*: Internet Societal Task Force. Web site: ISTF. Their mission is"To assure the open development, evolution and use of the Internet for the benefit of all people throughout the world".
- *W3c*: World Wide Web Consortium, sets standards for the web working with the IETF. W3C
- *Oasis*: Organization for the Advancement of Structured Information Standards. OASIS
- Internet2 Internet2 An Organization that supports internet related technologies including XML, DHTML, JAVA and more.
- *Irt*: Internet Related Technologies. Internet Related TechnologiesTheir website states"Internet2, led by over 180 U.S. universities working in partnership with industry and government, is developing and deploying advanced network applications and technologies, accelerating the creation of tomorrow's Internet."
- Graphic Communications Association A trade association that provides standards for the printing and publishing industries.

SYSTEM PROGRAMMING LANGUAGE

System programming languages are higher level and they are strongly typed languages. The term "higher level" means that many details are handled automatically so that programmers can write less code to get the same job done. System programming languages are well suited to building components where the complexity is in the data structures and algorithms.

System programming support following features:

- Register allocation is handled by the compiler so that programmers need not write code to move information between registers and memory.
- Programmers can use simple keywords such as while and if for control structures; the compiler generates all the detailed instructions to implement the control structures.
- Procedure calling sequences are generated automatically: programmers need not worry about moving arguments to and from the call stack.

EMBEDDED SYSTEM PROGRAMMING

Embedded System Programming was first used in Apollo guidance computer to guide Apollo. Technological advancement brought the price of embedded system (ICs) lower making it possible to use them for commercial purpose. Today embedded systems are widely used in various devices performing specific functions with drastic improvement in processing power. Embedded system programming has been derived from the word embedded system. An embedded system is nothing but a special purpose system in which the computer is fully encapsulated by the device it controls. Embedded software designs have advanced enough to produce widely used devices performing specific function devices such as ATM, PDA, mobile phones etc.

This widely used technological term in the field of Information Technology, is the combination of computer hardware and software which is either fixed in facility or programmable. In short it is purposely designed for a meticulous kind of application device. Systems that hosts this embedded systems are various industrial machines, automobiles, medical equipment, cameras, household appliances, and airplanes, vending machines, toys, cellular phone and PDA.

Seeing its importance and worth embedded systems programming has gained lot popularity and people are looking for companies providing this service. If you are looking for a company providing embedded systems programming then your search is over as Softage is there for you.

Softage is Russia's leading IT service provider providing best and advanced embedded systems programming. Embedded systems programming is specially dedicated to unequivocal tasks so that design engineers can optimize it by reducing the magnitude and cost of the product. In fact nowadays, embedded systems are frequently mass-produced. This has resulted in the cost savings that may be multiplied by millions of items. Apart from the other devices embedded systems also range from portable devices such as MP3 players, to large stationary installations like traffic lights or factory controllers.

According to the experts embedded systems are easily programmable and are provided with a programming interface. Embedded system programming is a tough and professional work which is efficiently handled by Softage. Backed by years of experience Softage hosts some of the best and professional programmers those are experts in embedded system software programming.

WINDOWS SYSTEM PROGRAMMING

In old days, the operating system programme executes the program's instructions in sequence one instruction after another as they arranged by the programmer. When the programme calls a function or interacts with the Operating System (OS) by calling one of the OS's service functions, the function's instructions executed in similar way and the execution continue sequentially until the end of the last instruction of the main programme. In this traditional way of programming the programme only need one main function to start the execution.

Nowadays, in event driven programming environment such as Windows, the interaction between the programme and the OS is a message-based interaction. In this interaction the programme start in a wait mode until the user create an event like for example, press a key or click a mouse button. The OS generates appropriate message and inserts it in application's message queue. The programme, when it ready, should dispatch the messages (read a message from the queue and send it back to the OS) one message after another for time scheduling purpose.

After that, the OS then send the message again to the programme and the programme respond by taking appropriate actions. In this kind of interaction, a simple programme need at least two functions, the main function that start the message loop (WinMain ()) and the other called by the OS (Windows Function())and respond to the passed message.

UNIX SYSTEMS PROGRAMMING

The Unix systems programming API has been standardised by a large number of POSIX standards documents from the IEEE. For the majority of programmers the most important of these is POSIX 1003.1 which covers process primitives and environments, directories and files, I/O primitives and device specific functions. Later standards cover other issues, such as Shells and Utilities (POSIX 1003.2) and Administration (POSIX 1387.2).

One of the unusual characteristics of POSIX 1003.1 is its use of the C language throughout. Whereas IEEE standards would normally be expected to be language independent, the history of Unix is so bound up with C that this was the only feasible route. The document claims that it will be the basis for definitions that are independent of particular programming languages. In fact, new language dependent versions have arisen, such as Ada (POSIX 1003.5) and Fortran.

Irrespective of the formal standards mechanisms, designers of libraries for other languages have used POSIX 1003.1 as the specification for their own libraries. For example, tcl [Ousterhout] and Perl [Wall] have well-developed Unix bindings that copy the syntax, and rely on the semantics, of POSIX 1003.1.

Java [Arnold] is the latest flavour in programming languages for all sorts of excellent reasons, despite some serious shortcomings. It is a full O/O language (although not as pure as SmallTalk or Eiffel); it is based on C/C++, but avoids the worst of both languages (not completely, though); by use of a virtual machine it is cross-platform (although some vendors have variant versions); it has a rich set set of libraries that deal with, for example, graphics and networking. These are combining to produce the "Web programming" environment where applications or applets are written once to run on any platform. Java extends the open authoring environment of HTML to an open programming environment.

How do Unix and Java co-exist? Very well in general terms. A Java application can do exactly the same things in a Unix environment that it can do in a Mac or Windows environment. With care, applications can even be written that transparently handle such issues as forward- versus back-slashes for directory separators.

Java currently lacks the depth of hooks into the POSIX API that tcl and Perl have. The standard must continue to have this lack or it will lose its universal applicability. However, *extensions* by *non-standard* libraries can supply this depth, as long as they are done in an appropriate manner.

This paper reports on a project to make the POSIX API available to Java applications or applets using a non-standard library. It encapulates POSIX calls within Java methods for a new set of classes in the posix package.

This project must be contrasted in aims and methods to the Microsoft policy with J++: their attempt is to make J++ the best environment for doing Windows programming in Java J++, and this implicitly rejects the notion of a cross-platform environment. It may even turn out to be difficult for the programmer using J++ to be certain of how general their code is. The statements from Microsoft do not seem to dispel any uncertainty.

This project, on the other hand, makes it explicit about the introduction of non-standard features, by placing all the new classes in a package that is non-standard. No application using the posix package will ever pass the "Java Pure" tests. On the other hand, this package will develop by an open process method: the source code will be freely available to all, and can be freely modified. If interest is high enough, it can be divorced from individual control and given to a suitable co-ordinating authority.

LINKERS

DEFINITION

In computer science, a linker is a programme that takes one or more objects generated by a compiler and assembles them into a single executable programme.

In IBM mainframe environments such as OS/360 this programme is known as a "linkage editor".

On Unix variants the term loader is often used as a synonym for linker. Because this usage blurs the distinction between the compile-time process and the run-time process, this article will use "linking" for the former and "loading" for the latter. However, in some operating systems the same programme handles both the jobs of linking and loading a programme; see "dynamic linking".

Computer programmes are typically comprised of several parts or modules; these parts, if not all contained within a single object file, refer to each other by means of symbols.

Typically, an object file can contain three kinds of symbols:

- Defined symbols, which allow it to be called by other modules.
- Undefined symbols, which call the other modules where these symbols are defined.
- Local symbols, used internally within the object file to facilitate relocation.

When a programme comprises multiple object files, the linker combines these files into a unified executable programme, resolving the symbols as it goes along.

Linkers can take objects from a collection called a "library". Some linkers do not include the whole library in the output; they only include its symbols that are referenced from other object files or libraries. Libraries exist for diverse purposes, and one or more system libraries are usually linked in by default.

The linker also takes care of arranging the objects in a program's address space. This may involve "relocating" code that assumes a specific base address to another base. Since a compiler seldom knows where an object will reside, it often assumes a fixed base location (for example, zero). Relocating machine code may involve re-targeting of absolute jumps, loads and stores.

The executable output by the linker may need another relocation pass when it is finally loaded into memory (just before execution). This pass is usually omitted on hardware offering virtual memory — every programme is put into its own address space, so there is no conflict even if all programmes load at the same base address. This pass may also be omitted if the executable is a position independent executable.

CONCEPT

The basic job of any linker is simple: it binds more abstract names to more concrete names, which permits programmers to write code using the more abstract names. That is, it takes a name written by a programmer such as get line and binds it to "the location 612 bytes from the beginning of the executable code in module iosys." Or it may take a more abstract numeric address such as "the location 450 bytes beyond the beginning of the static data for this module" and bind it to a numeric address.

A linkers is used in the development of computer programming in systems. The earliest computers were programmed entirely in machine language. Programmers would write out the symbolic programmes on sheets of paper, hand assemble them into machine code and then toggle the machine code into the computer, or perhaps punch it on paper tape or cards. If the programmer used symbolic addresses at all, the symbols were bound to addresses as the programmer did his or her hand translation.

If it turned out that an instruction had to be added or deleted, the entire programme had to be hand-inspected and any addresses affected by the added or deleted instruction adjusted. The problem was that the names were bound to addresses too early. Assemblers solved that problem by letting programmers write programmes in terms of symbolic names, with the assembler binding the names to machine addresses. If the programme changed, the programmer had to reassemble it, but the work of assigning the addresses is pushed off from the programmer to the computer.

Libraries of code compound the address assignment problem. Since the basic operations that computers can perform are so simple, useful programmes are composed of subprograms that perform higher level and more complex operations. Computer installations keep a library of pre-written and debugged subprograms that programmers can draw upon to use in new programmes they write, rather than requiring programmers to write all their own subprograms. The programmer then loads the subprograms in with the main programme to form a complete working programme. Programmers were using libraries of subprograms even before they used assemblers.

By 1947, John Mauchly, who led the ENIAC project, wrote about loading programmes along with subprograms selected from a catalog of programmes stored on tapes, and of the need to relocate the subprograms' code to reflect the addresses at which they were loaded.

Perhaps surprisingly, these two basic linker functions, relocation and library search, appear to predate even assemblers, as Mauchly expected both the programme and subprograms to be written in machine language. The relocating loader allowed the authors and users of the subprograms to write each subprogram as though it would start at location zero, and to defer the actual address binding until the subprograms were linked with a particular main programme. With the advent of operating systems, relocating loaders separate from linkers and libraries became necessary. Before operating systems, each programme had the machine's entire memory at its disposal, so the programme could be assembled and linked for fixed memory addresses, knowing that all addresses in the computer would be available.

But with operating systems, the programme had to share the computer's memory with the operating system and perhaps even with other programmes, This means that the actual addresses at which the programme would be running weren't known until the operating system loaded the programme into memory, deferring final address binding past link time to load time.

Linkers and loaders now divided up the work, with linkers doing part of the address binding, assigning relative addresses within each programme, and the loader doing a final relocation step to assign actual addresses. As systems became more complex, they called upon linkers to do more and more complex name management and address binding. Fortran programmes used multiple subprograms and common blocks, areas of data shared by multiple subprograms, and it was up to the linker to lay out storage and assign the addresses both for the subprograms and the common blocks. Linkers increasingly had to deal with object code libraries.

Including both application libraries written in Fortran and other languages, and compiler support libraries called implicitly from compiled code to handle I/O and other high-level operations.

Programmes quickly became larger than available memory, so linkers provided overlays, a technique that let programmers arrange for different parts of a programme to share the same memory, with each overlay loaded on demand when another part of the programme called into it. Overlays were widely used on mainframes from the advent of disks around 1960 until the spread of virtual memory in the mid-

1970s, then reappeared on microcomputers in the early 1980s in exactly the same form, and faded as virtual memory appeared on PCs in the 1990s. They're still used in memory limited embedded environments, and may yet reappear in other places where precise programmer or compiler control of memory usage improves performance.

With the advent of hardware relocation and virtual memory, linkers and loaders actually got less complex, since each programme could again have an entire address space. Programmes could be linked to be loaded at fixed addresses, with hardware rather than software relocation taking care of any load-time relocation.

But computers with hardware relocation invariably run more than one programme, frequently multiple copies of the same programme. When a computer runs multiple instances of one programme, some parts of the programme are the same among all running instance (the executable code, in particular), while other parts are unique to each instance. If the parts that don't change can be separated out from the parts that do change, the operating system can use a single copy of the unchanging part, saving considerable storage.

Compilers and assemblers were modified to create object code in multiple sections, with one section for read only code and another section for writable data, the linker had to be able to combine all of sections of each type so that the linked programme would have all the code in one place and all of the data in another. This didn't delay address binding any more than it already was, since addresses were still assigned at link time, but more work was deferred to the linker to assign addresses for all the sections.

LINKER ACTION

Programme Loading

Copy a programme from secondary storage (which since about 1968 invariably means a disk) into main memory so it's ready to run. In some cases loading just involves copying the data from disk to memory, in others it involves allocating storage, setting protection bits, or arranging for virtual memory to map virtual addresses to disk pages.

Relocation

Compilers and assemblers generally create each file of object code with the programme addresses starting at zero, but few computers let you load your programme at location zero. If a programme is created from multiple subprograms, all the subprograms have to be loaded at non-overlapping addresses. Relocation is the process of assigning load addresses to the various parts of the programme, adjusting the code and data in the programme to reflect the assigned addresses.

In many systems, relocation happens more than once. It's quite common for a linker to create a programme from multiple subprograms, and create one linked output programme that starts at zero, with the various subprograms relocated to locations within the big programme. Then when the programme is loaded, the system picks the actual load address and the linked programme is relocated as a whole to the load address.

Symbol Resolution

When a programme is built from multiple subprograms, the references from one subprogram to another are made using symbols; a main programme might use a square root routine called sqrt, and the math library defines sqrt. A linker resolves the symbol by noting the location assigned to sqrt in the library, and patching the caller's object code to so the call instruction refers to that location.

Although there's considerable overlap between linking and loading, it's reasonable to define a programme that does programme loading as a loader, and one that does symbol resolution as a linker. Either can do relocation, and there have been all-in-one linking loaders that do all three functions. The line between relocation and symbol resolution can be fuzzy. Since linkers already can resolve references to symbols, one way to handle code relocation is to assign a symbol to the base address of each part of the programme, and treat relocatable addresses as references to the base address symbols.

TWO-PASS LINKING PROCESS

Now we turn to the general structure of linkers. Linking, like compiling or assembling, is fundamentally a two pass process. A linker takes as its input a set of input object files, libraries, and perhaps command files, and produces as its result an output object file, and perhaps ancillary information such as a load map or a file containing debugger symbols.

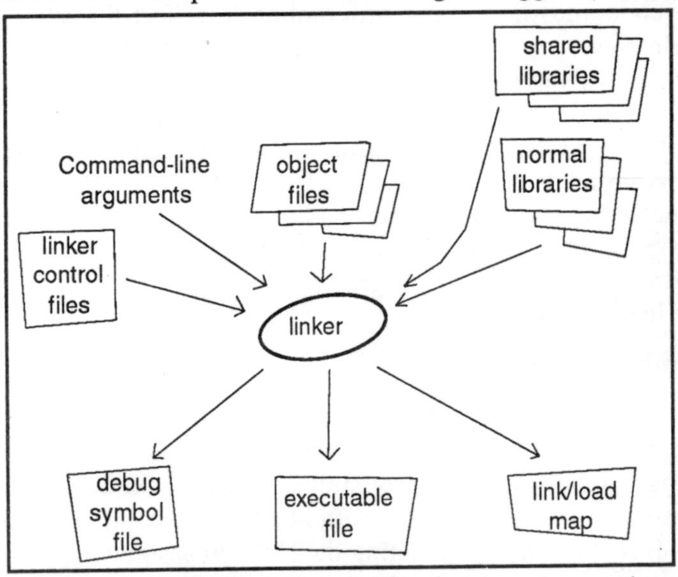

Each input file contains a set of *segments*, contiguous chunks of code or data to be placed in the output file. Each input file also contains at least one *symbol table*. Some symbols are exported, defined within the file for use in other files, generally the names of routines within the file that can be called from elsewhere. Other symbols are imported, used in the file but not defined, generally the names of routines called from but not present in the file. When a linker runs, it first has to scan the input files to find the sizes of the segments and to collect the definitions and references of all of the symbols It creates a segment table listing all of the segments defined in the input files, and a symbol table with all of the symbols imported or exported.

Using the data from the first pass, the linker assigns numeric locations to symbols, determines the sizes and location of the segments in the output address space, and figures out where everything goes in the output file. The second pass uses the information collected in the first pass to control the actual linking process. It reads and relocates the object code, substituting numeric addresses for symbol references, and adjusting memory addresses in code and data to reflect relocated segment addresses, and writes the relocated code to the output file.

It then writes the output file, generally with header information, the relocated segments, and symbol table information. If the programme uses dynamic linking, the symbol table contains the info the runtime linker will need to resolve dynamic symbols. In many cases, the linker itself will generate small amounts of code or data in the output file, such as "glue code" used to call routines in overlays or dynamically linked libraries, or an array of pointers to initialization routines that need to be called at programme startup time.

Whether or not the programme uses dynamic linking, the file may also contain a symbol table for relinking or debugging that isn't used by the programme itself, but may be used by other programmes that deal with the output file. Some object formats are relinkable, that is, the output file from one linker run can be used as the input to a subsequent linker run.

This requires that the output file contain a symbol table like one in an input file, as well as all of the other auxiliary information present in an input file. Nearly all object formats have provision for debugging symbols, so that when the programme is run under the control of a debugger, the debugger can use those symbols to let the programmer control the programme in terms of the line numbers and names used in the source programme. Depending on the details of the object format, the debugging symbols may be intermixed in a single symbol table with symbols needed by the linker, or there may be one table for the linker and a separate, somewhat redundant table for the debugger.

A few linkers appear to work in one pass. They do that by buffering some or all of the contents of the input file in memory or disk during the linking process, then reading the buffered material later. Since this is an implementation trick that doesn't fundamentally affect the two-pass nature of linking, we don't address it further here.

RELOCATION AND CODE MODIFICATION

The heart of a linker or loader's actions is relocation and code modification. When a compiler or assembler generates and object file, it generates the code using the unrelocated addresses of code and data defined within the file, and usually zeros for code and data defined elsewhere. As part of the linking process, the linker modifies the object code to reflect the actual addresses assigned. For example, consider this snippet of x86 code that moves the contents of variable a to variable b using the eax register.

```
mov a,%eax
mov%eax,b
```

If a is defined in the same file at location 1234 hex and b is imported from somewhere else, the generated object code will be: A1 34 12 00 00 mov a,%eax A3 00 00 00 00 mov%eax,b Each instruction contains a one-byte operation code followed by a fourbyte address. The first instruction has a reference to 1234 (byte reversed, since the x86 uses a right to left byte order) and the second a reference to zero since the location of b is unknown. Now assume that the linker links this code so that the section in which a is located is relocated by hex 10000 bytes, and b turns out to be at hex 9A12.

The linker modifies the code to be:

```
A1 34 12 01 00 mov a,%eax
A3 12 9A 00 00 mov%eax,b
```

That is, it adds 10000 to the address in the first instruction so now it refers to a's relocated address which is 11234, and it patches in the address for b. These adjustments affect instructions, but any pointers in the data part of an object file have to be adjusted as well. On older computers with small address spaces and direct addressing, the modification process is fairly simple, since there are only only one or two address formats that a linker has to handle. Modern computers, including all RISCs, require considerably more complex code modification.

No single instruction contains enough bits to hold a direct address, so the compiler and linker have to use complicated addressing tricks to handle data at arbitrary addresses. In some cases, it's possible to concoct an address using two or three instructions, each of which contains part of the address, and use bit manipulation to combine the parts into a full address.

In this case, the linker has to be prepared to modify each of the instructions appropriately, inserting some of the bits of the address into each instruction. In other cases, all of the addresses used by a routine or group of routines are placed in an array used as an "address pool", initialization code sets one of the machine registers to point to that array, and code loads pointers out of the address pool as needed using that register as a base register. The linker may have to create the array from all of the addresses used in a programme, then modify instructions that so that they refer to the appropriate address pool entry.

LINKER COMMAND LANGUAGES

Every linker has some sort of command language to control the linking process. At the very least the linker needs the list of object files and libraries to link. Generally there is a long list of possible options: whether to keep debugging symbols, whether to use shared or unshared libraries, which of several possible output formats to use.

Most linkers permit some way to specify the address at which the linked code is to be bound, which comes in handy when using a linker to link a system kernel or other programme that doesn't run under control of an operating system. In linkers that support multiple code and data segments, a linker command language can specify the order in which segments are to be linked, special treatment for certain kinds of segments, and other application-specific options. There are four common techniques to pass commands to a linker:

- *Command line:* Most systems have a command line or the equivalent, via which one can pass a mixture of file names and switches. This is the usual approach for Unix and Windows linkers. On systems with limited length command lines, there's usually a way to direct the linker to read commands from a file and treat them as though they were on the command line.

Intermixed with Object Files

Some linkers, such as IBM mainframe linkers, accept alternating object files and linker commands in a single input file. This dates from the era of card decks, when one would pile up object decks and hand-punched command cards in a card reader.

Embedded in Object Files

Some object formats, notably Microsoft's, permit linker commands to be embedded inside object files. This permits a compiler to pass any options needed to link an object file in the file itself. For example, the C compiler passes commands to search the standard C library.

Separate Configuration Language

A few linkers have a full fledged configuration language to control linking. The GNU linker, which can handle an enormous range of object file formats, machine architectures, and address space conventions, has a complex control language that lets a programmer specify the order in which segments should be linked, rules for combining similar segments, segment addresses, and a wide range of other options. Other linkers have less complex languages to handle specific features such as programmer-defined overlays.

LOADER

It is the Loader's function to fix absolute addresses for the relocated values in a relocatable module, thereby converting a relocatable module into an "executable" output file. The Loader is usually called automatically by the Linker but it may also be called separately by the user. As indicated below, several different Loaders are (optionally) available for use with Introl-C and, if the user has elected to obtain such optional Loaders, a variety of executable output file formats can be generated, depending on the Loader being used.

Each resident Introl-C compiler package, and each Introl-C cross-compiler package, nominally includes a single, specific type of Introl Loader which is considered as being the "standard" Loader for that compiler's particular host system configuration. For resident Introl-C Compiler packages, the 'standard' Loader that is furnished is an "operating system dependent" type of Loader which generates an output file that is executable on that particular Compiler's host system.

For cross-compiler versions of Introl-C, the "standard" Loader furnished is typically a "hex" type Loader that generates a file of output load records, which can be either Motorola S-Records, intel Hex, Tektronix Hex, or Tektronix Extended Hex at user option. Besides the "standard" Loader that accompanies any given Compiler type, it is also possible for the user to optionally obtain and use other compatible "cross-Loaders" which generate output formats unrelated to the Compiler's host operating system.

For example, "hex-type" Loaders are optionally available for use with resident versions of Introl-C; "operating system dependent" type Loaders are optionally available for use with cross-compiler versions; etc. There are, therefore, several different species of Loaders, (as well as several different types of related Standard Libraries) that may potentially be used under Introl-C.

The "standard" Loader supplied with your Introl-C package, as well as any other Loaders that may have been optionally ordered, are described in detail in the Loader Appendix of this Linker Reference Manual. This Loader section describes the general features that are common to all Loader types. Normally the input to the Loader is expected to be a relocatable file which has no unresolved external references; if unresolved references do exist in its input, loading will normally not be successful. A Loader option is provided, however, to force a file to be loaded even if it contains unresolved references.

Usually a relocatable file has to be linked before it can be used as input to the Loader. It is also possible, of course, to assemble a file which makes no external references and then use the relocatable output file produced by the Assembler directly as input to the Loader (ie without having actually linked it)

FUNCTIONS OF LOADER

- Allocate space in memory for the programme (allocation).
- Resolve symbolic references between object programmes (linking).
- Adjust all address dependent locations, such as address constraints, to correspond to the allocated space (relocation).
- Physically place the machine instruction and data into memory(loading) for execution.
- Loader: System programme that performs the loading function.
- Linker (or linkage editor): System programme that performs the linking operations (*i.e.* linking and relocation).

KINDS OF LOADER

Absolute loader

Performs Loading Only:

- Object programme contains:
  - H card (or record)
  - T cards (or record)
  - E card (or record)

- Check the starting address and memory size required (*i.e.* specified in H record), load Text records into memory sequentially, and then jump to the starting address specified by End record.

Absolute loader Algorithm

```
begin
read Header record
verify programme name and length
read first Text record
while record type '" 'E' do
begin
{if object code is in character form, convert
into
internal representation}
move object code to specified location in memory
read next object programme record
end
jump to address specified in End record
end
```

Relocatable loader

Perform allocation, relocation, and loading:

- Modification record: Used to describe the starting address and length of code to be modified.
- SIC computer: Most instructions use direct addressing. à Too many modification records are needed.
- Another approach: use relocation bit to indicate that the word should be modified or not.

Linkage editor

Performing linking only:

- Produce a linked version of the programme (called load module, executable image, or image programme).
- Solve external reference and library search, and perform relocation of all sections relative to the start of the linked programme.

- Although all linking has been performed, information concerning external reference is retained in the linked programme for further re-linking if necessary.

Linkage editor commands:

Example 1: new version of library routine

```
INCLUDE  PLANNER (PROGLIB)
DELETE  PROJECT
INCLUDE  PROJECT (NEWLY)
REPLACE   PLANNER (PROGLIB)
```

Example 2: combine subroutines into a package

```
INCLUDE   READR(FINLIB)
INCLUDE  WRITER(FIN LIB)
INCLUDE   BLOCK(FINLIB)
SAVE  FINIO(SUBLIB)
```

→The linked module name FINIO could be indexed in the directory of SUBLIB under the same name as the original subroutines.

- Linkage editor performs linking operation before the programme is loaded for execution. Linking loader perform linking operation at load time.
- Dynamic linking (or dynamic binding, load on call) perform linking operation until execution.
  - When a subroutine call is encountered and the subroutine is not resident in memory, load the subroutine into memory, perform linking, and finally jump to the subroutine.
  - Advantages: Load the routines when they are needed, the memory space will be saved.

Linking Loader

Perform allocation, linking, relocation, and loading:

- Modification record: Used to describe the starting address and length of code to be modified.
- SIC computer: Most instructions use direct addressing. à Too many modification records are needed.
- Another approach: use relocation bit to indicate that the word should be modified or not.

LOADER COMMAND LINE

The "standard" Loader supplied with your Introl-C package is normally automatically called by the Linker when the Linker pass finishes. However, linker command line options exist (see Linker Section of this manual) that mav be used to alternatively force the Linker to automatically call other optional Loaders. Situations also arise when it is desirable to explicitly call the Loader alone, without first executing the Linker. When such situations arise, the Loader may be independently called by the user with a loader command line of the general form:

`<c>ld <file> {<option>}`

where <c>ld represents the Introl filename of the specific Loader being called, <file> is the name of the (linked) relocatable module which is to be loaded, and (<option>) represents zero or more Loader option specifiers.

Each of the potentially usable Introl Loaders is uniquely identified by a 3-letter Loader filename, the last two letters of which are always "ld". The <c> designator indicated in the "<c>ld" loader call on the command line therefore represents the first letter in the three-letter Loader name. For example, to call the Introl hex type of Loader, which has the filename "hld", the "<c>ld" entry on the command line would actually become "hld". For further specifics on the names of the loaders which can be legally accessed. The relocatable file that is input to the Loader is expected to have a filenarne extension; if none is specified, the default filename extension ".RL" is assumed. Normally the name of the executable output file will be identical to the name of the input file, but with a filename extension typically added by the Loader. The filename extensions each Loader appends are discussed in the Loader Appendices to this manual.

LOADER OPTIONS

Each type of Loader available for use with the Introl-C has its own, generally unique set of options. When the Loader is being called separately, Loader options are specified directly on the loader command line when the Loader is being automatically called by the Linker, Loader options are specified on the link command line, together with the Linker options.

If Loader options are specified on the link command line, any such options (ie those that do not apply to the Linker) will be automatically sent on to the Loader. For the most part Linker and Loader option specifiers tend to be distinct, so that there is little ambiguity when Loader options are specified on the link command line.

LIBRARY FILES

A library file is a file which contains one or more linkable object modules of the type produced by the Introl Assembler. When a file is compiled and assembled, the result is exactly one linkable module which is placed into a file. This file is actually a library which happens to contain only a single module. When the user links a programme, one or more of these "libraries" are specified on the link command line.

Usually the "libraries" are those produced as a result of a compilation and contain only a single module, however, they may also contain several modules. The Library Manager, "libman", is a programme which allows the user to place several modules into a single library file. When the user has a large set of modules which are commonly used in programmes, it is usually convenient to place them all in one library and then simply specify the library once on the link command line.

The Linker will extract only those modules it requires in order to satisfy the external references of the programme. The Linker is designed to automatically search the "Standard Library", libc.R, if it still has external references to satisfy after it has exhausted all the alternatives provided by the modules specified an the link command line. For many C programmes, the Standard Library is usually where most of the external references are satisfied. Many users find it useful to add to, or modify routines in, the Standard Library. The Library Manager is the utility programme which allows the user to create new libraries and also to maintain existing ones.

MODES OF OPERATION

The Library Manager has three modes of operation: Direct Mode, Interactive Mode, and Command File Mode. The most convenient to use for simple additions and deletions to the library is the Direct Mode. For more extensive modifications the user may instead wish to use Interactive mode. The third mode is the Command File mode which causes the Library Manager to read its commands from a file rather than getting them from the user terminal.

Direct Mode: In Direct Mode the user is permitted to specify a single command on the library manager command line. When the Library Manager is called, it executes this single command function and then immediately exits from the Library Manager. When modifying libraries, however, a single command function is often all that is necessary to accomplish the change desired by the user.

When Direct Mode is being used, the desired command is specified right on the command line, following the <lib> library specification. Any Library Manager command may be used in the Direct Mode. Interactive Mode: if no command is specified on the Library Manager call line, the Library Manager will enter its Interactive Mode of operation. In Interactive Mode the Library Manager will print a colon (".") as a promet and will accept a succession of commands directly from the user terminal.

Interactive Mode is useful when the user must make extensive changes to a library, or when the user wishes to step through the library checking and/or changing modules in an "interactive" manner. Once selected, the Interactive Mode will remain in effect until the user enters a "quit" or "omit" command.

Command File Mode: One of the commands which the user can specify as an Interactive code or a Direct Mode command entry is the "Comfile" command. This command instructs the Library Manager to read subsequent instructions from a command file. When a "Comfile command is entered, the Library Manager will read from the file specified until it reads a "quit" or "omit" command or, alternatively, until it reaches the end of the file. when exiting the Command File Mode, the Library Manager will return to whatever mode it was in before the Command File Mode was entered. If the

Command File Mode was entered as the result of a Direct Mode command, then the Library Manager will terminate when Command File Mode is exited. If entered from the Interactive Mode, it will return to the Interactive Mode.

ASSEMBLER

DEFINITION

An assembler is a programme that converts simple commands into machine code. The simple commands, written in an assembly language, are used in groups to perform more complicated tasks.

FUNCTION

The function of the assembler is to translate programmes written in the assembler language into object modules. The code will then be in a suitable form for processing by the Linkage Editor. The assembler language is a symbolic representation of machine language.

The correspondence between the two can be best understood by examining the listings produced by an assembler. The assembler, like the linkage editor, is supplied as part of VSE, CMS, and MVS, and executes under control of the appropriate control programme. It accepts, as input, a source programme written in the Assembler Language.

This consists of three types of instructions:

1. C Machine instructions.
2. C Assembler instructions.
3. C Macro instructions.

As expected with an IBM language, code can also be copied in from a source statement library (VSE) or a pds (MVS) or MACLIB (CMS).

SEGMENTS AND OFFSETS IN ASSEMBLER

The original designers of the 8088, decided that nobody

will every need to use more that one megabyte of memory. So they built the machine so it couldn't access above that. The problem is to access a whole megabyte 20 bits are needed (one bit being either a one or a zero.

Registers only have 16 bits, and they didn't want to use two because that would be 32 bits and that was too much for anyone. They decided to do the addressing with two registers but not 32 bits. Is this confusing? Blame the designers of the 8088.

```
OFFSET = SEGMENT * 16
SEGMENT = OFFSET/ 16 (the lower 4 bits are lost)
SEGMENT * 16 |0010010000010000—| range (0 to 65535) * 16
+OFFSET |—0100100000100010| range (0 to 65535)
=20 bit address |00101000100100100010| range 0 to 1048575 (1 MEG)

====== DS ======
====== SI ======
```

(note DS and SI overlap). This is how DS:SI is used to make a 20 bit address. The segment is in DS and the offset is in SI.

Segment registers are: CS, DS, ES, SS. On the 386+ there are also FS & GS

Offset registers are: BX, DI, SI, BP, SP, IP. In 386+ protected mode, ANY general register (not a segment register) can be used as an Offset register. (Except IP, which you can't access.)

REGISTERS

- *AX*: This is split into half - into AL and AH (for low and high). They store the high part and the low part of the number in ax.
- *BX (BH/BL)*: same as AX
- *CX (CH/CL)*: Same as AX (used for loops)
- *DX (DH/DL)*: Same as AX (used for multiplication/ division)
- *DI and SI*: are index registers and can be used as offset registers.

- *SP*: Stack Pointer. Does just that. Points to the current position in the stack. *Don't* alter unless you REALLY know what you are doing.

INTERPRETER

DEFINITION

- An interpreter runs programme code by converting it to machine code on the fly. You save some time in the front by avoiding the compiling and linking steps, but interpreters generally run slower because they have to convert the same code (in a loop, say) again and again. An example of a common interpreter is the one that executes.bat files.
- An *interpreter* is also a programme that translates a high-level language into a low-level one, but it does it at the moment the programme is run. You write the programme using a text editor or something similar, and then instruct the interpreter to run the programme. It takes the programme, one line at a time, and translates each line before running it: It translates the first line and runs it, then translates the second line and runs it etc. The interpreter has no "memory" for the translated lines, so if it comes across lines of the programme within a loop, it must translate them afresh every time that particular line runs.
  Consider this simple Basic programme:
- 10 FOR COUNT = 1 TO 1000
- 20 PRINT COUNT * COUNT
- 30 NEXT COUNT
- Line 20 of the programme displays the square of the value stored in COUNT and this line has to be carried out 1000 times. The interpreter must also translate that line 1000 times, which is clearly an inefficient process. However, interpreted languages do have their uses, as we will see in a later section.
- Examples of interpreted languages are Basic, JavaScript and LISP

- The Interpreter pattern discusses: defining a domain language (*i.e.* problem characterization) as a simple language grammar, representing domain rules as language sentences, and interpreting these sentences to solve the problem. The pattern uses a class to represent each grammar rule. And since grammars are usually hierarchical in structure, an inheritance hierarchy of rule classes maps nicely.
- An abstract base class specifies the method interpret(). Each concrete subclass implements interpret() by accepting (as an argument) the current state of the language stream, and adding its contribution to the problem solving process.

STRUCTURE

- Interpreter suggests modeling the domain with a recursive grammar. Each rule in the grammar is either a "composite" (a rule that references other rules) or a terminal (a leaf node in a tree structure). Interpreter relies on the recursive traversal of the Composite pattern to interpret the "sentences" it is asked to process.

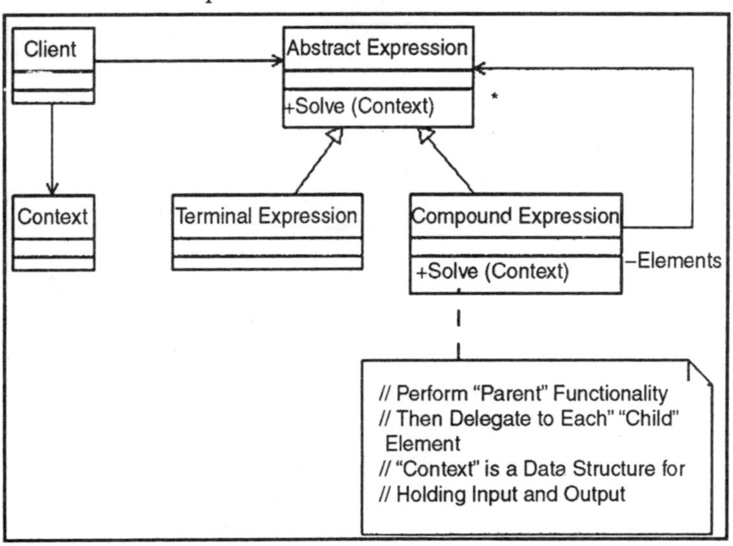

Example

- The Interpreter pattern defines a grammatical representation for a language and an interpreter to interpret the grammar. Musicians are examples of Interpreters. The pitch of a sound and its duration can be represented in musical notation on a staff. This notation provides the language of music. Musicians playing the music from the score are able to reproduce the original pitch and duration of each sound represented.

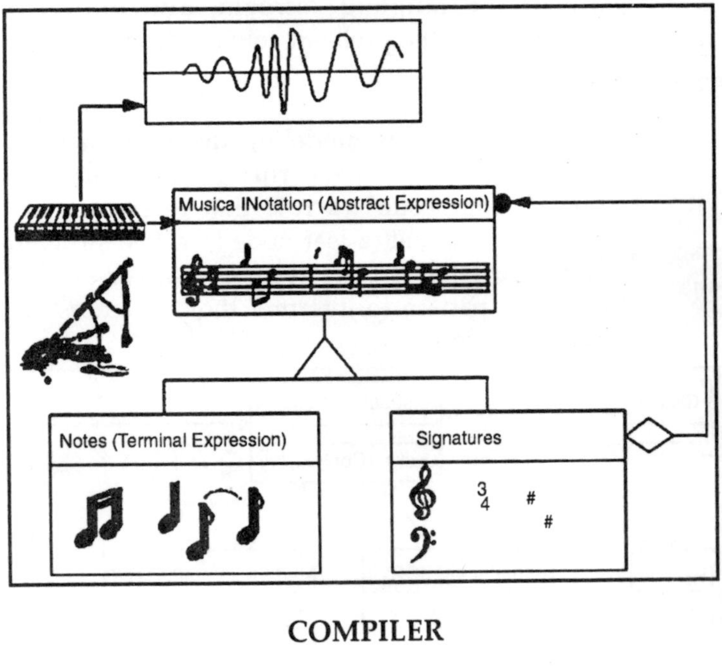

COMPILER

DEFINITION

A compiler completely converts programme code to machine code once. The computer user runs the machine code in the form of an executable command, ending in.exe say. Because the translation is complete before execution, compiled code is much faster.

The translation process should also report the presence of errors in the source programme.

Source Programme → Compiler → Target Programme

↓

Error Messages

There are two parts of compilation. The analysis part breaks up the source programme into constant piece and creates an intermediate representation of the source programme.

The synthesis part constructs the desired target programme from the intermediate representation. *Compilers* were the first sort of translator programme to be written. The idea is simple: You write the programme, then hand it to the compiler which translates it. Then run the result.

The compiler takes the file that you have written and produces another file from it. In the case of Pascal programmes, for instance, you might write a programme called my Prog.pas and the Pascal compiler would translate it into the file myProg.exe which you could then run. If you tried to examine the contents of myProg.exe using, say, a text editor, then it would just appear as gobbledy-gook.

The compiler has another task apart from translating your programme. It also checks it to make sure that it is grammatically correct. Only when it is sure that there are no grammatical errors does it do the translation. Any errors that the compiler detects are called compile-time errors or syntax errors. If it finds so much as one syntax error, it stops compiling and reports the error to you. Here is an example of the C++ compiler reporting a whole list of errors:

COMPILER PHASES

The compiler has a number of phases plus symbol table manager and an error handler:

Input Source Programme

↓

Lexical Analyser

↓

Syntax Analyser

↓

Symbol Table Manager — Semantic Analyser — Error Handler

↓

Intermediate Code Generator

↓

Code Optimizer

↓

Code Generator

↓

Out Target Programme

The cousins of the compiler are:

- Preprocessor.
- Assembler.
- Loader and Link-editor.

Front End vs Back End of a Compilers. The phases of a compiler are collected into front end and back end. The front end includes all analysis phases end the intermediate code generator. The back end includes the code optimization phase and final code generation phase. The front end analyses the source programme and produces intermediate code while the back end synthesizes the target programme from the intermediate code.

A naive approach (front force) to that front end might run the phases serially:

- Lexical analyser takes the source programme as an input and produces a long string of tokens.
- Syntax Analyser takes an out of lexical analyser and produces a large tree.
- Semantic analyser takes the output of syntax analyser and produces another tree.
- Similarly, intermediate code generator takes a tree as an input produced by semantic analyser and produces intermediate code.

Minus Points

- Requires enormous amount of space to store tokens and trees.
- Very slow since each phase would have to input and output to and from temporary disk

Remedy

- use syntax directed translation to inter leaves the actions of phases.
- Compiler construction tools.

Parser Generators

The specification of input based on regular expression. The organization is based on finite automation.

Scanner Generator

The specification of input based on regular expression. The organization is based on finite automation.

Syntax-Directed Translation

It walks the parse tee and as a result generate intermediate code.

Automatic Code Generators

Translates intermediate rampage into machine language.

Data-Flow Engines

It does code optimization using data-flow analysis.

WORKING OF COMPILER

Compiling a programme takes several stages of processing, which outlined as shown. The principles which are explained below also apply to interpreters, with the exception that the interpreters translate each programme one line at a time before running it, and then moving on to the next line.

Tokenising

This part of the process is also sometimes called *Lexical*

Analysis. It involves turning the programme from a series of characters into a series of *tokens* that represent the building blocks of a programme. The tokens are keywords of the language *i.e.* important words such as *if, print* or *repeat*), variable names and mathematical operators (+, *, brackets etc.).

The tokeniser takes each of the characters in turn, and as soon as it recognises a legitimate token, it reports it to the next stage of the process. Each token has a label and a type, so a variable "count" in a programme would have the label corresponding to its name ("count") and the type "variable name". The tokeniser is also responsible for ignoring comments in the programme - these are words and phrases inserted purely for the benefit of any human reading the programme, and they have no function.

Syntax Analysis

Syntax means "grammar" and the syntax analyser in a compiler checks that the right tokens appear in the right order to make grammatically correct instructions. For instance, in C++, the instruction xyz++; is syntactically correct, but the instruction +;xyz+is not - the order of the tokens is wrong.

Semantic Analysis

The word "semantics" refers to *meaning*, and the semantic analyser checks the meaning of the programme. This refers to aspects such as whether the variables have been declared, *e.g.* xyz++; may be syntactically correct, but if the variable xyz has not been declared, then it is semantically incorrect!

The semantic analyser checks not only variable declarations and scope, but whether the programme has entered or left loops, or subroutines, whether classes are accessed correctly etc.

ADVANTAGES

Choosing the right C compiler for your embedded-system projects may be a bigger challenge than you expect. The embedded-system-industry trend is moving from using assembly to using the higher level languages. Assembly language gives you more control over your code size and execution speeds. However, embedded C is easy to understand and portable from platform to platform. Another benefit is that developing code in C generally improves your product time to market. These features are advantageous if you expect your firmware to have longevity or if your staff changes periodically.

A variety of embedded-C compilers is available in the market today. Embedded-C compilers are available as shareware from controller- or processor-IC vendors; or from high-end, reputable software companies whose selling prices often reflect the sophistication of the software. Some compiler-software companies have great advertisements and competitive prices but inferior products. So, how do you choose your compiler software for now and for the future?

There are many issues to consider when choosing your compiler. The most important are ANSI compliance, size and speed optimizations, portability, and supporting tools.

Adherence to the ANSI standard for the C language is critical for about 80 to 85% of code. This feature facilitates portability from part to part, as well as from software platform to software platform. ANSI-compliant software also integrates easy-to-understand code into your library.

This type of code—if it is well-written—will have a shelf life like a good red wine. Even if portability is not an issue, it is important to understand how the compiler differs from ANSI and whether those differences will impact your development.

If the compiler of interest is ANSI-compliant, you should then examine the software's machine-code-generation capability. You might ask whether the compiler output code is optimized for small code (because memory is precious in controllers or processors) or whether the application executes in a timely or time-accurate manner. These features are somewhat mutually exclusive, but the compiler software should be able to optimize one or the other. Portability between platforms is critical in larger companies that have a diverse range of products. However, it can also be convenient in smaller companies that may want the flexibility to quickly change controllers during development. Portability allows you to change quickly from one controller to another during application development. It also makes your code libraries more valuable over time.

If you want to easily complete your programming projects, the compiler cannot stand on its own. Every compiler needs an integrated suite of other tools. This tool suite should have, at a minimum, an integrated development environment that comes complete with a simulator and a hardware-debugging interface. Sometimes, you can mix and match these tools from other vendors, but use the vendor for your compiler as a first source. It can be difficult and frustrating to mix and then match tools from various vendors.

Some other characteristics that make up a good compiler are the availability of code libraries and library support. This concept does not fit into organizations with the NIH (not-invented-here) philosophy. An NIH organization deserves everything it gets (or doesn't get). Libraries with code that implements useful functions help expedite your projects to completion. Many times, these libraries have gone through evaluations and debugging to ensure their value.

Some of the final details in your compiler evaluation have to do with customer service. You need to ask whether your compiler company supports your questions and helps with its software bugs. You will find this information in the company's application-notes library, discussion forums, and software-release history. Although frequent releases can be a sign of responsiveness, they can also be an indication of serious stability concerns. The ideal compiler vendor has more support than you'll ever need.

In the past, most firmware designers would write embedded-firmware programmes in assembly language. The embedded-C compiler transforms your source code into machine code. The C compiler you use determines the size as well as the execution time of your code. Many ways exist for determining these factors, so running your own test programmes is also important. Don't depend on the results from a compiler-software company that runs its own tests. Many times, these companies can consciously or unconsciously skew the results.

5

Role of Linux

MEMORY AND FILE MANAGEMENT

MEMORY

Memory is the electronic holding place for instructions and data that the computer's microprocessor can reach quickly. When the computer is in normal operation, its memory usually contains the main parts of the operating system and some or all of the application programmes and related data that are being used. Memory is often used as a shorter synonym for random access memory (RAM). This kind of memory is located on one or more microchips that are physically close to the microprocessor in the computer.

Most desktop and notebook computers sold today include at least 16 megabytes of RAM, and are upgradeable to include more. The more RAM you have, the less frequently the computer has to access instructions and data from the more slowly accessed hard disk form of storage.

Memory is sometimes distinguished from storage, or the physical medium that holds the much larger amounts of data that won't fit into RAM and may not be immediately needed there. Storage devices include hard disks, floppy disks, CD-ROM, and tape backup systems. The terms auxiliary storage, auxiliary memory, and secondary memory have also been used for this kind of data repository.

Additional kinds of integrated and quickly accessible memory are read-only memory (ROM), programmable ROM (PROMO), erasable programmable ROM (EPROM). These are used to keep special programmes and data, such as the basic input/output system, that need to be in the computer all the time.

The memory is a resource that needs to be managed carefully. Most computers have a memory hierarchy, with a small amount of very fast, expensive, volatile cache memory, some number of megabytes of medium-speed, medium-price, volatile main memory (RAM), and hundreds of thousands of megabytes of slow, cheap, non-volatile disk storage. It is the job of the operating system to coordinate how these memories are used.

The part of the operating system that manages the memory hierarchy is the memory manager. It keeps track of parts of memory that are in use and those that are not in use, to allocate memory to processes when they need it and de-allocate it when they are done, and to manage swapping between main memory and disk when main memory is too small to hold all the processes.

Systems for managing memory can be divided into two categories: the system of moving processes back and forth between main memory and disk during execution (known as swapping and paging) and the process that does not do so (that is, no swapping and ping).

Mono Programming without Swapping or Paging

The most simple memory management scheme is to run one programme at a time, sharing the memory between that programme and the operating system. As shown in the diagram bellow, there are three variations of this type. The operating system may be at the bottom of the memory in TAM (random access memory), as shown in the diagram 1, or it may be in ROM (read-only memory) at the top of the memory, as shown in diagram 2, or the device drivers may be at the top of the memory in a ROM and the rest of the system in RAM down bellow

With the system organised in this way, only one process at a time can be running. As soon as the user types a command, the operating system copies the request programme from a disk to memory and executes it. When the process finishes, the operating system displays a prompt character and waits for a new command. When it receives the command, it loads a new programme into memory overwriting the first one.

Mono Programming with Fixed Partitions

It is often desirable to allow multiple processes to run at the same time, even on simple operating systems in which multiprogramming is sometimes used. On time-sharing systems, having multiple processes in memory at once means that when one process is blocked waiting for the I/O to finish, another one can use the CPU. This way, multiprogramming increases the CPU utilisation. It is however preferable to be able to run two or more programmes at once even on personal computers.

Swapping

The process of organising memory into fixed partitions on batch system is simple compared to time sharing systems or graphically oriented personal computers. On batch systems, each job is loaded into a partition when it gets to the head of the queue. It stays in memory until it has finished. As long as enough jobs can be kept in memory to keep the CPU busy all the time, there is no reason to use anything more complicated. On time-sharing machines, sometimes there is not enough main memory to hold all the currently active processes, therefore excess processes must be kept on disk and brought in to run dynamically.

Swapping as an approach to memory management consists of bringing each process in its entirety, running it for a while, then putting it back on the disk.

THE SCENARIO

The problem we are trying to overcome is simply this: You want to develop some kind of file or text editor, and you want your programme to be able to load, edit and save files of any size. In fact, you want your programme to load and edit the largest sized file possible. Under 32bit Windows this is a 4Gb file. (Actually, Windows NT supports 18 exabyte files with its 64bit NTFS file system, but I will talk about this type of file later in the series.

Your file editor needs be able to load a 4Gb file in a fraction of a second. In addition, insertions and deletions to and from the file must be as fast for a 4Gb file as they are for a 1Kb file. This series of articles (I haven't decided exactly how many articles there will be yet) will take you through the design decisions and algorithms necessary to accomplish these goals. At the end of the series you will have enough information to develop your own file-handling functions, which will be as powerful and flexible as those used in my HexEdit application.

MEMORY MANAGEMENT

Let's forget about actually editing a large file for the moment, and concentrate just on loading a file into your application. So, your have a 4Gb file saved on your hard disk, and you want to load this file so you can preview any portion of it. Let's assume that our first application will be a simple hex file viewer, with no editing capabilities.

The first decision to take is what memory facilities we will use to gain access to the file's contents. To make this decision, we need to know what memory facilities are available to our programme, and base our decision on that. Because our file viewer will be a 32bit Windows programme capable of running under Windows 9x and NT/ 2000, we have the following facilities at our disposal.

VIRTUAL MEMORY

Another strategy for managing memory is the virtual memory, which allows programmes to run even when they are only partially in main memory. The basic idea behind this strategy is that the combine size of the programme, data, and stack may exceed the amount of physical memory available for it. The operating system keeps those parts of the programme currently in use in main memory, and the rest on the disk. Virtual memory can also work in a multiprogramming system, with bits and pieces pf many programmes in memory at once. While a programme is waiting for a part of itself to be brought in, it is waiting for I/O and cannot run, so the CPU can be given to another process, the same way as for any other multiprogramming system. Most virtual memory systems use a technique called paging.

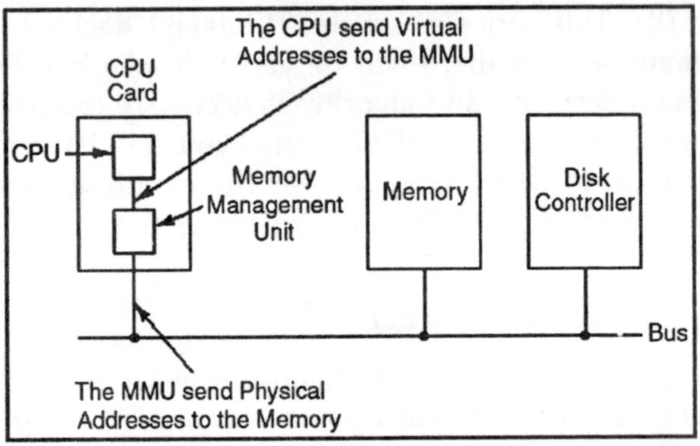

Every 32bit process in Windows has a 4Gb virtual address space, regardless of the amount of physical RAM you have installed. Of this total virtual space, only 2Gb is available for an application's private use. Actually, the available space slightly less than this - 128Kb less in WinNT and 4Mb less in Win9x). There are a variety of methods to allocate memory from this 2Gb region of space. All depend on how much memory needs to be allocated, and what its intended use is.

Malloc and new

The simplest is to use the standard C or C++ memory allocation routines (malloc and new[], respectively). Both of these methods use the memory allocation facilities provided by the operating system. In Visual C++ 6.0, malloc and new[] use VirtualAlloc internally. Anyway, malloc and new[] are only really meant for allocating lots of small objects, not one gigantic memory region.

HeapAlloc

The second method to allocate memory in Windows is

to use the Heap function – HeapAlloc (or the older LocalAlloc and GlocalAlloc). These functions are also meant for allocating many small objects though - just like malloc and new[] - and are also implemented by calls to VirtualAlloc.

VirtualAlloc

The third way to allocate memory in Windows is to use VirtualAlloc directly. This method is much more flexible because it allows you to specify where you want the memory to be in your address space, and allows you to reserve a region of memory without actually allocating any space from it.

Memory-Mapped-Files

The forth way to allocate memory is by using Memory Mapped Files. Rather than allocating memory, a memory-mapped file is a reserved region of the 2Gb address space, which has mapped into it a region a file stored on disk. The great thing about memory-mapped-files is that they free the programmer from having to do any direct file reading or writing. Simply reading and writing to the memory-mapped view causes the file's contents to be accessed. The operating system provides clever page caching to make memory-mapped files a very quick way to read/write to a file.

DOS

DEFINITION

DOS (Disk Operating System) was the first widely-installedo perating system for personal computers. (Earlier, the same name had been used for an IBM operating system for a line of business computers.)

The first personal computer version of DOS, called PC-DOS, was developed for IBM by Bill Gates and his new Microsoft Corporation. He retained the rights to market a Microsoft version, called MS-DOS. PC-DOS and MS-DOS are almost identical and most users have referred to either of them as just "DOS." DOS was (and still is) a non-graphical line-oriented command- or menu-driven operating system, with a relatively simple interface but not overly "friendly" user interface. Its prompt to enter a command looks like this:

C:>

The first Microsoft Windows operating system was really an application that ran on top of the MS-DOS operating system. Today, Windows operating systems continue to support DOS (or a DOS-like user interface) for special purposes by emulating the operating system.

In the 1970s before the personal computer was invented, IBM had a different and unrelated DOS (Disk Operating System) that ran on smaller business computers. It was replaced by IBM's VSE operating system. DOS stands for Disk Operating System. DOS controls the computer's hardware and provides an environment for programmes to run. Everything you can do with a GUI can be done at the DOS prompt. There are many flavours of *DOS operating system*like MS-DOS, PC DOS, DR DOS, FreeDOS, etc. There are two types of commands in DOS, internal and external. Internal commands are part of the command processor, whereas external commands exist as executable files. The entire operating system is small enough to fit on a floppy disk.

Booting

To run DOS on a computer, it should be the first programme to be executed when the computer is switched on. This led to a problem for the designers: "How can DOS be loaded and executed when there is no DOS programme running to load and execute *it*??!!". Well, just as the fictional Baron Munchausen managed to pull himself up by his own bootstraps, the computer manages this seemingly impossible trick, and the term "bootstrapping", or "booting up" is applied to this process.

Communicating with DOS

DOS is an entirely text based system. All it provides for the user is a prompt: "C:>" or "A:>", where the user can type in commands from the keyboard. The system is entirely case insensitive: so either "ForMAt C:" or "format c:" would erase your hard disk... The latter example is of course a small warning: with DOS comes power, you can very easily mess up your system if you use powerful commands in the wrong way. The commands you should be careful of are: "Format", "Recover", and "Del". All of these perform useful functions, when used correctly, and all the others are pretty much safe to use.

Working of DOS

DOS works within a file, directory and disk drive structure. This means that all programme and data files are named, and grouped together in named directories on disks. 'Directories' are just lists of files.

Naming of Files

While newer versions of DOS support longer filenames, the standard DOS filename format remains: 1-8 letter name, period, 3 letter extension eg:

```
PROGRAMME.EXE      DATA.DAT      LETTER.DOC
```

The extension to a file's name is there to allow files of a similar type to be grouped together. Ie. all wordprocessor files might have the extension.DOC, while all picture files might have the extension.PIC While these extensions can be specified by the user, many programmes have used them to differentiate between formats, and so they have gradually become standardised. For example you would expect a ".TXT" file to be a file containing unformatted text, or a ".BMP" file to be in a bit mapped graphics file format.

To completely specify a file on your computer you must specify its drive and directory path, and its filename. However a file does not always have to be specified in this complete form: If it is in the current directory, then you can just enter its filename.

Naming Directories

Every disk drive has a root directory which can have subdirectories which are named in the same format as filenames, (though generally without any extension). The subdirectories can have subdirectories and so on. Eg: a floppy disk might contain the following directory structure:

- Pictures
- Holiday
- Italy
- France
- Family
- Pets
- Text
- Letters
- E-mail

A directory path name includes the disk drive and all subdirectories needed to specify a directory on a disk. The disk drive is specified by a single letter. Eg: The floppy disk drive is A and the hard disk drive is C.

The drive letter, is followed by a colon, the directory path names are separated by backward slashes (\), (*Not* forward slashes like internet addresses). Eg. In the above example "A:\PICTURES\HOLIDAY\FRANCE" would be more than likely to contain pictures of a few baguettes and onions.

Uses of DOS

When you type anything at the DOS prompt, and press enter, you are telling DOS to run a programme. It will first look to see if there is an internal command programme which has that name, and if it does not find one, then it will look to see if there is a file on disk with that name.

If it finds an external file with the extension.COM (command), or.EXE (executable), then the programme is loaded and run. At this point DOS looses control of the computer until the programme has ended. However parts of it are still used by the programmes as they are running, eg to load and save files etc.

Some very useful internal DOS commands:

A: Change current directory path to the floppy disk drive

C: Change current directory path to the hard disk drive

DIR: Display current directory (show all files and sub-directories).

MD: Make a new directory, eg: MD C:\E-MAIL

CD: Change current directory, eg. CD C:\E-MAIL

COPY: Copy file(s) from one place to another.

Del: Delete/erase a file

Any other text on the input line after the file name, is passed to the programme. This means that in the command "Copy help.txt help.bak", the text, "help.txt and help.bak" is passed to the copy programme which will in this case use it to specify source and destination files for a copy.

WINDOWS OPERATING SYSTEM

Microsoft first started developing the Interface Manager (later renamed Microsoft Windows) in September 1981. While the first prototypes used Multiplan and Word-like menus at the bottom of the screen, the interface was modified in 1982 to utilize pull-down menus and dialogues, as used on the Xerox Star.

On November 10, 1983, at the Plaza Hotel in New York City, Microsoft Corporation officially announced Microsoft Windows, a next-generation operating system that would supply a graphical user interface (GUI) and a multitasking environment for IBM computers. This was after the release of the Apple Lisa, and prior to Digital Research announcing GEM, and DESQ from Quarterdeck and the Amiga Workbench, or GEOS/GeoWorks Ensemble, IBM OS/2, NeXTstep or even DeskMate from Tandy. Windows assured an easy-to-use graphical interface, device-independent graphics and multitasking support. The development was held up several times, however, and the Windows 1.0 arrive at store shelves in November 1985. The selection of applications was thin, however, and Windows sales were moderate.

Windows 1.0 package, included: MS-DOS Executive, Calendar, Cardfile, Notepad, Terminal, Calculator, Clock, Reversi, Control Panel, PIF (Programme Information File) Editor, Print Spooler, Clipboard, RAMDrive, Windows Write,

Windows Paint. Microsoft Windows version 1.0 was viewed as buggy, rough, and sluggish. This bumpy start was made sorrier by a threatened lawsuit from Apple Computers. In September 1985, Apple lawyers warned Bill Gates that Windows 1.0 infringed on Apple copyrights and patents, and that his corporation had stolen Apple's trade secrets. Microsoft Windows had similar drop-down menus, tiled windows and mouse support.

Bill Gates and his head counsel Bill Neukom, chose to make an offer to license features of Apple's operating system. Apple concurred and a contract was drawn up. The key to this is: Microsoft wrote the licensing agreement to include use of Apple features in Microsoft Windows version 1.0 and all future Microsoft software programmes. As it turned out, this move by Bill Gates was as intelligent as his decision to purchase QDOS from Seattle Computer Products and his persuading IBM to let Microsoft keep the licensing rights to MS-DOS. Windows 1.0 fluttered on the market until January 1987, when a Windows-compatible programme called Aldus PageMaker 1.0 was brought out. PageMaker was the first WYSIWYG desktop-publishing programme for the PC. Later that year, Microsoft released a Windows-compatible spreadsheet called Excel. Other popular and functional software like Microsoft Word and Corel Draw helped advance Windows, yet, Microsoft recognized that Windows required further development.

Microsoft Windows version 2.0 came out in December 1987, and evidenced somewhat more popular than its predecessor. A great deal of the popularity for Windows 2.0 came through its inclusion as a "run-time version" with Microsoft's new graphical applications, Excel and Word for Windows. They could be operated from MS-DOS, executing Windows for the length of their activity, and shutting down Windows upon exit.

Microsoft Windows incurred a major boost about this time when Aldus PageMaker came out in a Windows version, having previously run exclusively on Macintosh. Some computer historians date this, the introduction of a significant and non-Microsoft application for Windows, as the start of the success of Windows.

Versions 2.0x used the real-mode memory model, which held it to a maximum of 1 megabyte of memory. In such a form, it could run under a different multitasker like DESQview, which used the 286 Protected Mode. Subsequently, two new versions were published: Windows/286 2.1 and Windows/386 2.1.Like preceding versions of Windows, Windows/286 2.1 used the real-mode memory model, but was the first version to support the HMA.

Windows/386 2.1 had a protected mode kernel with LIM-standard EMS emulation, the predecessor to XMS which would at last shift the topology of IBM PC computing. All Windows and DOS-based applications at the time were real mode, running over the protected mode kernel by using the virtual 8086 mode, which was new with the 80386 processor.

After Versions 2.0 and beyond were released, Apple began filing suit against IBM for various copyright infringements. In their defence, Microsoft claimed that their licensing agreement actually afforded them the rights to use Apple features. Apple claimed that Microsoft had encroached on 170 of their copyrights. After a four-year court case, Microsoft won. The courts stated that the licensing agreement gave Microsoft the rights to use all but nine of the copyrights, and Microsoft later convinced the courts that the other nine copyrights shouldn't be covered by copyright law. Bill Gates asserted that Apple had acquired ideas from the graphical user interface developed by Xerox for Xerox's Alto and Star computers. On June 1, 1993, Judge Vaughn R. Walker of the U.S. District Court of Northern California ruled in Microsoft's favour in the Apple vs. Microsoft and Hewlett-Packard copyright suit. The judge granted Microsoft's and Hewlett-Packard's motions to dismiss the last remaining copyright infringement claims against Microsoft Windows versions 2.03 and 3.0, as well as HP NewWave.

What would have occurred if Microsoft had lost the lawsuit? Microsoft Windows might never have become the predominant operating system that it is today.

FEATURES

Some individuals with disabilities require assistive technology (AT) in order to access computers. Hundreds of Windows AT third-party products are available, making it possible for almost anyone to use Windows® applications, regardless of their disabilities. The Microsoft® Windows® operating systems also provides a core set of basic accessibility features and AT applications, which can be deployed on all computers in a computer lab or classroom without additional cost. These applications provide students with basic accessibility features from any workstation, maximizing the inclusiveness of the learning environment. It should be noted that the AT applications that are bundled with Windows provide only a minimum level of accessibility, not the full set of features that many users require for equal access to the operating system, educational programmes, and other software applications. Therefore, many educational entities deploy the standard set of Windows AT on all workstations by default, but addditionally 1) provide a small number of dedicated workstations that are equipped with commonly requested third party AT, and 2) are prepared to purchase and install additional AT as needed by specific students. It should also be noted that the availability of AT does not itself guarantee accessibility. Software applications must be designed in a way that is compatible with AT and other accessibility features of the operating system. The following is a list of basic accessibility features that are included with Windows XP. Previous versions of Windows also included several of these same features.

Display and Readability

These features are designed to increase the visibility of items on the screen.

- *Font style, colour, and size of items on the desktop*: Using the Display options, choose font colour, size and style combinations.
- *Icon size*: Make icons larger for visibility, or smaller for increased screen space.

- *Screen resolution*: Change pixel count to enlarge objects on screen.
- *High contrast schemes*: Select colour combinations that are easier to see.
- *Cursor width and blink rate*: Make the cursor easier to locate, or eliminate the distraction of its blinking.
- *Microsoft Magnifier*: Enlarge portion of screen for better visibility.

Sounds and Speech

These features are designed to make computer sounds easier to hear or distinguish - or, visual alternatives to sound. Speech-to-text options are also available.

- *Sound Volume*: Turn computer sound up or down.
- *Sound Schemes*: Associate computer sounds with particular system events.
- *ShowSounds*: Display captions for speech and sounds.
- *SoundSentry*: Display visual warnings for system sounds.
- *Notification*: Get sound or visual cues when accessibility features are turned on or off.
- *Text-to-Speech*: Hear window command options and text read aloud.

Keyboard and Mouse

These features are designed to make the keyboard and mouse faster and easier to use.

Mouse Options:

- *Double-Click Speed*: Choose how fast to click the mouse button to make a selection.
- *ClickLock*: Highlight or drag without holding down the mouse button.
- *Pointer Speed*: Set how fast the mouse pointer moves on screen.
- *Snapto*: Move the pointer to the default button in a dialog box.
- *Cursor Blink Rate*: Choose how fast the cursor blinks—or, if it blinks at all.

- *Pointer Trails*: Follow the pointer motion on screen.
- *Hide Pointer While Typing*: Keep pointer from hiding text while typing.
- *Show Location of Pointer*: Quickly reveal the pointer on screen.
- *Reverse the function of the right and left mouse buttons*: Reverse actions controlled by the right and left mouse buttons.
- *Pointer schemes*: Choose size and colour options for better visibility.

Keyboard Options

- *Character Repeat Rate*: Set how quickly a character repeats when a key is struck.
- *Dvorak Keyboard Layout*: Choose alternative keyboard layouts for people who type with one hand or finger.
- *Sticky Keys*:Allow pressing one key at a time (rather than simultaneously) for key combinations.
- *Filter Keys*: Ignore brief or repeated keystrokes and slow down the repeat rate.
- *Toggle Keys*: Hear tones when pressing certain keys.
- *MouseKeys*: Move the mouse pointer using the numerical keypad.
- *Extra Keyboard Help*: Get ToolTips or other keyboard help in programmes that provide it.

Accessibility Wizard

The Accessibility Wizard is designed to help new users quickly and easily set up groups of accessibility options that address visual, hearing and dexterity needs all in one place. The Accessibility Wizard asks questions about accessibility needs.

Then, based on the answers, it configures utilities and settings for individual users. The Accessibility Wizard can be run again at any time to make changes, or changes can be made to individual settings through Control Panel.

LINUX

FUNDAMENTAL OF LINUX

If you truly enjoy working with computers, Linux is the operating system of your dreams. It is more fun than any other computer operating system around. Linux is a computer hobbyist's paradise.

However, the reason why Linux is truly revolutionary is that it is Open Software. Our science and technology work owing to the free availability of information, peer review, public critique, and the capablitiy to pick up ideas and modify or extend them. Open Software is an implementation of the scientific method into the field of software development. The freedom to pick-up, modify and extend, that comes with the Linux licence, offers a promise that the software development under Linux licence will continue in the way that science does.

The making of horseshoes, good glass, or measuring time were once closely guarded trade secrets. Science and technology exploded 500 years ago thanks to the sharing of knowledge by the means of printing, and thus breaking the monopoly of the few on the know-how. Why were the science and technology relatively stagnant before the printing era? Because the "trade secret" approach to growth has its limits: the development continues until the rate of learning equals the rate of forgetting.

Moving the know-how to the public domain (printed on paper) shifted the position of the equilibrium to a higher level, which, after 500 years of turbulent development, we are still to achieve. For interested, I can present equations, borrowed from chemical equilibrium field, that describe this in a more formal way. The main point is that printing increased the audience, and allowed passing information across space and time. In the early days of printing, many of those who dared to share were assassinated for revealing "trade secrets." Linux is for the computer age what Gutenberg was for writing. Hopefully there will be no assassinations this time:-). Linux does clash, violently at times, with those who claim the "ownership" of information, trying to push time back 500 years. Open Source Linux has also implications for computer security. Imagine a plane based on secret "scientific laws" and built to an unreviewed design, a plane at internals of which nobody but the manufacturer could inspect. Would you believe that this new, unique, completely proprietary plane, obviously built by clever and well-financed marketers in their basement, is any safer than one built in the open world, under the eyes of thousands of critical engineers and curious hobbyists with no association to the manufacturer?

Then why would you trust a secret computer programme? Open-source Linux is ideally suited for a mission-critical application—its security and power are based on robust solutions which are reviewed with no restrictions whatsoever, and continuously improved upon.

Linux is quite different from MS Windows, so do not expect that if you can get around MS Windows, then Linux will be straightforward for you. You may need to learn. On the other hand, if you come from UNIX, Linux will be easy for you.

BENEFITS OF LINUX

Linux can give you:

o A modern, very stable, multi-user, multitasking environment on your inexpensive PC hardware, at no (or almost no) monetary cost for the software. Linux is a rich and powerful platform—don't think of it as a "poor people" operating system. Out-of-box Linux has as much capability as MS Windows NT with $5000 in software add-ons, is more stable, and requires less powerful hardware for comparable tasks.

- Standard platform. Linux is VERY standard—it is essentially a POSIX compliant UNIX. (Yes, Linux is a best-of-the-breed UNIX. The word "UNIX" is not used in conjunction with Linux because "UNIX" is a registered trademark of "The Open Group".) Linux includes all the tools and utilities typically associated with UNIX, plus more, significantly more than even the most expensive commercial UNIX implementations.

To run Linux software, UNIX vendors these days implement "Linux compatiblity layers" into their platforms.

- Unsurpassed computing power, portability, flexibility, and customizibility. A Linux cluster recently (April 1999) beat a Cray supercomputer in a standard benchmark. Linux is most popular on Intel-based PCs (price of the hardware), but it runs very well on numerous other hardware platforms, from toy-like to mainframes. One distribution (Debian) expresses the idea like this: "Linux, The Universal Operating System." Linux can be customised to perform almost any computing task.
- Advanced graphical user interface. Linux uses a standard, network-transparent X-windowing system with a "window manager" (typically KDE or GNOME). The graphical desktop under Linux can be made to look like MS Windows (or probably ANY other graphical user interface of your choice).
- Dozens of excellent, free, general-interest desktop applications. These include a range of web browsers, e-mail programmes, word processors, spreadsheets, bitmap and vector graphics programmes, file managers, audio players, CD writers, some good games, etc.
- Thousands of free applets, tools, and smaller programmes. "Small is beautiful" goes well with Linux philosophy. The small Linux tools and applets often work in tandem to perform more complex tasks.
- Hundreds of specialized applications built by researchers around the world (astronomy, information technology, chemistry, physics, engineering, linguistics, biology...). In many fields, Linux seems like "the only" operating system in existence (try to find out what your friend astronomer runs on her computer). The software in this category is typically not very easy to use, but if

you want the power, it is the best software that humanity has in these areas.

- Scores of top-of-the line commercial programmes including all the big databases (*e.g.*, Oracle, Sybase, but no Microsoft's). Many (most?) of these are offered free for developers and for personal use.
- A truly great learning platform. If you are a parent, you should be really glad your daughter/son does Linux—s/he will surely learn something of lasting value. If you are a teacher, you should consider the installation of Linux at your school. "It is indeed a strange world when educators need to be convinced that sharing information, as opposed to concealing information, is a good thing". You select Linux if you care to provide education, not training. The better the university, the greater the chance their computer department uses Linux in teaching. For example, under Linux, you can immediately begin modifying and compiling for yourself a spreadsheet application which is in every bit as advanced and capable as MS Excel. Linux puts you right on the cutting edge (in technology, project management, QA, methodology of science). Many teachers won't use Linux in schools because they are lacking in computer education themselves.
- Excellent networking capability built into your operating system. You think you don't need a network? Once you try home networking, you will never be able to live without it! How about connecting the two or more computers that you have at home and sharing your hard drives, CDROM(s), sound card(s), modem, printer(s), etc.? How about browsing the net on two or more machines at the same time using a single Internet connection? How about playing a game with your son over your home network? Even your old 386 with Win3.11 may become useful again when connected to your Linux Pentium server and when it is able to use your

network resources. All necessary networking software comes with standard Linux, free, just setup is required. And it is not second-rate shareware—it is exactly the same software that runs most of the Internet (the Apache software runs more than 50% of all Internet web servers and Sendmail touches some 70% of all e-mail). The pleasure of home networking is something I was able to discover only owing to Linux.

- Connectivity to Microsoft, Novel, and Apple proprietary networking. Reading/writing to your DOS/MS Windows and other disk formats. This includes "transparent" use of data stored on the legacy MS Windows partition of your hard drive(s).
- State-of-the-art development platform with many best-of-the-kind programming languages and tools coming free with the operating system. Access to all the operating system source codes, should you require it, is also free. The "C" compiler that comes standard with Linux can compile code for more platforms than (probably) any other compiler on earth. Perl, Python, Guile, Tcl, Ruby, powerful "shell" scripting, and even assembler tools also come as standard with Linux.
- Freedom from viruses, "backdoors" to your computer, software manufacturer "features," invasion of privacy, forced upgrades, proprietary file formats, licensing and marketing schemes, product registration, high software prices, and pirating. How is this? Linux has no viruses worth mentioning because it is too secure an operating system for the viruses to spread with any degree of efficiency. The rest follows from the open-source and non-commercial nature of Linux: Linux evolved itself by "bazaar-like" mechanisms to encapsulate the best computing practices, code legibility and correctness, security, flexibility, usefulness, coolness, and performance.

- The operating platform that is guaranteed "here-to-stay." Since Linux is not owned, it cannot possibly be put out of business. The Linux General Public License (GPL) insures that development/maintenance will be provided as long as there are Linux users. There are a great number of highly-educated Linux users and tens of thousands of actively developed projects.
- A platform which will technically develop at a rapid pace. This is insured by the modern, open-software development model which Linux implements: "build-on-the-back-of-the-previous-developer" and "peer-review-your-code" (as opposed to the anachronistic closed-software model: "always-start-from-scratch" and "nobody-will-see-my-code"). Even if the current "Linux hype" died out, Linux will develop as it did before the media hype started. Open source development does have its peculiarities: the development appears rather slow (vertically) but it proceeds on a very wide front, dangerous security bugs are fixed almost upon discovery, there are typically several alternatives for a programme of similar functionality. Linux depth cannot be overestimated.

LINUX AND UNIX

Command-line-wise, almost none, although this has been changing (for better or worse). Linux has a much larger market appeal and following than any commercial UNIX. GUI-wise there are also no major differences—Linux, as most other UNIXes, uses an X-Windowing system.

The major differences:

- Linux is free, while many UNICES (this is supposed to be the plural of UNIX), are very expensive. The same for applications—many good applications are available on Linux free. Even the same commercial application (if you wanted to buy one) typically costs much more for a commercial UNIX than for Linux.

- Linux runs on many hardware platforms, the commodity Intel-x86/IBM-spec personal computers being the most prominent. In contrast, a typical UNIX is proprietary-hardware-bonded (and this hardware tends to be much more expensive than a typical PC clone).
- With Linux, you are in charge of your computer, whereas on most UNICES you are typically confined to be an "l-user" (some administrators pronounce it "loser").
- Linux feels very much like DOS/Win in the late 80s/90s, but is much sturdier and richer, while a typical UNIX account feels like a mainframe from the 60s/70s.
- Some UNICES may be more mature in certain areas (for example, security, some engineering applications, better support of cutting-edge hardware). Linux is more for the average Joe who wants to run his own server or engineering workstation.

LINUX AND MS WINDOWS

Mouse-click-wise, almost none, once Linux is properly installed. Linux installation can be a challenge though, whereas MS Windows comes, most likely, pre-installed with your computer.

The major differences

Linux is free, whereas MS Windows costs money. Same for applications. If MS Windows or Office comes preinstalled with the computer it is unlikely it is free. Ask in the store to take it off your computer and you are likely to obtain a discount, at least in smaller stores.

- Linux file formats are free, so you can access them in a variety of ways. On MS Windows, the common practice is to make you lock your own data in secret formats that can only be accessed with tools leased to you at the vendor's price. How corrupt (or incompetent?) must be the politicians who lock our public records into these formats! "What we will get with Microsoft is a three-year lease on a health record we need to keep for 100 years" [http://news.bbc.co.uk/hi/english/health/newsid_1694000/1694372.stm].

- With Linux, you are unlikely to violate any licence agreement—all the software is happily yours. With MS Windows you likely already violate all kinds of licenses and you could be pronounced a computer pirate if only a smart lawyer was after you (don't worry, most likely none is after you).
- MS Windows tries to be the "lowest-common-denominator" operating system (for better or worse), whereas Linux is built for more sophisticated, feature-hungry computer users (for better or worse).
- MS Windows is based on DOS; Linux is based on UNIX. MS Windows Graphical User Interface (GUI) is based on Microsoft-owned specifications. Linux GUI is based on an industry-standard network-transparent X-Windowing system.
- Linux beats Windows hands down on network features, as a development platform, in data processing capabilities, and as a scientific workstation. MS Windows desktop has a more polished appearance, smoother general business applications, and many more games for kids (these are not better games though—Linux games tend to be more sophisticated).
- Linux is more feature-rich than you could imagine. Heard on the Internet: "Two big products came from the University of California: UNIX and LSD. And I don't think it's a coincidence." MS Windows is simpler.

LINUX IS A GOOD

The Linux community has repeatedly been labeled "religious zealots" by journalists whose well-established computer magazines received massive feedback after they had published highly unfair articles on Linux. So yes, the Linux community is numerous, literate, and willing to express its opinions. And many computer journalists/magazines know that Linux means less money for them (users pay less for their computing and the associated advertisement, while expecting more). Does this explain the "zealots"? Face it, you salespeople pretending to be journalists. There is hardly any integrity left in the computing press. How many words on Linux did your PC Magazine (or any other IT magazine) publish by 1999-01-01? Wasn't Linux at least an interesting technology by that time? It surely was, yet you conspired to keep your readership in the dark, selling your journalistic integrity for a few dollars. And now, after Linux has surfaced in the mainstream (non-computer) media, you keep writing misleading articles about it saying "yah, but it will/cannot/may...." whatever (trying the "fear, uncertainty and doubt" tactics to kill it).

And adding "Microsoft is already...", continuing to write about the vaporware and the future paradise in the face of the increasingly stealthy, unstable, pricey, architecturally unsound computer platform, whose greatest achievement has been exhorting unheard-of-before money by denying inter-operatibility, and killing any existing or proposed standard (by "embracing" and then proprietary-extending it). Whom do you serve? Surely not your readers. You think "self-serving" is OK in business? How pathetic must your business be then! I always thought that business was a social contract in which we exchange good values, for a mutual benefit. As I read history, societies use to hang/ guillotine/ electrocute those members who really persisted in their self-serving business. Well, times have changed. A bit for the better, a bit for the worse:)) To be fair, there seems to be a number of hard-core devotees around any computer programme/platform, and Linux might have accummulated a fair share of them. Oh, well, you may be religious about whatever you like.

COMPARISON OF LINUX WITH MS-DOS AND WINDOWS

LINUX VS MS-DOS

DOS was the first operating system I learned to use. I

remember a test by my tutor in which one had to create a hierarchical set of directories. This probably sounds trivial to anyone familiar with graphical user interfaces, but then the scenario was very different. It even looks ancient by today's standards.

Windows 95 hadn't been released at that time, and Linux was unheard of in India. I liked DOS much better than Windows 3.1, which looked quite flimsy and unstable, not to mention that it was a big memory hog. DOS is quite different from Linux in many ways.

DOS does not provide any graphical user interface and you have to learn at least a dozen commands with its numerous options to do some basic tasks like copying a file or moving between the directories. Even a minor spelling mistake can result in a "Bad command or file name" error.

DOS does not support the concept of multi-users; each and every user has to customise the system according to his need every time he wants to work on it. It was also not a multitasking system. This meant that you could not check out the value of a calculation when typing a letter without closing that application first.

DOS also does not have any in built security features. This was acceptable as long as you did not want a networking system. There was other variants of MS-DOS, like PC-DOS from IBM and some others, which tried to add the missing features. Some of the deficiencies have been resolved using third party utilities but basic limitations like the arcane 640kb-memory limit and single-tasking were not acceptable to many.

Now in case you are wondering why anyone would care to use DOS, I will point out some advantages. Basically DOS has had very different goals from that of Linux. It was a very cheap system (as far as cost is concerned) and it was quite usable with its minimalist set of features. It was a simple system to work with. There weren't too many complications to worry about if you didn't want to develop anything on it. It was arguably the world's most popular operating system and it had a comfortable number of applications for common tasks.

Files and Directories

The files in Linux can be very long, up-to 255 characters like Windows, and they do not always have extensions. The executable files are identified through an attribute rather than the extension. File extensions are less important to Linux than for DOS and Windows, since Linux usually identifies files by a unique identification code called the magic number that depends on the file type.

Directories are similar to that of DOS and follow a hierarchical structure. The path names are separated by forward slashes (/)in Linux whereas DOS and Windows uses back slashes (\).

For example:

```
% cd/mnt/cdrom
```

A/ denotes the root and.. stands for the parent directory, similar to DOS. In bash shells, the ~ symbol maybe used to jump to the home directory quickly. For example:

```
;% cd ~
```

Linux shell

Several of the DOS commands have Linux equivalents. The Linux shell is similar to the DOS command line but is far more powerful, and I found that it was also more workable with features like colour highlighting and friendlier navigation capabilities, depending on the particular shell you are using.

Most Linux distributions come with the Bash (Bourne Again SHell) as the default. There are several others, like the Korn shell and the C shell. They are usually similar. It's recommended that you learn to work with one shell completely before trying out the others. Things usually get complicated if you want to run shell scripts, which are similar to batch files (files with the.bat extension) under DOS.

Running DOS programmes under Linux

There is a DOS emulator called dosemu www. dosemu.org for Linux that is capable of running DOS programmes under the Linux operating system. This software is still under development; you may wish to try it out though. It is known to be fairly usable at least for some applications. If you are looking for Linux just to use DOS programmes for free then try using FreeDOS www.freedos.org. That should be much better than Linux.

LINUX VS. WINDOWS

As I have said before Windows is more or less similar to Linux. When people are introduced to Linux they are at first intimidated by the system. It has different kinds of graphical interfaces and things don't always work as they are expected to. When users look at me in a puzzled manner I demonstrate in some easy ways how common tasks like changing the desktop wallpaper or playing a song is similar to Windows. The problem with this kind of approach is that the users complain very soon that Linux doesn't offer them much more than Windows does:-).

I agree with them to a certain extent on this. There are some limitations to what you can expect from an operating system. You just can't expect Linux to work like a 3D-shooter game or something. Of course, there are many differences in the shell, the choice of user interfaces and the philosophy and goals of the operating system. Linux is developed as a open system in which the source code of the core Linux system (kernel) is available for anyone for free but how this could affect the end user is difficult to explain initially.

The user interface is probably the first thing you notice when you begin to use the Linux system. Windows offers a single, monolithic user interface, which is more or less the same across all the versions. In contrast, Linux has two major desktop environments called KDE and Gnome. KDE has a built-in window manager, while Gnome is supported by many, such as Sawfish and Enlightenment.

The decision of choosing one among the desktop environments and windows managers is left to you. Some of them can run efficiently in a system with low amounts of memory and some of them are designed to look like a game console. KDE would be more similar to Windows, and Gnome with the Enlightenment window manager was fancy enough for me. Try out some of the popular ones before making the decision. Let's take a look at Windows in more detail so that you can clearly make out the differences.

Versions of Windows

Windows has two major series, a desktop oriented series (Windows 9x) And a network oriented series Windows.There are also other versions like Windows CE for embedded systems.

Windows 9x Series

Before Windows 95 was released, all versions of Windows until version 3.1 were graphical platforms on top of DOS. This offered limited capability for multitasking and the Programme Manager interface was cluttered with no distinct hierarchy. Windows 95 was a 32-bit operating system and a major improvement in user interface with its"Desktop" concept adapted from the Macintosh user interface. It also offered limited compatibility with previous versions of Windows and DOS. Stability was also improved Windows 98 and Windows ME offered some more features though nothing major was added. The more recent version called Windows XP is considerably more stable due to incorporating the Windows 2000 kernel, and is comparatively friendlier and easier due to an attractive interface.

Windows NT Series

Windows NT is considerably stable but demands more resources. It supports the Intel architecture, and at one time the Digital alpha and MIPS processors, but I believe those have been dropped now. It managed to replace UNIX in small-scale networks due to the similarity to the popular Windows 95 interface. The latest incarnation called Windows 2000 provides a few more administrative utilities and services.

6

Global Network

USE OF COMPUTER

The Internet is a global network of computers. Every computer that is connected to the Internet is considered a part of that network. This means even your home computer. It's all a matter of degrees, you connect to your ISP's network, then your ISP connects to a larger network and so on. At the top of the tree is the high-capacity backbones, all of these interconnect at'Network Access Points''NAPs' at important regions around the world. The entire Internet is based on agreements between these backbone providers who set in place all the fibre optics lines and other technical aspects of the Internet. The first high speed backbone was created by the'National Science Foundation' in 1987.

The Internet was first created by the Advanced Research Projects Agency (ARPA) of the U.S. government in 1960's, and was first known as the ARPANet. At this stage the Internet's first computers were at academic and government institutions. They were mainly used for accessing files and to send e-mail. From 1983 onwards the Internet as we know it today started to form with the introduction of the communication protocol TCP/IP to ARPANet.

Since 1983 the Internet has accommodated alot of changes and continues to keep developing. The last two decades has seen the Internet accommodate such things as network LANs and ATM and frame switched services. The Internet continues to evolve with it becoming available on mobile phones and pagers and possibly on televisions in the future.

The actual term"Internet" was finally defined in 1995 by FNC (The Federal Networking Council). The resolution created by the The Federal Networking Council (FNC) agrees that the following language reflects our definition of the term"Internet"."Internet" refers to the global information system that,

EVOLUTION

The underpinnings of the Internet are formed by the global interconnection of hundreds of thousands of otherwise independent computers, communications entities and information systems. What makes this interconnection possible is the use of a set of communication standards, procedures and formats in common among the networks and the various devices and computational facilities connected to them. The procedures by which computers communicate with each other are called"protocols." While this infrastructure is steadily evolving to include new capabilities, the protocols initially used by the Internet are called the"TCP/IP" protocols, named after the two protocols that formed the principal basis for Internet operation.

On top of this infrastructure is an emerging set of architectural concepts and data structures for heterogeneous information systems that renders the Internet a truly global information system. In essence, the Internet is an architecture, although many people confuse it with its implementation. When the Internet is looked at as an architecture, it manifests two different abstractions. One abstraction deals with communications connectivity, packet delivery and a variety of end-end communication services. The other abstraction deals with the Internet as an information system, independent of its underlying communications infrastructure, which allows creation, storage and access to a wide range of information resources, including digital objects and related services at various levels of abstraction.

Interconnecting computers is an inherently digital problem. Computers process and exchange digital information, meaning that they use a discrete mathematical "binary" or"two-valued" language of 1s and 0s. For communication purposes, such information is mapped into continuous electrical or optical waveforms. The use of digital signaling allows accurate regeneration and reliable recovery of the underlying bits. We use the terms"computer,""computer resources" and"computation" to mean not only traditional computers, but also devices that can be controlled digitally over a network, information resources such as mobile programmes and other computational capabilities.

The telephone network started out with operators who manually connected telephones to each other through"patch panels" that accepted patch cords from each telephone line and electrically connected them to one another through the panel, which operated, in effect, like a switch. The result was called circuit switching, since at its conclusion, an electrical circuit was made between the calling telephone and the called telephone.

Conventional circuit switching, which was developed to handle telephone calls, is inappropriate for connecting computers because it makes limited use of the telecommunication facilities and takes too long to set up connections. Although reliable enough for voice communication, the circuit-switched voice network had difficulty delivering digital information without errors.

For digital communications, packet switching is a better choice, because it is far better suited to the typically"burst" communication style of computers. Computers that communicate typically send out brief but intense bursts of data, then remain silent for a while before sending out the next burst. These bursts are communicated as packets, which are very much like electronic postcards. The postcards, in reality packets, are relayed from computer to computer until they reach their destination.

The special computers that perform this forwarding function are called variously"packet switches" or"routers" and form the equivalent of many bucket brigades spanning continents and oceans, moving buckets of electronic postcards from one computer to another. Together these routers and the communication links between them form the underpinnings of the Internet.

Without packet switching, the Internet would not exist, as we now know it. Going back to the postcard analogy, postcards can get lost. They can be delivered out of order, and they can be delayed by varying amounts. The same is true of Internet packets, which, on the Internet, can even be duplicated. The Internet Protocol is the postcard layer of the Internet. The next higher layer of protocol, TCP, takes care of re-sending the"postcards" to recover packets that might have been lost, and putting packets back in order if they have become disordered in transit.

Of course, packet switching is about a billion times faster than the postal service or a bucket brigade would be. It also has to operate over many different communications systems, or substrata. The authors designed the basic architecture to be so simple and undemanding that it could work with most communication services. Many organizations, including commercial ones, carried out research using the TCP/IP protocols in the 1970s. E-mail was steadily used over the nascent Internet during that time and to the present. It was not until 1994 that the general public began to be aware of the Internet by way of the World Wide Web application, particularly after Netscape Communications was formed and released its browser and associated server software.

Thus, the evolution of the Internet was based on two technologies and a research dream. The technologies were packet switching and computer technology, which, in turn, drew upon the underlying technologies of digital communications and semiconductors. The research dream was to share information and computational resources. But that is simply the technical side of the story. Equally important in many ways were the other dimensions that enabled the Internet to come into existence and flourish. This aspect of the story starts with cooperation and far-sightedness in the U.S. Government, which is often derided for lack of foresight but is a real hero in this story. It leads on to the enthusiasm of private sector interests to build upon the government funded developments to expand the Internet and make it available to the general public. Perhaps most important, it is fueled by the development of the personal computer industry and significant changes in the telecommunications industry in the 1980s, not the least of which was the decision to open the long distance market to competition. The role of workstations, the Unix operating system and local area networking (especially the Ethernet) are themes contributing to the spread of Internet technology in the 1980s into the research and academic community from which the Internet industry eventually emerged.

Many individuals have been involved in the development and evolution of the Internet covering a span of almost four decades if one goes back to the early writings on the subject of computer networking by Kleinrock, Licklider, Baran, Roberts, and Davies. The ARPANET, described below, was the first wide-area computer network. The NSFNET, which followed more than a decade later under the leadership of Erich Bloch, Gordon Bell, Bill Wulf and Steve Wolff, brought computer networking into the mainstream of the research and education communities. It is not our intent here to attempt to attribute credit to all those whose contributions were central to this story, although we mention a few of the key players

ROLE OF DARPA

Modern computer networking technologies emerged in the early 1970s. In 1969, The U.S. Defence Advanced Research Projects Agency (variously called ARPA and DARPA), an agency within the Department of Defence, commissioned a wide-area computer network called the ARPANET. This network made use of the new packet switching concepts for interconnecting computers and initially linked computers at universities and other research institutions in the United States and in selected NATO countries.

At that time, the ARPANET was essentially the only realistic wide-area computer network in existence, with a base of several dozen organizations, perhaps twice that number of computers and numerous researchers at those sites. The programme was led at DARPA by Larry Roberts. The packet switches were built by Bolt Beranek and Newman (BBN), a DARPA contractor. Others directly involved in the ARPANET activity included the authors, Len Kleinrock, Frank Heart, Howard Frank, Steve Crocker, Jon Postel and many many others in the ARPA research community.

Back then, the methods of internetworking (that is interconnecting computer networks) were primitive or non-existent. Two organizations could interwork technically by agreeing to use common equipment, but not every organization was interested in this approach. Absent that, there was jury-rigging, special case development and not much else. Each of these networks stood on its own with essentially no interaction between them - a far cry from today's Internet.

In the early 1970s, ARPA began to explore two alternative applications of packet switching technology based on the use of synchronous satellites (SATNET) and ground-based packet radio (PRNET). The decision by Kahn to link these two networks and the ARPANET as separate and independent networks resulted in the creation of the Internet programme and the subsequent collaboration with Cerf. These two systems differed in significant ways from the ARPANET so as to take advantage of the broadcast and wireless aspects of radio communications.

The strategy that had been adopted for SATNET originally was to embed the SATNET software into an ARPANET packet switch, and interwork the two networks through memory-to-memory transfers within the packet switch. This approach, in place at the time, was to make SATNET an"embedded" network within the ARPANET; users of the network would not even need to know of its existence. The technical team at Bolt Beranek and Newman (BBN), having built the ARPANET switches and now building the SATNET software, could easily produce the necessary patches to glue the programmes together in the same machine.

Indeed, this is what they were under contract with DARPA to provide. By embedding each new network into the ARPANET, a seamless internetworked capability was possible, but with no realistic possibility of unleashing the entrepreneurial networking spirit that has manifest itself in modern day Internet developments. A new approach was in order.

The Packet Radio (PRNET) programme had not yet gotten underway so there was ample opportunity to change the approach there. In addition, up until then, the SATNET programme was only an equipment development activity. No commitments had been obtained for the use of actual satellites or ground stations to access them. Indeed, since there was no domestic satellite industry in the U.S. then, the only two viable alternatives were the use of Intelsat or military satellites. The time for a change in strategy, if it was to be made, was then.

INTERNET ARCHITECTURE

The authors created architecture for interconnecting independent networks that could then be federated into a seamless whole without changing any of the underlying networks. This was the genesis of the Internet, as we know it today.

In order to work properly, the architecture required a global addressing mechanism (or Internet address) to enable computers on any network to reference and communicate with computers on any other network in the federation. Internet addresses fill essentially the same role as telephone numbers do in telephone networks. The design of the Internet assumed first that the individual networks could not be changed to accommodate new architectural requirements; but this was largely a pragmatic assumption to facilitate progress.

The networks also had varying degrees of reliability and speed. Host computers would have to be able to put disordered packets back into the correct order and discard duplicate packets that had been generated along the way. This was a major change from the virtual circuit-like service provided by ARPANET and by then contemporary commercial data networking services such as Tymnet and Telenet. In these networks, the underlying network took responsibility for keeping all information in order and for re-sending any data that might have been lost. The Internet design made the computers responsible for tending to these network problems.

A key architectural construct was the introduction of gateways (now called routers) between the networks to handle the disparities such as different data rates, packet sizes, error conditions, and interface specifications. The gateways would also check the destination Internet addresses of each packet to determine the gateway to which it should be forwarded.

These functions would be combined with certain end-end functions to produce the reliable communication from source to destination. A draft paper by the authors describing this approach was given at a meeting of the International Network Working Group in 1973 in Sussex, England and the final paper was subsequently published by the Institute for Electrical and Electronics Engineers, the leading professional society for the electrical engineering profession, in its Transactions on Communications in May, 1974.

DARPA contracted with Cerf's group at Stanford to carry out the initial detailed design of the TCP software and, shortly thereafter, with BBN and University College London to build independent implementations of the TCP protocol (as it was then called - it was later split into TCP and IP) for different machines. BBN also had a contract to build a prototype version of the gateway.

These three sites collaborated in the development and testing of the initial protocols on different machines. Cerf, then a professor at Stanford, provided the day-to-day leadership in the initial TCP software design and testing. BBN deployed the gateways between the ARPANET and the PRNET and also with SATNET. During this period, under Kahn's overall leadership at DARPA, the initial feasibility of the Internet Architecture was demonstrated.

The TCP/IP protocol suite was developed and refined over a period of four more years and, in 1980, it was adopted as a standard by the U.S. Department of Defence. On January 1, 1983 the ARPANET converted to TCP/IP as its standard host protocol. Gateways (or routers) were used to pass packets to and from host computers on"local area networks." Refinement and extension of these protocols and many others associated with them continues to this day by way of the Internet Engineering Task Force.

RUNNING THE INTERNET

The Domain Name System

The Internet evolved as an experimental system during the 1970s and early 1980s. It then flourished after the TCP/IP protocols were made mandatory on the ARPANET and other networks in January 1983; these protocols thus became the standard for many other networks as well. Indeed, the Internet grew so rapidly that the existing mechanisms for associating the names of host computers (*e.g.* UCLA, USC-ISI) to Internet addresses (known as IP addresses) were about to be stretched beyond acceptable engineering limits. Most of the applications in the Internet referred to the target computers by name.

These names had to be translated into Internet addresses before the lower level protocols could be activated to support the application. For a time, a group at SRI International in Menlo Park, CA, called the Network Information Center (NIC), maintained a simple, machine-readable list of names and associated Internet addresses which was made available on the net. Hosts on the Internet would simply copy this list, usually daily, so as to maintain a local copy of the table. This list was called the"host.txt" file (since it was simply a text file). The list served the function in the Internet that directory services (*e.g.* 411 or 703-555-1212) do in the US telephone system - the translation of a name into an address.

As the Internet grew, it became harder and harder for the NIC to keep the list current. Anticipating that this problem would only get worse as the network expanded, researchers at USC Information Sciences Institute launched an effort to design a more distributed way of providing this same information. The end result was the Domain Name System (DNS) which allowed hundreds of thousands of"name servers" to maintain small portions of a global database of information associating IP addresses with the names of computers on the Internet.

The naming structure was hierarchical in character. For example, all host computers associated with educational institutions would have names like"stanford.edu" or"ucla.edu". Specific hosts would have names like"cs.ucla.edu" to refer to a computer in the computer science department of UCLA, for example. A special set of computers called"root servers" maintained information about the names and addresses of other servers that contained more detailed name/address associations.

The designers of the DNS also developed seven generic"top level" domains, as follows:

- *Education*: EDU
- *Government*: GOV
- *Military*: MIL
- *International*: INT
- *Network*: NET
- *Organization*: ORG
- *Commercial*: COM

Under this system, for example, the host name"UCLA" became"UCLA.EDU" because it was operated by an educational institution, while the host computer for"BBN" became"BBN.COM" because it was a commercial organization. Top-level domain names also were created for every country: United Kingdom names would end in".UK," while the ending".FR" was created for the names of France.

The Domain Name System (DNS) was and continues to be a major element of the Internet architecture, which contributes to its scalability. It also contributes to controversy over trademarks and general rules for the creation and use of domain names, creation of new top-level domains and the like. At the same time, other resolution schemes exist as well. One of the authors (Kahn) has been involved in the development of a different kind of standard identification and resolution scheme that, for example, is being used as the base technology by book publishers to identify books on the

Internet by adapting various identification schemes for use in the Internet environment. For example, International Standard Book Numbers (ISBNs) can be used as part of the identifiers. The identifiers then resolve to state information about the referenced books, such as location information (*e.g.* multiple sites) on the Internet that is used to access the books or to order them. These developments are taking place in parallel with the more traditional means of managing Internet resources. They offer an alternative to the existing Domain Name System with enhanced functionality.

The growth of Web servers and users of the Web has been remarkable, but some people are confused about the relationship between the World Wide Web and the Internet. The Internet is the global information system that includes communication capabilities and many high level applications. The Web is one such application.

The existing connectivity of the Internet made it possible for users and servers all over the world to participate in this activity. Electronic mail is another important application. As of today, over 60 million computers take part in the Internet and about 3.6 million web sites were estimated to be accessible on the net. Virtually every user of the net has access to electronic mail and web browsing capability. E-mail remains a critically important application for most users of the Internet, and these two functions largely dominate the use of the Internet for most users.

INTERNET STANDARDS PROCESS

Internet standards were once the output of research activity sponsored by DARPA. The principal investigators on the internetting research effort essentially determined what technical features of the TCP/IP protocols would become common. The initial work in this area started with the joint effort of the two authors, continued in Cerf's group at Stanford, and soon thereafter was joined by engineers and scientists at BBN and University College London. This informal arrangement has changed with time and details can be found elsewhere.

At present, the standards efforts for Internet are carried out primarily under the auspices of the Internet Society (ISOC). The Internet Engineering Task Force (IETF) operates under the leadership of its Internet Engineering Steering Group (IESG), which is populated by appointees approved by the Internet Architecture Board (IAB) which is, itself, now part of the Internet Society.

The IETF comprises over one hundred working groups categorized and managed by Area Directors specializing in specific categories. There are other bodies with considerable interest in Internet standards or in standards that must interwork with the Internet.

Examples include the International Telecommunications Union Telecommunicationsstandards group (ITU-T), the International Institute of Electrical and Electronic Engineers (IEEE) local area network standards group (IEEE 801), the Organization for International Standardization (ISO), the American National Standards Institute (ANSI), the World Wide Web Consortium (W3C), and many others.

As Internet access and services are provided by existing media such as telephone, cable and broadcast, interactions with standards bodies and legal structures formed to deal with these media will become an increasingly complex matter. The intertwining of interests is simultaneously fascinating and complicated, and has increased the need for thoughtful cooperation among many interested parties.

MANAGING THE INTERNET

Perhaps the least understood aspect of the Internet is its management. In recent years, this subject has become the subject of intense commercial and international interest, involving multiple governments and commercial organizations, and recently congressional hearings. At issue is how the Internet will be managed in the future, and, in the process, what oversight mechanisms will insure that the public interest is adequately served.

In the 1970s, managing the Internet was easy. Since few people knew about the Internet, decisions about almost everything of real policy concern were made in the offices of DARPA. It became clear in the late 1970s, however, that more community involvement in the decision-making processes was essential. In 1979, DARPA formed the Internet Configuration Control Board (ICCB) to insure that knowledgeable members of the technical community discussed critical issues, educated people outside of DARPA about the issues, and helped others to implement the TCP/IP protocols and gateway functions. At the time, there were no companies that offered turnkey solutions to getting on the Internet.

It would be another five years or so before companies like Cisco Systems were formed, and while there were no PCs yet, the only workstations available were specially built and their software was not generally configured for use with external networks; they were certainly considered expensive at the time.

In 1983, the small group of roughly twelve ICCB members was reconstituted (with some substitutions) as the Internet Activities Board (IAB), and about ten"Task Forces" were established under it to address issues in specific technical areas. The attendees at Internet Working Group meetings were invited to become members of as many of the task forces as they wished.

The management of the Domain Name System offers a kind of microcosm of issues now frequently associated with overall management of the Internet's operation and evolution. Someone had to take responsibility for overseeing the system's general operation. In particular, top-level domain names had to be selected, along with persons or organizations to manage each of them. Rules for the allocation of Internet addresses had to be established. DARPA had previously asked the late Jon Postel of the USC Information Sciences Institute to take on numerous functions related to administration of names, addresses and protocol related matters.

With time, Postel assumed further responsibilities in this general area on his own, and DARPA, which was supporting the effort, gave its tacit approval. This activity was generally referred to as the Internet Assigned Numbers Authority (IANA). In time, Postel became the arbitrator of all controversial matters concerning names and addresses until his untimely death in October 1998.

It is helpful to consider separately the problem of managing the domain name space and the Internet address space. These two vital elements of the Internet architecture have rather different characteristics that colour the management problems they generate. Domain names have semantics that numbers may not imply; and thus a means of determining who can use what names is needed. As a result, speculators on Internet names often claim large numbers of them without intent to use them other than to resell them later. Alternate resolution mechanisms, if widely adopted, could significantly change the landscape here.

The rapid growth of the Internet has triggered the design of a new and larger address space (the so-called IP version 6 address space); today's Internet uses IP version 4. However, little momentum has yet developed to deploy IPv6 widely. Despite concerns to the contrary, the IPv4 address space will not be depleted for some time. Further, the use of Dynamic Host Configuration Protocol (DHCP) to dynamically assign IP addresses has also cut down on demand for dedicated IP addresses. Nevertheless, there is growing recognition in the Internet technical community that expansion of the address space is needed, as is the development of transition schemes that allow interoperation between IPv4 and IPv6 while migrating to IPv6.

In 1998, the Internet Corporation for Assigned Names and Numbers (ICANN) was formed as a private sector, non-profit, organization to oversee the orderly progression in use of Internet names and numbers, as well as certain protocol related matters that required oversight. The birth of this organization, which was selected by the Department of Commerce for this function, has been difficult, embodying as it does many of the inherent conflicts in resolving discrepancies in this arena. However, there is a clear need for an oversight mechanism for Internet domain names and numbers, separate from their day-to-day management. Many questions about Internet management remain. They may also prove difficult to resolve quickly. Of specific concern is what role the U.S. government and indeed governments around the world need to play in its continuing operation and evolution. This is clearly a subject for another time.

ADVANTAGES OF INTERNET

There are many advantages of using the Internet, such as:

Global Audience

Content published on the World Wide Web is immediately available to a global audience of users. This makes the World Wide Web a very cost-effective medium to publish information. Reaching more than 190 countries.

Operates 24 hours and 365 days

You don't need to wait until resources are available to conduct business. From a consumer's perspective as well as a provider's business can be consummated at any time. The fact that the Internet is operational at all times makes it the most efficient business machine to date.

Relatively Inexpensive

It is relatively inexpensive to publish information on the Internet. At a fraction of the cost to publish information by traditional methods, various organizations and individuals can now distribute information to millions of users. It costs only a few thousand dollars to establish an Internet presence and publish content on the Internet.

Product Advertising

You can use the World Wide Web to advertise various products. Before purchasing a product, customers will be able to look up various product specification sheets and find out additional information. You can use the multimedia capabilities of the World Wide Web to make available not only various product specification sheets but also audio files, images, and even video clips of products in action. The beauty of the Web is that it allows customers to explore products in as much detail as they desire. If the client just wants a general overview, he or she can look at the advertising information. For those wanting more in depth information, you can provide white papers and product descriptions for download. The Web allows a business to provide timely information, you can simply place the information on the Web page and it is available immediately for your customers.

Distribute Product Catalogs

The World Wide Web is a very effective medium for distributing product catalogs. In the old days, putting together a product catalog used to be very costly in terms of time and money needed to publish and distribute it. The World Wide Web changes all this by allowing content developers to put together a sales catalog and make it available to millions of users immediately. Furthermore, unlike printed product catalogs that are usually updated around once a month, product catalogs on the World Wide Web can be updated as needed to respond to various changing market conditions.

Online Surveys

Traditional methods of performing surveys are often relatively slow and expensive compared to online surveys conducted on the Internet. For example, in order to fill out various needs of customers or what they would like to see in a future product, it's often necessary to compile a list of address and mail a questionnaire to many customers. The success of such an attempt is not always guaranteed and can be very costly in terms of mailing the questionnaires and entering responses to a databases and analyzing it.

On the other hand, you can use the World Wide Web to automate the whole process. For example, you can set up a CGI script to conduct online surveys. Results of such a survey can be automatically updated to a database. This database can then be used to keep a pulse on various opinions and needs of customers.

Announcements

With the World Wide Web, you can distribute various announcements to millions of users in a timely manner. Because there is virtually no time lag from the time it takes to publish information to making the information available to users, the Web is an ideal medium to publicize announcements. As more people discover the virtues of the Web and get connected to the Internet, the Web will become the medium of choice for many organizations and individuals to publicize various announcements.

Provide Technical Support

You can also use Web site to provide technical support to users. Because Web pages can be updated immediately with new information, various technical support literature can be immediately modified in light of new findings and developments. This can be accomplished without having to distribute changes to all users affected by any changes using traditional mediums of information distribution, which are often quite costly compared to the World Wide Web.

Create Online Discussion Forums

By using applications such as WebBoard, it's possible to set up online discussion forums on the Web.

Obtain Customer Feedback

The interactive nature of the World Wide Web is ideal for obtaining customer feedback. You can easily set up a CGI script to obtain customer feedback about a product or service. Because customer feedback submitted by customers can be read immediately, it's possible to respond to various customer concerns in a timely manner, increasing customer satisfaction and quality of customer service.

Immediate Distribution of Information

When information is added to a Web site, it's immediately available for browsing by millions of Internet users. The World Wide Web is an ideal medium of information distribution because it takes away the time lag associated with publishing content and actually making it available to users

Easy Integration with Internal Information Systems

Internet information systems deployed on the Internet can be easily integrated with internal information systems managed with office productivity applications such as Microsoft Office.

Powerful Content Publishing Tools

A new breed of Internet aware applications will start emerging in software stores by the time you read this. These applications will enable users to develop content for the World Wide Web by simply saving as an HTML file. In addition to software developers making existing applications Internet aware, various new, powerful, and easy-to use Internet content publishing applications are also being developed. These applications will make the task of publishing content on the Internet even easier. Most of these applications are developed for Windows users.

Multimedia

The capability to incorporate multimedia into Web pages is a major advantage of using World Wide Web to publish information. For example, many Web sites use sounds and video clips to make the content easier and more interesting to browse.

Formatting Capabilities

Content published on the World Wide Web can be richly formatted by using various HTML tags and graphic formats. The capability to do this is a major reason for the success of the World Wide Web. In addition to using HTML tags and various multimedia formats in Web pages, various interactive controls can also be added to a web page. This capability allows Web site content developers to create"active" Web sites. For example, before a user sends some information to a Web server for processing, a VBScript or JavaScript subroutine can be used to verify information typed in by the user. Various formatting capabilities, along with technologies such as Java and VBScript, make the World Wide Web a richly interactive medium that you can use to distribute information to millions of users.

DISADVANTAGES OF INTERNET

Many fear the Internet because of its disadvantages. They claim to not use the Internet because they are afraid of the possible consequences or are simply not interested. People who have yet connected to the Internet claim they are not missing anything. Today's technological society must realise, it is up to them to protect themselves on the Internet.

Children using the Internet has become a big concern. Most parents do not realise the dangers involved when their children log onto the Internet. When children are online, they can easily be lured into something dangerous. When children talk to others online, they do not realise they could actually be talking to a harmful person. In addition, children may also receive pornography online by mistake; therefore, causing concern among parents everywhere.

Whether surfing the Web, reading newsgroups, or using e-mail, children can be exposed to extremely inappropriate material. Pornographic sites tend to make sure they are the first sites to be listed in any search area. Some critics say that parents are responsible for their own children on the Internet because there are available services to protect children. To keep children safe, parents and teachers must be aware of the dangers. They must actively guide and guard their children online.There are a number of tools available today that may help keep the Internet environment safer for children.

Musicians are also concerned with disadvantages to the Net such as, accessibility and freedom. They are upset because the Internet provides their music online at no charge to consumers. File-sharing software, such Kazaa, Emule and may others provides copyrighted songs to all Internet users. The main concern is - the music is free! Musicians feel"they are not getting paid for their work". It is almost impossible to close down all file-sharing services; there are too many of them to count.

Another major disadvantage of the Internet is privacy. Electronic messages sent over the Internet can be easily snooped and tracked, revealing who is talking to whom and what they are talking about. As people surf the Internet, they are constantly giving information to web sites. People should become aware that the collection, selling, or sharing of the information they provide online increases the chances that their information will fall into the wrong hands. When giving personal information on the Internet, people should make sure the Web site is protected with a recognizable security symbol. On the other hand, this does not mean they are fully protected because anyone may obtain a user's information.

Today, not only are humans getting viruses, but computers are also. Computers are mainly getting these viruses from the Internet; yet, viruses may also be transmitted through floppy disks. However, people should mainly be concerned about receiving viruses from the Internet. Some of these dangerous viruses destroy the computer's entire hard drive, meaning that the user can no longer access the computer. Virus protection is highly recommended

In conclusion, today's society is in the middle of a technological boom. People can either choose to take advantage of this era, or simply let it pass them by. The Internet is a very powerful tool. It has many advantages; however, people need to be extremely aware of the disadvantages as well.

7

Intra-Network

For such an extensive and involved subject, which includes so many different technologies, hardware devices and protocols, the definition of networking is actually quite simple. A network is simply a collection of computers or other hardware devices that are connected together, either physically or logically, using special hardware and software to allow them to exchange information and cooperate. Networking is the term that describes the processes involved in designing, implementing, upgrading, managing and otherwise working with networks and network technologies.

Networks are used for an incredible array of different purposes. In fact, the definitions above are so simple for the specific reason that networks can be used so broadly, and can allow such a wide variety of tasks to be accomplished. While most people learning about networking focus on the interconnection of PCs and other"true" computers, you use various types of networks every day. Each time you pick up a phone, use a credit card at a store, get cash from an ATM machine, or even plug in an electrical appliance, you are using some type of network.

In fact, the definition can even be expanded beyond the world of technology altogether: I'm sure you've heard the term"networking" used to describe the process of finding an employer or employee by talking to friends and associates. In this case too, the idea is that independent units are connected together to share information and cooperate.

The widespread networking of personal computers is a relatively new phenomenon. For the first decade or so of their existence, PCs were very much"islands unto themselves", and were rarely connected together. In the early 1990s, PC networking began to grow in popularity as businesses realised the advantages that networking could provide. By the late 1990s, networking in homes with two or more PCs started to really take off as well.

This interconnection of small devices represents, in a way, a return to the"good old days" of mainframe computers. Before computers were small and personal, they were large and centralized machines that were shared by many users operating remote terminals. While having all of the computer power in one place had many disadvantages, one benefit was that all users were connected because they shared the central computer.

Individualized PCs took away that advantage, in favour of the benefits of independence. Networking attempts to move computing into the middle ground, providing PC users with the best of both worlds: the independence and flexibility of personal computers, and the connectivity and resource sharing of mainframes. in fact, networking is today considered so vital that it's hard to conceive of an organization with two or more computers that would not want to connect them together!

TYPES OF NETWORKING

The word"networking" strikes fear into legions of otherwise intrepid job hunters. It conjures up one of three images: calling everyone in your address book to see whether anyone knows anyone who may know anyone who may give you an informational interview, attending club meetings with other job hunters or having your friends come up with ideas and contacts instead of advising you to get out there and network. But there is no need to fear because there are many different types of networking techniques you can use to help with your job search and references.

Obviously number three doesn't always work. But the other two aren't so appealing either. Who enjoys calling total strangers and asking them to meet with you when there's nothing in it for them? If they're successful in what they do - and why else would you want to meet with them? - they're likely to be busy doing it.

STRONG-CONTACT NETWORKS

Structured explicitly to pass business referrals among members, they allow only one member per profession. Strong-contact networks are particularly good for developing in-depth relationships because you see the same members week after week and pass referrals as a part of each meeting.

CASUAL-CONTACT NETWORKS

Bring businesspeople together in a less-structured context than strong-contact networks, but for many they are a primary source of referrals; membership is not limited by profession. These groups are good for developing breadth in your network, but deep, long-lasting relationships can be formed as well.

SERVICE ORGANIZATIONS

Associations that exist to provide and support humanitarian efforts and good works in the community and larger venues. They also bring people together in settings that facilitate referral and knowledge networking. Like casual-contact groups, they help you add breadth and diversity to your network.

PROFESSIONAL ASSOCIATIONS

Established to exchange information and ideas among those in a given industry, as well as to promote and support that industry. These networks often include direct competitors, but they also provide contacts in related, non-competing businesses as well.

SOCIAL/BUSINESS ORGANIZATIONS

Combine social activities with business networking and can provide a variety of networking opportunities; many tend to resemble singles bars.

WOMEN'S NETWORKING GROUPS

Still important networking organizations, but are slowly disappearing as women enter the business mainstream, especially as professionals, entrepreneurs, and small-business owners.

ONLINE NETWORKS

A new phenomenon covering a wide range of interests.

TYPES OF COMPUTER NETWORKS

A computer network is two or more computers connected together using a telecommunication system for the purpose of communication and sharing resources". Ask any computer network expert to simplify this definition to you and you will start a debate on how it should not be just two computers but three. Simply put a network is a means of communication between computers. Within a given network, computers can send files, e-mails and other correspondence to each other. Even things like instant messaging, is set up within a computer's network.

LAN

LAN or Local Area Network is the most common kind of network set up. There are two ways to connect a LAN network. The simplest and easiest way is the peer-to-peer connection network. This is when two or more computers are directly connected to each other.

For example if there were four computers in the network, computer 1 would be connected to computer 2, computer 2 would be connected to computer 3 and computer 3 would be connected to computer 4. This means each computer is dependent on the other.

And if there were a network problem with any one computer, all of them would be affected. The other type if the client server connection. This is the type of connection where all the computers in a given network are connected to one central computer. This is a more complicated network but one that is much more efficient that peer-to-peer.

A local area network, or LAN, is a network of connected computers in a room, building, or set of buildings. Local area networks have been around since the beginning of computer use. A LAN is defined as a user network whereby data is sent at high rates between people located relatively close to each other. LANs do not usually make use of leased communication lines, but only means of communication that are provided by the installer of the network.

The Internet is a wide area network, or WAN, which is distinct from a LAN. In contrast to the term Internet, local area networks are often called intranets, though sometimes this term refers to a cluster of LANs associated with a particular company or organization but not connected to the larger Internet. A local area network uses a hub or router to connect computers together. The means of communication is the omnipresent Ethernet cable or wireless wi-fi technology. These technologies offer data transfer rates running between 10 to 10000 Mbit/s.

Larger, more important LANs have redundant lines or other backup protocols. In networked computers, the most popular communication protocol is TCP/IP. Smaller LANs may be temporary and used between friends to play computer games over the network. Over a network, users can share files, view files, make changes to data on other computers if permitted, play movies or music on multiple computers at once, chat with instant messaging, send e-mails to each other, play games, and so on. All the advantages of the Internet apply, although they only include others on the LAN, and the data transfer rates are high.

Perhaps the most frequently employed use of a LAN is to connect users to the Internet with only one connected router. In modern times, we use broadband cable or DSL modems to connect to the Internet, and it would be clumsy to have a modem associated with every computer, so we simply plug the modem into a router and link the router to computers with Ethernet cables. Configuring a LAN can be intimidating at first, but contemporary operating systems have programmes that do most of the necessary configurations automatically, so setting up a local area network is pretty easy. A local area network (LAN) supplies networking capability to a group of computers in close proximity to each other such as in an office building, a school, or a home. A LAN is useful for sharing resources like files, printers, games or other applications. A LAN in turn often connects to other LANs, and to the Internet or other WAN.

Most local area networks are built with relatively inexpensive hardware such as Ethernet cables, network adapters, and hubs. Wireless LAN and other more advanced LAN hardware options also exist.

Examples

The most common type of local area network is an Ethernet LAN. The smallest home LAN can have exactly two computers; a large LAN can accommodate many thousands of computers. Many LANs are divided into logical groups called subnets. An Internet Protocol (IP)"Class A" LAN can in theory accommodate more than 16 million devices organized into subnets.

The High Performance Network

The HPN is used for the exchange of large amounts of operational data. Two Force10 E600 Routers, interconnected via 4-way 10-Gigabit Ethernet aggregated links, provide connectivity between the High Performance Computing Facility (HPCF) and the Data-Handling System (DHS). The HPCF network nodes are connected via 10-Gigabit Ethernet and all DHS nodes via Gigabit Ethernet aggregated links.

The General Purpose Network

The GPN is used for all other traffic. It has at its core two Foundry BigIron RX-16 routers and at the edge seven Foundry Super-X switches. The core routers are interconnected via 4-way 10-Gigabit Ethernet aggregated links and have multiple Gigabit Ethernet uplinks to the edge routers. The core also includes two further Super-X switches that are dual-attached to the RX-16s via 10-Gigabit Ethernet.

The GPN provides connectivity to:

- The HPCF, the DHS and additional servers via Gigabit Ethernet ports in the core.
- The user desktops and laptops via Gigabit Ethernet ports on the edge switches.
- The firewalls (for the Wide Area Network and the Demilitarized Zone (DMZ) via Gigabit Ethernet ports in the core. The DMZ includes ECaccess, web servers, the mail gateway and DNS (Domain Name Servers).

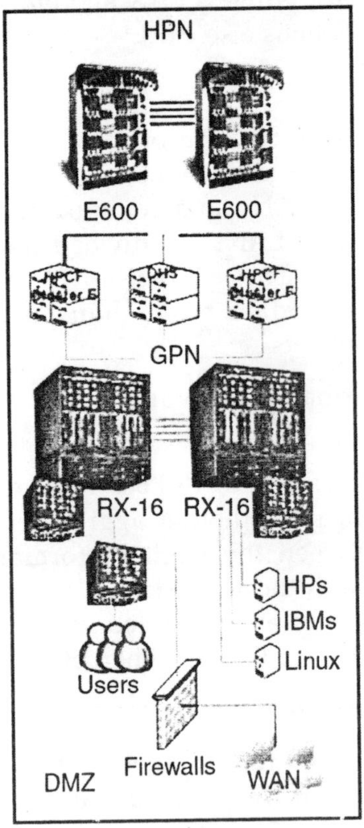

The Hardware

Both the Force10 E600 chassis are populated with 24 10-Gigabit-Ethernet and 144 Gigabit Ethernet ports. For resiliency there are four power supplies, two CPU modules and nine switching fabric modules. Both the RX-16 chassis are populated with 8 10-Gigabit Ethernet ports and 144 Gigabit Ethernet ports. For resiliency there are seven power supplies, two CPU modules and four switching fabric modules. The Super-X chassis each contain up to 156 Gigabit Ethernet ports and dual power-supplies.

WAN

Definition

The wide area network, often referred to as a WAN, is a communications network that makes use of existing technology to connect local computer networks into a larger working network that may cover both national and international locations. This is in contrast to both the local area network and the metropolitan area network, which provides communication within a restricted geographic area. Here is how the wide area network functions, and why it is so important to communications today.

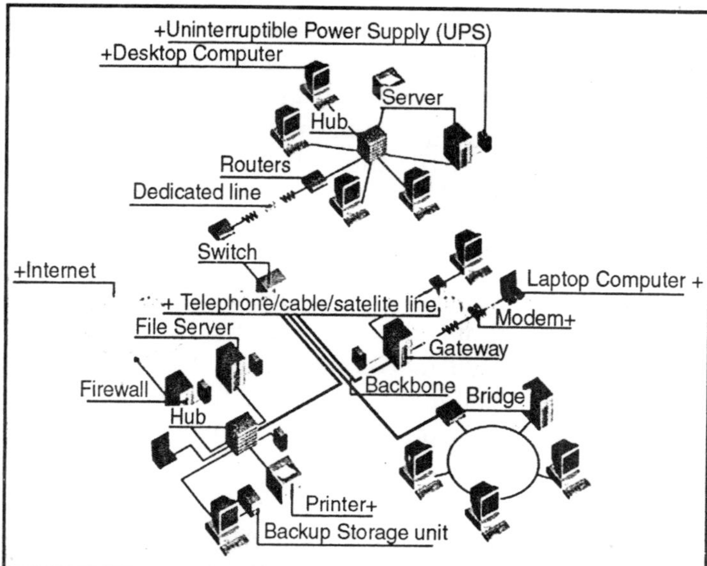

The concept of linking one computer network with another is often desirable, especially for businesses that operate a number of facilities. Beginning with the local area network and going up to the wide area network, this is most easily accomplished by using existing telephony technology. Essentially, fibre optics are used to create the link between networks located in different facilities.

Often, this means using standard phone lines, referred to as POTS, or employing PSTN (public switched telephone network) technology. During the 1990s, a third option, that of ISDN (integrated services digital network) solutions for creation a wide area network gained a great deal of popularity, mainly because the concept made it more cost effective to extend the network beyond national boundaries.

With coverage in a broad area, a wide area network allows companies to make use of common resources in order to operate. For example, many retail drugstores make use of a wide area network as part of their support to customers who fill prescriptions with one of their stores. Once in the common customer database for the pharmacy, the client is free to fill a prescription at any of the company's locations, even while vacationing in another state.

Companies also make good use of the wide area network as well. Internal functions such as sales, production and development, marketing and accounting can also be shared with authorized locations through this sort of broad area network application. The concept of a wide area network as a means of taking individual location based computer networks and using them to create a unified computer network for the entire corporation means that employees can work from just about anywhere. Should one facility be damaged or rendered inaccessible due to natural disaster, employees simply move to another location where they can access the unified network, and keep on working.

OVERVIEW

WAN or Wide Area Network is when several LANs or independent computers are connected to a single, wider network. The Internet is the perfect example of WAN. E-mails, Chat Rooms and IMs all connect to the WAN of the Internet.

WAN is much more complex and requires connecting devices or hubs from all over the world.

The term Wide Area Network (WAN) usually refers to a network which covers a large geographical area, and use communications circuits to connect the intermediate nodes. A major factor impacting WAN design and performance is a requirement that they lease communications circuits from telephone companies or other communications carriers. Transmission rates are typically 2 Mbps, 34 Mbps, 45 Mbps, 155 Mbps, 625 Mbps (or sometimes considerably more).

Numerous WANs have been constructed, including public packet networks, large corporate networks, military networks, banking networks, stock brokerage networks, and airline reservation networks. Some WANs are very extensive, spanning the globe, but most do not provide true global coverage. Organizations supporting WANs using the Internet Protocol are known as Network Service Providers (NSPs). These form the core of the Internet.

Wide Area Networks, or WANs, connect a geographically diverse group of computers within a state, country, or even across several states or countries. WANs typically are connected by telephone lines, other types of communication lines, or radio waves. Quite often, smaller local area networks (LANs) are linked together to form a WAN. This is accomplished via dedicated private lines, leased from telecommunications firms like Sprint and AT&T, or by Switched Multi-Megabit Data Services (SMDS) technology, developed in 1995 to eliminate the need for a leased line.

WAN technology has been refined over a period of several decades. It first emerged in the mid-twentieth century with the advent of networks like ARPAnet. Developed in 1969 by the Department of Defence, ARPAnet and several other networks eventually evolved into the Internet, the largest WAN in the world. The packet switching technology most commonly used with WANs surfaced in the 1960s, and standard packet switching protocol, known as X.25, was developed in 1976. To increase network speed, packet switching allows for the parceling of data into smaller chunks, known as packets, prior to transmission. These packets can travel independently via alternate routes, and they are reassembled once they reach their target. Although X.25 remained the most popular WAN packet switching protocol for years, other packet switching protocols used with increasing frequency by WAN developers and administrators include the Internet standard, Transmission Control Protocol/ Internet Protocol (TCP/IP), and Frame Relay, used most often by WANs connected via high speed T-1 and T-3 lines.

WANs are used for a variety of purposes. A corporation with offices in several locations may use a WAN to form an intranet. Quite often, the individual offices will use their own LANs for things like internal messaging, data processing functions, and hardware and software sharing. When these LANs are joined together to form a WAN, similar data sharing and messaging capabilities become possible across a much broader geographic area.

Businesses wanting to link up with their suppliers or distributors may create a WAN as a means of establishing an extranet. For example, an extranet could provide a sales representative with electronic access to information in about the time it might take to deliver a product, or the availability of a product. Some WANs bring together various types of communications, such as data, video, and voice. Some organizations, including companies, universities, research centers, hospitals, and libraries, use WANs to connect to the Internet.

By connecting the NSP WANs together using links at Internet Packet Interchanges (sometimes called"peering points") a global communication infrastructure is formed. NSPs do not generally handle individual customer accounts (except for the major corporate customers), but instead deal with intermediate organizations whom they can charge for high capacity communications. They generally have an agreement to exchange certain volumes of data at a certain"quality of service" with other NSPs. So practically any NSP can reach any other NSP, but may require the use of one or more other NSP networks to reach the required destination. NSPs vary in terms of the transit delay, transmission rate, and connectivity offered.

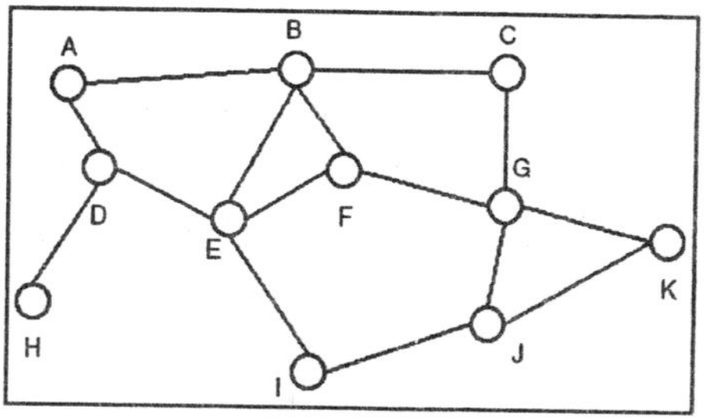

Fig. Typical"mesh" connectivity of a Wide Area Network

A typical network is shown in the figure above. This connects a number of End Systems (ES) (*e.g.* A, C, H, K) and a number of Intermediate Systems (IS) (*e.g.* B, D, E, F, G, I, J) to form a network over which data may be communicated between the End Systems (ES). The characteristics of the transmission facilities lead to an emphasis on efficiency of communications techniques in the design of WANs. Controlling the volume of traffic and avoiding excessive delays is important. Since the topologies of WANs are likely to be more complex than those of LANs, routing algorithms also receive more emphasis. Many WANs also implement sophisticated monitoring procedures to account for which users consume the network resources. This is, in some cases, used to generate billing information to charge individual users.

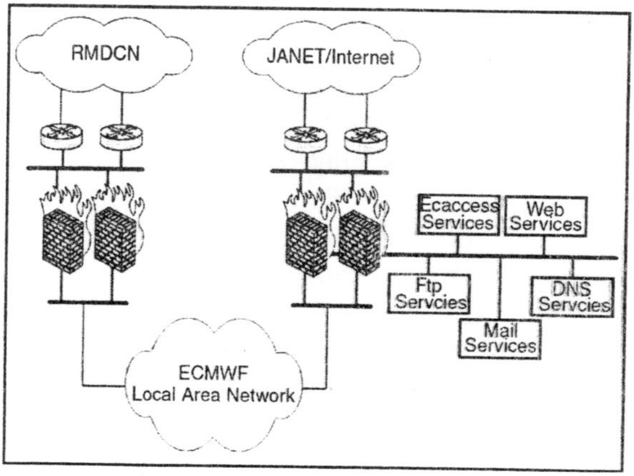

The size of a network is limited due to size and distance constraints.

However networks may be connected over a high-speed communications link (called a WAN link) to link them together and thus becomes a WAN.

WAN links are usually:

- Dial up connection
- Dedicated connection - It is a permanent full time connection. When a dedicated connection is used, the cable is leased rather than a part of the cable bandwidth and the user has exclusive use.
- Switched network - Several users share the same line or the bandwidth of the line.

There are two types of switched networks:

- Circuit switching - This is a temporary connection between two points such as dial-up or ISDN.
- Packet switching - This is a connection between multiple points. It breaks data down into small packets to be sent across the network.

A virtual circuit can improve performance by establishing a set path for data transmission. This will shave some overhead of a packet switching network. A variant of packet switching is called cell-switching where the data is broken into small cells with a fixed length.

WAN CONNECTION TECHNOLOGIES

- X.25: This is a set of protocols developed by the CCITT/ITU which specifies how to connect computer devices over an internet work. These protocols use a great deal of error checking for use over unreliable telephone lines. They establish a virtual communication circuit. It uses a store and forward method which can cause about a half second delay in data reception when two way communications are used. Their speed is about 64Kbps. Normally X.25 is used on packed switching PDNs (Public Data Networks). A line must be leased from the LAN to a PDN to connect to an X.25 network. A PAD (packet assembler/disassembler) or an X.25 interface is used on a computer to connect to the X.25 network. CCITT is an abbreviation for International Telegraph and Telephone Consultative Committee. The ITU is the International Telecommunication Union.

- *Frame Relay*: Devices at both sides of the connection handle Error checking. Frame relay uses frames of varying length and it operates at the data link layer of the OSI model. A permanent virtual circuit (PVC) is established between two points on the network. Frame relay speed is between 56Kbps and 1.544Mbps. Frame relay networks provide a high-speed connection up to 1.544Mbps using variable-length packet switching over digital fibre-optic media. Frame relay does not store data and has less error checking than X.25.
- *Switched Multi-megabit Data Service (SMDS)*: Uses fixed length cell switching and runs at speeds of 1.533 to 45Mbps. It provides no error checking and assumes devices at both ends provide error checking.
- Telephone connections
  - Dial up
  - *Leased lines*: These are dedicated analog lines or digital lines. Dedicated digital lines are called digital data service (DDS) lines. A modem is used to connect to analog lines, and a Channel Service Unit/Data Service Unit or Digital Service Unit(CSU/DSU) is used to connect to digital lines. The DSU connects to the LAN and the CSU connects to the line.
  - *T Carrier lines*: Multiplexors are used to allow several channels on one line. The T1 line is basic T Carrier service. The available channels may be used separately for data or voice transmissions or they may be combined for more transmission bandwidth. The 64Kbps data transmission rate is referred to as DS-0 (Digital Signal level 0) and a full T1 line is referred to as DS-1.

Signal	System	Total Kbps	Channels	Number of equivalent T1 lines
DS-1	T1	1544	24	1
DS-2	T2	6312	96	4
DS-3	T3	44736	672	28
DS-4	T4	274760	4032	3668

– T1 and T3 lines are the most common lines in use today. T1 and T2 lines can use standard copper wire. T3 and T4 lines require fibre-optic cable or other high-speed media. These lines may be leased partially called fractional T1 or fractional T3, which means a customer, can lease a certain number of channels on the line. A CSU/ DSU and a bridge or router is required to connect to a T1 line.

– Integrated Services Digital Network (ISDN) - Comes in two types and converts analog signals to digital for transmission. It is a dial up service

- Basic Rate ISDN (BRI) - Two 64Kbps B-channels with one 16Kbps D channel. The D-channel is used tor call control and setup.
- Primary Rate ISDN (PRI) - 23 B-channels and one D channel.

A device resembling a modem (called an ISDN modem) is used to connect to ISDN. The computer and telephone line are plugged into it.

– Switched-56 - A switched line similar to a leased line where customers pay for the time they use the line. Speed is 56Kbps. It is not dedicated and will not work to connect a WAN.

- Asynchronous Transfer Mode (ATM) - May be used over a variety of media with both baseband and broadband systems.

It is used for audio, video, and data. It uses fixed length data packets of 53 8 bit bytes called cell switching. 5 bytes contain header information. The cell contains path information that the packet is to use. It uses hardware devices to perform the switching of the data. Speeds from 155Mbps to 622 Mbps are achieved. Error checking is done at the receiving device, not by ATM. A permanent virtual connection or circuit (PVC) is established.

It may also use a switched virtual circuit (SVC). Service classes:

- Constant bit rate for data.
- Variable bit rate for audio or video.
- Connection less for data.
- Connection oriented for data.

ATM can be embedded in other protocols such as ATM-25, T1, T3, OC-1, OC-3, OC-12, and OC-48.

Some ATM technologies include:

- ATM-25 - 25Mbps speed.
- STS-3 - 155Mbps on fibre or category 5 cable.
- STS-12 - 620 Mbps on fibre cable for campus wide network.
- STS-48 - 2.2 Gbps on fibre cable on a MAN.
- STS-192 - 8.8 Gbps on fibre cable on intercity long distance. Phone companies normally use this.

Synchronous Optical Network (SONET) - A physical layer standard that defines voice, data, and video delivery methods over fibre optic media. It defines data rates in terms of optical carrier (OC) levels. The transmission rate of OC-1 is 51.8 Mbps. Each level runs at a multiple of the first. The OC-5 data rate is 5 times 51.8 Mbps which is 259 Mbps. SONET also defines synchronous transport signals (STS) for copper media which use the same speed scale of OC levels. STS-3 runs at the same speed of OC-3. Mesh or ring topology is used to support SONET. SONET uses multiplexing. The ITU has incorporated SONET into their Synchronous Digital Hierarchy (SDH) recommendations.

NETWORKING TOPOLOGIES

DEFINITION

Network topology refers to the way that your computer network is arranged. The network can have a physical or a logical topology. The physical topology describes the layout of computers and where the workstations are positioned. The logical network topology describes how the information flows through the network.

Choosing your physical topology is important because if it is not chosen correctly, this could cause your network to not operate properly. There are several terms that describe the type of physical topology that a network can have. The most common topologies are bus, ring, star, and mesh.

In a bus topology, all of the computers are attached to a single cable using terminators. The terminators work to absorb the energy from the signals in the network. The bus topology is easy to install, but it is not reliable because a single default can bring down your network.

In a ring topology, each computer is connected directly to two other computers on the network. As with a bus topology, a single fault can disrupt a ring network. This type of network does have advantages, however, and does not require a network server.

In a star topology, each computer is connected using its own separate cable. This set up is more reliable than a bus topology because its design makes it fault tolerant and susceptible to errors. The information on the network is transmitted from one system to another and the data flows in one single direction. The topology is expensive to maintain and is not reliable because removing one computer can disrupt your entire network.

In a mesh topology, a path is present from one computer to another computer in the network. The mesh topology is usually used in internet structure. The mesh topology can be complicated to construct because it has multiple connection between locations. For every computer that you have you will need at least one and a half connections for each one. This contributes to the expensive structure.

In choosing a network topology, understand that each one has its advantages and disadvantages. Research each one and see which one fits within your budget and which one fits your network layout. Also consider the amount of maintenance required in each topology. When setting up a network at home, consider a network topology that is simple and easy to maintain. You will also want a topology that is inexpensive to set up. If you are choosing a topology for a business, you will want to consider a topology that is reliable and resistant to errors. Your customers will need a network that is free of downtime; therefore, be sure that your topology is one that withstands disruption.

TYPES OF NETWORKING TOPOLOGIES

BUS TOPOLOGY

A bus topology is a method of transmission on networks that uses a common vehicle for transmissions and thus it is categorized as shared communication. Imagine a bus picking up various people from one stop and dropping of people as it travels and then picking a few more. That is what happens in a bus network exactly. A bus network uses a multi-drop transmission medium, all node on the network share a common bus and thus share communication. This allows only one device to transmit at a time. A distributed access protocol determines which station is to transmit. Data frames contain source and destination addresses, where each station monitors the bus and copies frames addressed to itself.

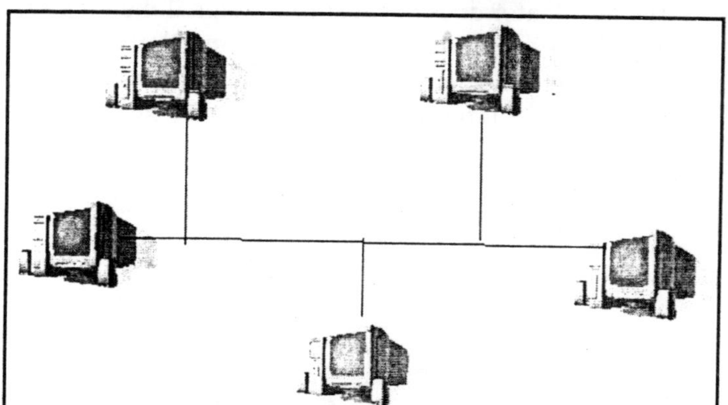

A bus topology connects each computer (nodes) to a single segment trunk (a communication line, typically coax cable, that is referred to as the'bus'. The signal travels from one end of the bus to the other. A terminator is required at each to absorb the signal so as it does not reflect back across the bus.

A media access method called CSMA/MA is used to handle the collision that occur when two signals placed on the wire at the same time. The bus topology is passive. In other words, the computers on the bus simply'listen' for a signal; they are not responsible for moving the signal along.

However in a Bus topology only one device is allowed to transmit at a given point of time. The DAP or the Distribute Access Protocol has the information about which station has to transmit the data. The data that is being transmitted have frames that will have the source name and the network address.

Function of Bus Topology

The bus topology connects each computer on the network into something called the segment trunk. A bus is usually referred to a cable that connects end to end and this is used to transmit the signals from one end to the other end. At every end a terminator is placed so that it understands in which direction the data is traveling and also the terminator is used to absorb the signals.

If the terminator does not absorb the signal then the same signal is reflected back to the bus confusing the whole data flow. The bus is considered to be a passive network because the computers are largely dependant on the signal that is being transmitted.

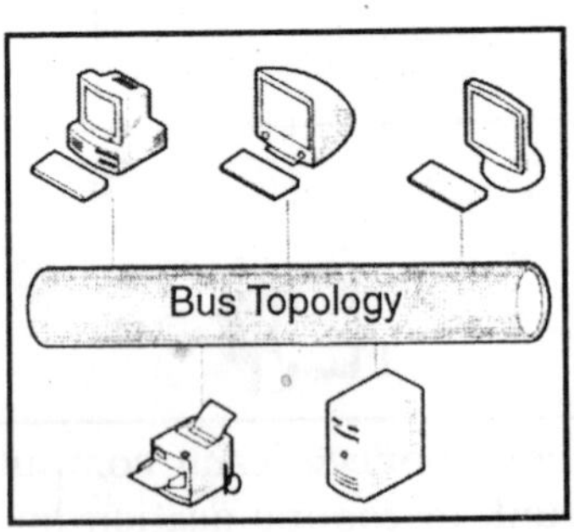

Advantages

The advantage of the Bus network is that if one computer fails in the network the others are still not affected and they continue to work. Bus network is very simple and easy to set up. If there is an urgent need to set up a network and perhaps be used on a short term basis then the Bus network is the best possibility. Bus networks use the least amount of cable to set up making it cost effective.

Limitations

In the bus network you will need a network connection in order to determine if the data is being transferred between two nodes. If the data transfer rate is high then the Bus network does not perform very well because the data travels in a stream and cannot be overloaded. The bus network is a bit challenging when you have to troubleshoot the problems. Bus networks are not suitable as large networks as there are limitations to the number of nodes you can set up for one single cable. As the number of computers increase in the network the data transfer rate goes down accordingly and noticeably.

Conclusion

The bus networks in spite of its limitations is considered to be the easiest and the fastest network that can be set up compared to the other kinds of network. In bus networks there is a collision handling system which ensures that data travels without errors and data is delivered correctly.

There is a bus master on the network which ensures that data is flowing in the right direction and order. All the computers on the bus network however listen for the signals and they do not hold the responsibility to move the signal forward.

The signal carries forward on its own. So if one computer is not receiving any signals the signal still carries forward without stopping at the computer that has failed. These days bus networks are less common due to the advancement of networks and there are much lesser complicated networks that are easy to operate and efficient. However even these newer technologies derive their basics from older technologies like the Bus Topology.

RING TOPOLOGY

Definition

A ring topology is a network topology or circuit arrangement in which each network device is attached along the same signal path to two other devices, forming a path in the shape of a ring. Each device in the network that is also referred to as node handles every message that flows through the ring. Each node in the ring has a unique address. Since in a ring topology there is only one pathway between any two nodes, ring networks are generally disrupted by the failure of a single link.

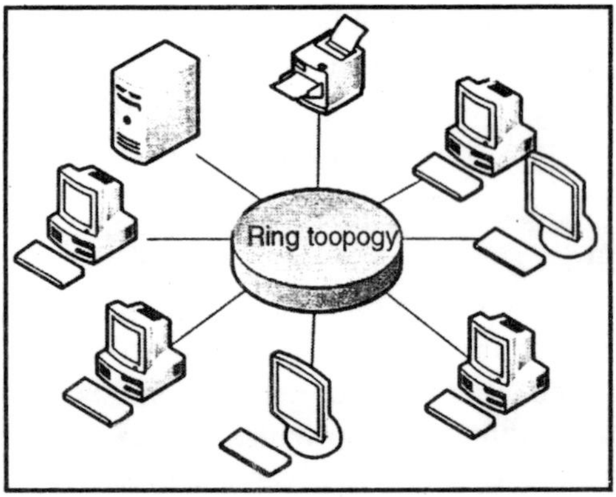

The redundant topologies are used to eliminate network downtime caused by a single point of failure. All networks need redundancy for enhanced reliability. Network reliability is achieved through reliable equipment and network designs that are tolerant to failures and faults. The FDDI networks overcome the disruption in the network by sending data on a clockwise and a counterclockwise ring. In case there is a break in data flow,the data is wrapped back onto the complementary ring before it reaches the end of the cable thereby maintaining a path to every node within the complementary ring. Ring network connects computers in a circle of point-to-point connections, with no central server, such as a series of desktop computers in an office. Each node handles its own applications and also shares resources over the entire network. If one node becomes inoperative, the other nodes are still able to maintain contact with one another. Such a network is best for decentralized systems in which no priorities are required

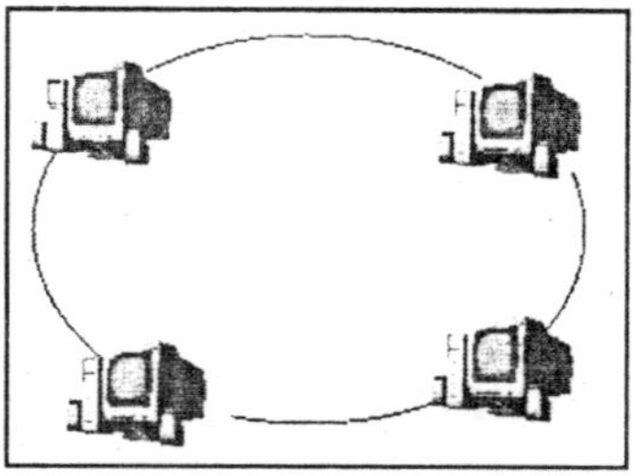

Under the network, a signal is transferred sequentially via a"token" fro one station to the next. When a station wants to transmit, it"grabs" the token, attaches data and an address to it, and then sends it around the ring. The token travels along the ring until it reaches the destination address. The receiving computer acknowledges receipt with a return message to the sender. The sender then releases the token for the token for use by another computer. Each station on the ring has equal access but only one station can talk at a time. To allow an orderly access to the ring, a single electronic token passes from one computer to the next around the ring as seen in (token ring). A computer can only transmit data when it capture the token.

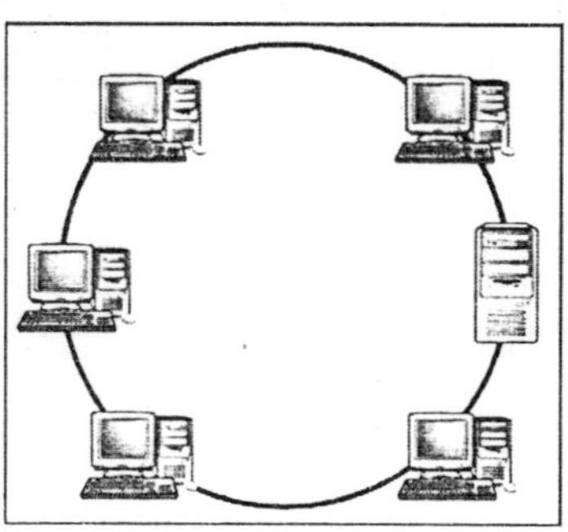

In a true ring topology, if a single computer or section of cable fails, there is an interruption in the signal. The entire network becomes inaccessible. Network disruption can also occur when computers are added or removed from the network, making it an impractical network design in environments where there is constant change to the network.

Ring networks are most commonly wired in a star configuration. In a Token Ring network, a multistation access unit (MSAU) is equivalent to a hub or switch on an Ethernet network. The MSAU performs the token circulation internally. To create the complete ring, the ring in (RI) port on each MSAU is connected to the ring out (RO) port on another MSAU. The last MSAU in the ring is then connected to the first, to complete the ring.

TOKEN RING TOPOLOGY

Unlike Ethernet, Token Ring uses a ring topology whereby the data is sent from one machine to the next and so on around the ring until it ends up back where it started. It also uses a token passing protocol which means that a machine can only use the network when it has control of the Token,.this ensures that there are no collisions because only one machine can use the network at any given time.

Figure below shows the basic of a Token Ring Topology. Although 16Mbps is the standard ring speed these days (and Fast Token Ring is being developed) we will consider a 4Mbps Token Ring in this tutorial to explain the basic concepts.

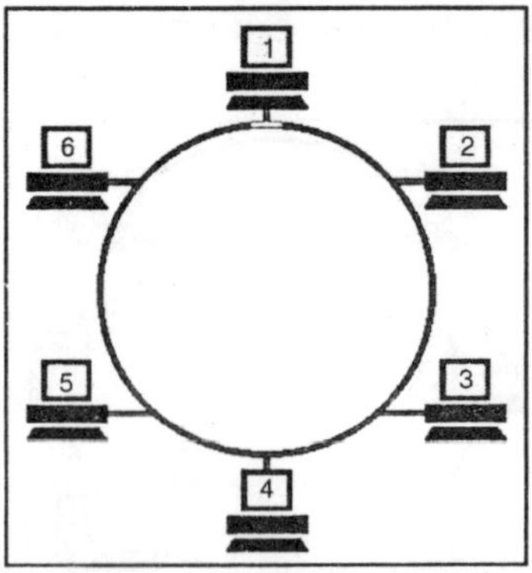

At the start, a free Token is circulating on the ring, this is a data frame which to all intents and purposes is an empty vessel for transporting data. To use the network, a machine first has to capture the free Token and replace the data with its own message.

In the example above, machine wants to send some data to machine, so it first has to capture the free Token. It then writes its data and the recipient's address onto the Token.

The packet of data is then sent to machine who reads the address, realises it is not its own, so passes it on to machine Machine does the same and passes the Token on to machine. This time it is the correct address and so number reads the message.

It cannot, however, release a free Token on to the ring, it must first send the message back to number with an acknowledgement to say that it has received the data (represented by the purple flashing screen).

The receipt is then sent to machine who checks the address, realises that it is not its own and so forwards it on to the next machine in the ring, number.Machine does the same and forwards the data to number, who sent the original message. Machin erecognizes the address, reads the acknowledgement from number (represented by the purple flashing screen) and then releases the free Token back on to the ring ready for the next machine to use.

That's the basics of Token Ring and it shows how data is sent, received and acknowledged, but Token Ring also has a built in management and recovery system which makes it very fault tolerant. Below is a brief outline of Token Ring's self maintenance system.

Token Ring Self Maintenance

When a Token Ring network starts up, the machines all take part in a negotiation to decide who will control the ring, or become the'Active Monitor' to give it its proper title. This is won by the machine with the highest MAC address who is participating in the contention procedure, and all other machines become'Standby Monitors'. The job of the Active

Monitor is to make sure that none of the machines are causing problems on the network, and to re-establish the ring after a break or an error has occurred. The Active Monitor performs Ring Polling every seven seconds and ring purges when there appears to be a problem.

The ring polling allows all machines on the network to find out who is participating in the ring and to learn the address of their Nearest Active Upstream Neighbour (NAUN). Ring purges reset the ring after an interruption or loss of data is reported.

Each machine knows the address of its Nearest Active Upstream Neighbour. This is an important function in a Token Ring as it updates the information required to re-establish itself when machines enter or leave the ring.

When a machine enters the ring it performs a lobe test to verify that its own connection is working properly, if it passes, it sends a voltage to the hub which operates a relay to insert it into the ring.

If a problem occurs anywhere on the ring, the machine that is immediately after the fault will cease to receive signals. If this situation continues for a short period of time it initiates a recovery procedure which assumes that its NAUN is at fault, the outcome of this procedure either removes its neighbour from the ring or it removes itself.

Token Ring Operation using a Hub

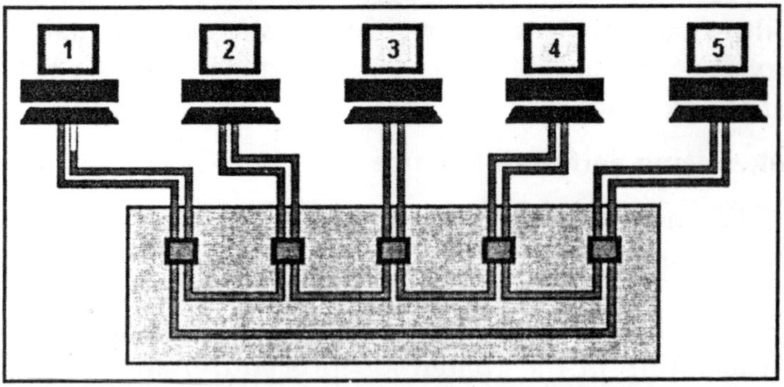

A Token Ring hub simply changes the topology from a physical ring to a star wired ring. The Token still circulates around the network and is still controlled in the same manner, however, using a hub or a switch greatly improves reliability because the hub can automatically bypass any ports that are disconnected or have a cabling fault.

Further advancements have been made in recent years with regard to Token Ring technology, such as early Token release and Token Ring switching but as this site is primarily concerned with cabling issues we will not go into any more detail here.

STAR TOPOLOGY

Star topology is the most commonly used physical technology in Ethernets LANS, when installed, the star topology resembles spokes I n a bicycle wheel. The star topology is made up of a central connection point that is a device such as a hub, switch, or router, where all the cabling segments meet.

Each host in the network is connected to the central devices with its own cables although a physical star topology costs more to implement than the physical bus topology, the advantage of star topology make it worth the additional cost. Because each host it connected to the central device with its own cable.

When that cable has a problem, only that host is affected, the rest of the network remains operational this benefit is extremely important and is why virtually every newly designed Ethernet a central connection point might be desirable for security or restricted access, but this is also a main disadvantage of a star topology.

If the central device fails, the whole network become disconnected.when a star network is expanded to include an additional networking device that is connected for the main networking device, it is called an extended star topology.

Description

A star topology is designed with each node (file server, workstations, and peripherals) connected directly to a central network hub or concentrator as shown in figure below:

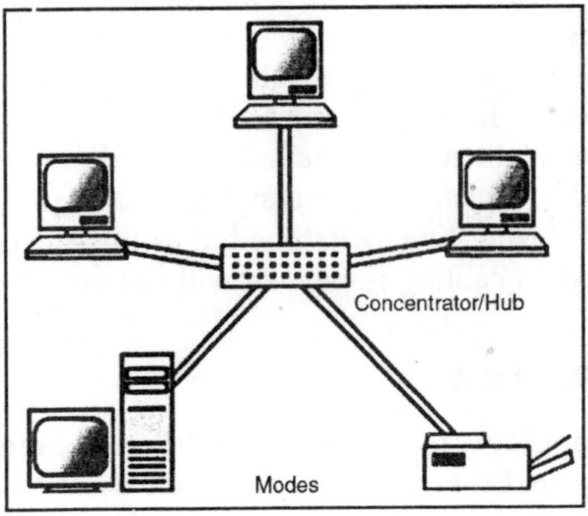

Data on a star network passes through the hub or concentrator before continuing to its destination. The hub or concentrator manages and controls all functions of the network. It also acts as a repeater for the data flow. This configuration is common with twisted pair cable; however, it can also be used with coaxial cable or fibre optic cable.

Many businesses and home networks use the star topology. A star network features a central connection point called a"hub" that may be an actual hub or a switch as shown below:

Devices typically connect to the hub with Unshielded Twisted Pair (UTP) Ethernet cables also known as RJ45 cables. Compared to the bus topology, a star network generally requires more cable, but a failure in any star network cable will only take down one computer's network access and not the entire LAN. (If the hub fails, however, the entire network also fails.)

Star topology has the following advantages:

- Easy to manage
- Easy to locate problems (cable/workstations)
- Easier to expand than a bus or ring topology
- Easy to Install and Wire
- No disruptions to the network then connecting or removing devices.
- Easy to detect faults and to remove parts.

Star topology has following disadvantages:

- It is susceptible to a single point of failure be it the server or hub/switch
- With Increased devices and traffic can make the network slow
- Requires more Cable Length.
- If the hub or concentrator fails, nodes attached are disabled.
- More expensive than linear bus topologies because of the cost of the concentrators.

TREE TOPOLOGY

Among all the Network Topologies we can derive that the Tree Topology is a combination of the bus and the Star Topology. The tree like structure allows you to have many servers on the network and you can branch out the network in many ways.

This is particularly helpful for colleges, universities and schools so that each of the branches can identify the relevant systems in their own network and yet connect to the big network in some way.

A Tree Structure suits best when the network is widely spread and vastly divided into many branches. Like any other topologies, the Tree Topology has its advantages and disadvantages.

A Tree Network may not suit small networks and it may be a waste of cable to use it for small networks. Tree Topology has some limitations and the configuration should suit those limitations.

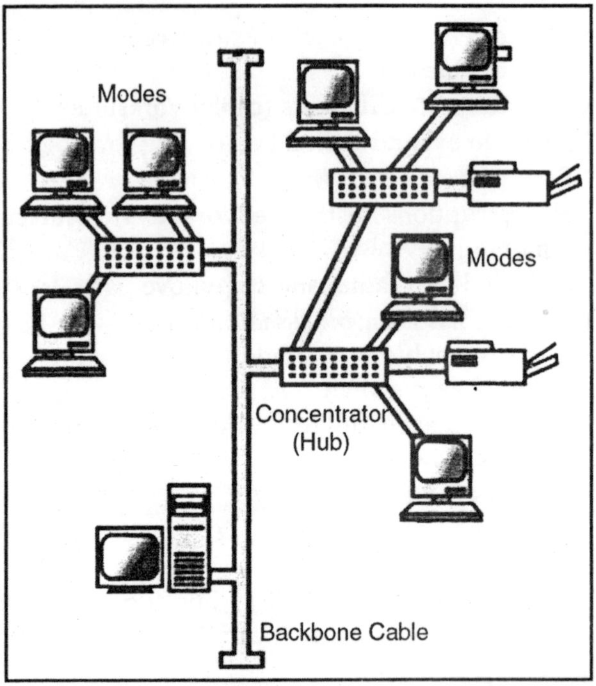

Benefits

A Tree Topology is supported by many network vendors ad even hardware vendors. A point to point connection is possible with Tree Networks. All the computers have access to the larger and their immediate networks. Best topology for branched out networks.

Limitations

In a Network Topology the length of the network depends on the type of cable that is being used. The Tree Topology network is entirely dependant on the trunk which is the main backbone of the network. If that has to fail then the entire network would fail.

Since the Tree Topology network is big it is difficult to configure and can get complicated after a certain point. The Tree Topology follows a hierarchical pattern where each level is connected to the next higher level in a symmetrical pattern.

Each level in the hierarchy follows a certain pattern in connecting the nodes. Like the top most level might have only one node or two nodes and the following level in the hierarchy might have few more nodes which work on the point to point connectivity and the third level also has asymmetrical node to node pattern and each of these levels are connected to the root level in the hierarchy.

Think of a tree that branches out in various directions and all these branches need the roots and the tree trunk to survive. A Tree Structured network is very similar to this and that is why it is called the Tree Topology.

Features

There will be at least three levels of hierarchy in the Tree Network Topology and they all work based on the root node.

The Tree Topology has two kinds of topology integral in it, the star and the linear way of connecting to nodes. The Tree Topology functions by taking into account the total number of nodes present in the network.

It does not matter how many nodes are there on each level. Nodes can be added to any level of the hierarchy and there are no limitations a far as the total number of nodes do not exceed.

The higher levels in the hierarchy are expected to perform more functions than the lower levels in the network.

Advantages of a Tree Topology

- Point-to-point wiring for individual segments.
- Supported by several hardware and software venders.

Disadvantages of a Tree Topology

- Overall length of each segment is limited by the type of cabling used.
- If the backbone line breaks, the entire segment goes down.
- More difficult to configure and wire than other topologies.

MESH TOPOLOGY

A type of network setup where each of the computers and network devices are interconnected with one another, allowing for most transmissions to be distributed, even if one of the connections go down. This type of topology is not commonly used for most computer networks as it is difficult and expensive to have redundant connection to every computer. However, this type of topology is commonly used for wireless networks. The mesh topology incorporates a unique network design in which each computer on the network connects to every other, creating a point-to-point connection between every device on the network. The purpose of the mesh design is to provide a high level of redundancy. If one network cable fails, the data always has an alternative path to get to its destination.

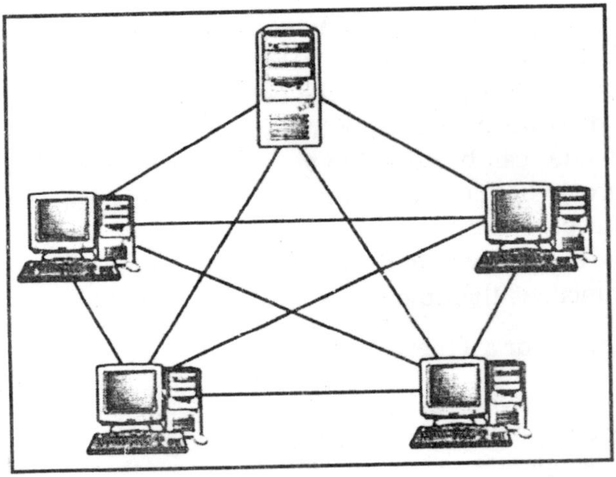

As seen in the above figure, the wiring for a mesh network can be very complicated. Further, the cabling costs associated with the mesh topology can be high, and troubleshooting a failed cable can be tricky. Because of this, the mesh topology is rarely used. A variation on a true mesh topology is the hybrid mesh. It creates a redundant point-to-point network connection between only specific network devices.

Wireless Mesh Networks

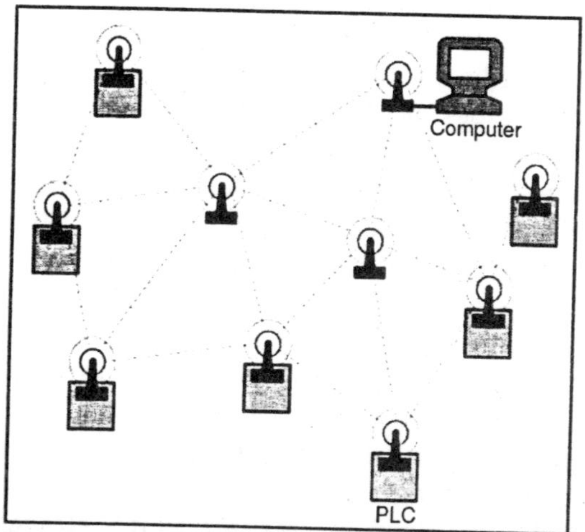

Wireless Mesh Networks work based on the radio frequencies and was originally developed by the army to be able to communicate. The reliability factor is high in any kind of Mesh Network.

There are three types of wireless Mesh Topologies:

1. Fixed Wireless Connections
2. Peer to Peer or Adhoc Networks
3. Node to Node

Fixed Mesh Networks

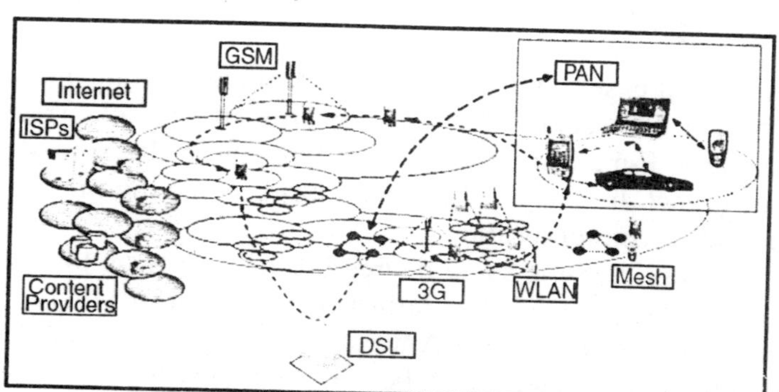

The fixed Mesh Networks will work only in the specified location and they are not mobile networks. They are meant to be used in a limited surrounding with boundaries. The location of nodes in affixed Mesh Network is all pre determined and they are not interchangeable.

The fixed Mesh Network does not work on line of sight like the other types of Mesh Networks. The total number of hops in a fixed Mesh Network is usually fixed and also short. There may not be many nodes as this kind of Mesh Networks exist within an office or building. More often than not the data travels ion a specific direction.

Peer to Peer Mobile Networks

In a peer to peer mobile network the individual devices connect to each other using the Mesh Network. The peer does not require connecting to the main node and they can still communicate from one device to another device by taking the shortest possible data transfer route. However many experts believe that in the peer to peer Mesh Networks the problems with scalability in terms of time taken for data transfer is questionable. The device has to know to transmit the data in the most optimal path and the entire data transfer or depends on this single factor. If the device is incapable then the whole purpose of using it in a peer to peer connection is lost.

E-MAIL

DEFINITION

E-mail is simply the shortened form of electronic mail, a protocol for receiving, sending and storing electronic messages. E-mail has gained popularity with the spread of the Internet. In many cases, e-mail has become the preferred method of communication.

Though there is some degree of uncertainty as to when e-mail was invented, the father of the modern version is generally regarded to be American Ray Tomlinson. Before Tomlinson, messages could be sent between users but only those connected to the same computer. They could not be targeted to a particular individual. Tomlinson devised a way to address e-mail to certain users and thus was credited for one of the most important communication inventions in the 20th century.

Tomlinson's idea was to identify the name of the user and the computer at which they were located. As a result, the basic formula for addressing an e-mail was username@usercomputer.

This standard has not changed over the years, other than the user computer now commonly being replaced by the name of an e-mail provider. In many cases, this is the same as the user's Internet service provider.

The influence of e-mail cannot be overstated. The United States Postal Service, for example, notes that it handles 212 billion pieces of mail per year. Many sources have nearly that many e-mails being sent back and forth every single day. In other words, e-mail handles more than 300 times the amount of mail of the largest postal system in the world.

In many cases, users receive, send and store e-mail based on one of two standards, SMTP or POP. SMTP stands for simple message transfer protocol. POP stands for Post Office Protocol. Though there is some amount of confusion over what these two protocols mean, the explanation is rather simple. POP is a protocol for storage of e-mail. SMTP is a protocol for sending and receiving.

WORKING WITH E MAIL

In reality, sending your message off into the network cloud is a bit like sending Little Red Riding Hood into the deep dark woods. You never know what might happen. In this diagram, the sender is a human being using their company account to send an e-mail to someone at a different company.

Step A: Sender creates and sends an e-mail

The originating sender creates an e-mail in their Mail User Agent (MUA) and clicks'Send'. The MUA is the application the originating sender uses to compose and read e-mail, such as Eudora, Outlook, etc.

Step B: Sender's MDA/MTA routes the e-mail

The sender's MUA transfers the e-mail to a Mail Delivery Agent (MDA). Frequently, the sender's MTA also handles the responsibilities of an MDA. Several of the most common MTAs do this, including sendmail and qmail (which Kavi uses). The MDA/MTA accepts the e-mail, then routes it to local mailboxes or forwards it if it isn't locally addressed. In our diagram, an MDA forwards the e-mail to an MTA and it enters the first of a series of"network clouds," labeled as a"Company Network" cloud.

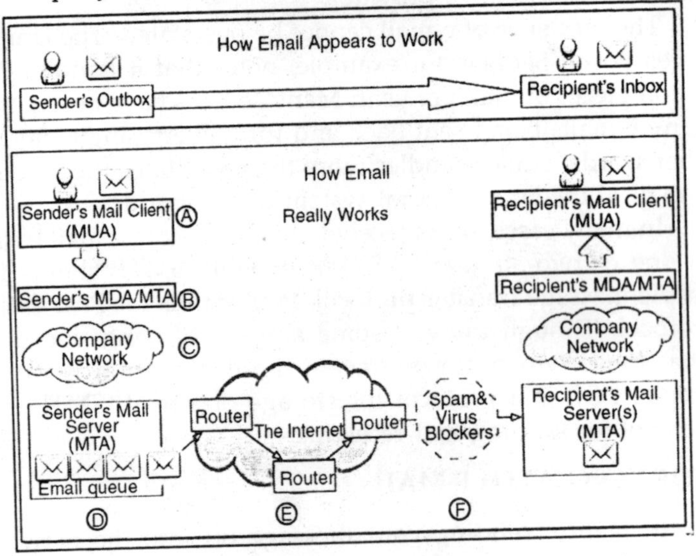

Step C: Network Cloud

An e-mail can encounter a network cloud within a large company or ISP, or the largest network cloud in existence: the Internet. The network cloud may encompass a multitude of mail servers, DNS servers, routers, lions, tigers, bears (wolves!) and other devices and services too numerous to mention.

These are prone to be slow when processing an unusually heavy load, temporarily unable to receive an e-mail when taken down for maintenance, and sometimes may not have identified themselves properly to the Internet through the Domain Name System (DNS) so that other MTAs in the network cloud are unable to deliver mail as addressed. These devices may be protected by firewalls, spam filters and malware detection software that may bounce or even delete an e-mail. When an e-mail is deleted by this kind of software, it tends to fail silently, so the sender is given no information about where or when the delivery failure occurred.

E-mail service providers and other companies that process a large volume of e-mail often have their own, private network clouds. These organizations commonly have multiple mail servers, and route all e-mail through a central gateway server (*i.e.*, mail hub) that redistributes mail to whichever MTA is available. E-mail on these secondary MTAs must usually wait for the primary MTA (*i.e.*, the designated host for that domain) to become available, at which time the secondary mail server will transfer its messages to the primary MTA.

Step D: E-mail Queue

The e-mail in the diagram is addressed to someone at another company, so it enters an e-mail queue with other outgoing e-mail messages. If there is a high volume of mail in the queue-either because there are many messages or the messages are unusually large, or both-the message will be delayed in the queue until the MTA processes the messages ahead of it.

Step E: MTA to MTA Transfer

When transferring an e-mail, the sending MTA handles all aspects of mail delivery until the message has been either accepted or rejected by the receiving MTA.

As the e-mail clears the queue, it enters the Internet network cloud, where it is routed along a host-to-host chain of servers. Each MTA in the Internet network cloud needs to"stop and ask directions" from the Domain Name System (DNS) in order to identify the next MTA in the delivery chain. The exact route depends partly on server availability and mostly on which MTA can be found to accept e-mail for the domain specified in the address. Most e-mail takes a path that is dependent on server availability, so a pair of messages originating from the same host and addressed to the same receiving host could take different paths. These days, it's mostly spammers that specify any part of the path, deliberately routing their message through a series of relay servers in an attempt to obscure the true origin of the message.

To find the recipient's IP address and mailbox, the MTA must drill down through the Domain Name System (DNS), which consists of a set of servers distributed across the Internet. Beginning with the root nameservers at the top-level domain (.tld), then domain nameservers that handle requests for domains within that.tld, and eventually to nameservers that know about the local domain.

DNS resolution and transfer process

- There are 13 root servers serving the top-level domains (*e.g.*.org.com.edu.gov.net, etc.). These root servers refer requests for a given domain to the root name servers that handle requests for that tld. In practice, this step is seldom necessary.
- The MTA can bypass this step because it has already knows which domain name servers handle requests for these.tlds. It asks the appropriate DNS server which Mail Exchange (MX) servers have knowledge of the subdomain or local host in the e-mail address. The DNS server responds with an MX record: a prioritized list of MX servers for this domain.

An MX server is really an MTA wearing a different hat, just like a person who holds two jobs with different job titles (or three, if the MTA also handles the responsibilities of an MDA). To the DNS server, the server that accepts messages is an MX server. When is transferring messages, it is called an MTA.

- The MTA contacts the MX servers on the MX record in order of priority until it finds the designated host for that address domain.

- The sending MTA asks if the host accepts messages for the recipient's username

Step F: Firewalls, Spam and Virus Filters

The transfer process described in the last step is somewhat simplified. An e-mail may be transferred to more than one MTA within a network cloud and is likely to be passed to at least one firewall before it reaches it's destination.

An e-mail encountering a firewall may be tested by spam and virus filters before it is allowed to pass inside the firewall. These filters test to see if the message qualifies as spam or malware. If the message contains malware, the file is usually quarantined and the sender is notified. If the message is identified as spam, it will probably be deleted without notifying the sender. Spam is difficult to detect because it can assume so many different forms, so spam filters test on a broad set of criteria and tend to misclassify a significant number of messages as spam, particularly messages from mailing lists. When an e-mail from a list or other automated source seems to have vanished somewhere in the network cloud, the culprit is usually a spam filter at the receiver's ISP or company. This explained in greater detail in Virus Scanning and Spam Blocking.

INPUT/OUTPUT INTERFACE

Input and output in IF/Prolog take place using device drivers which are managed on the basis of a driver model. A device driver is responsible for operations for a particular stream type, *e.g.* files, character strings or pipes. Prolog can manage different streams with the same set of generic built-in predicates.

Prolog provides the following built-in devices:

- File is the device for operating system files
- Null is the "bit bucket" device
- Pipe is the device for operating system pipes
- Standard is the device for the standard streams of the Prolog system
- String is the device for input/output using character strings

- Socket is the device for interprocess communication The I/O-related COM interfaces which are defined by header files in the oskit/io directory.

Most of these interfaces are fairly generic and can be used in a wide variety of situations. Some of these interfaces, such as the bufio interface, are extensions to other more primitive interfaces, and allow objects to export the same functionality in different forms, permitting clients to select the service that most directly meets their needs thereby reducing interface crossing overhead and increasing overall performance.

MACHINE LANGUAGE

DEFINITION

A language that need not be modified, translated, or interpreted before the processor for which it was designed can use it. The arithmetic and control unit circuits of the processor for which the language is designed can directly sense the operation codes and addresses used in instructions written in machine language.

It is also called as the Instructions written in an assembly language or a high-level language must be translated into machine language before a processor can execute them.

Sometimes referred to as machine code or object code, machine language is a collection of binary digits or bits that the computer reads and interprets. Machine language is the only language a computer is capable of understanding. Computer designers rather than computer users usually use machine languages.

A system of codes directly understandable by a computer's CPU is termed this CPU's native or machine language. Although *machine code* may seem similar to *assembly language* they are in fact two different types of languages. *Assembly code* consists of both binary numbers and simple words whereas *machine code* is composed only of the two binary digits 0 and 1. Every CPU has its own machine language, although there is considerabie overlap between some. If CPU *A* understands the full language of CPU *B* it is said that *A* is compatible with *B*. CPU *B* may not be compatible with CPU *A*, as *A* may know a few codes that *B* does not.

The "words" of a machine language are called *instructions*; each of these gives a basic command to the CPU. A programme is just a long list of instructions that are *executed* by a CPU. Older processors executed instructions one after the other, but newer super scalar processors are capable of executing several instructions at once. Programme flow may be influenced by special *jump* instructions that transfer execution to an instruction other than the following one. Conditional jumps are taken (execution continues at another address) or not (execution continues at the next instruction) depending on some condition.

Instructions are simply a pattern of bits — different patterns correspond to different commands to the machine. The more readable rendition of a machine language is called assembly language.

Some languages give all their instructions the same number of bits, while the instruction length differs in others. How the patterns are organised depends largely on the specific language. Common to most is the division of an instruction into *fields*, of which one or more specify the exact operation (for example "add"). Other fields may give the type of the operands, their location, or their value directly (operands contained in an instruction are called *immediate*).

ASSEMBLY LANGUAGE

DEFINITION

Assembly language is nothing more than a symbolic representation of machine code, which also allows symbolic designation of memory locations. Thus, an instruction to add the contents of a memory location to an internal CPU register called the accumulator might be add a number instead of a string of binary digits (bits).

No matter how close assembly language is to machine code, the computer still cannot understand it. The assembly-language programme must be translated into machine code by a separate programme called an assembler. The assembler programme recognizes the character strings that make up the symbolic names of the various machine operations, and substitutes the required machine code for each instruction. At the same time, it also calculates the required address in memory for each symbolic name of a memory location, and substitutes those addresses for the names.

The final result is a machine-language programme that can run on its own at any time; the assembler and the assembly-language programme are no longer needed. To help distinguish between the "before" and "after" versions of the programme, the original assembly-language programme is also known as the source code, while the final machine-language programme is designated the object code. If an assembly-language programme needs to be changed or corrected, it is necessary to make the changes to the source code and then re-assemble it to create a new object programme.

OVERVIEW

Although the numbers of the above programme make perfect sense to a computer, they are about as clear as mud to a human. Who would have guessed that they put a dollar sign on the screen? Clearly, entering numbers by hand is a lousy way to write a programme. It doesn't have to be this way, though. A long time ago, someone came up with the idea that computer programmes could be written using words instead of numbers. A special programme called an *assembler* would then take the programmer's words and convert them to numbers that the computer could understand. This new method, called writing a programme in *assembly language,* saved programmers thousands of hours, since they no longer had to look up hard-to-remember numbers in the backs of programming books, but could use simple words instead.

The programme above, written in assembly language, looks like this:

- MOV AX, 47104

- MOV DS, AX
- MOV [3998], 36
- INT 32

When an assembler reads this sample programme, it converts each line of code into one CPU-level instruction. This programme uses two types of instructions, MOV and INT. On Intel processors, the MOV instruction moves data around, while the INT instruction transfers processor control to the device drivers or operating system.

The programme still isn't quite clear, but it is much easier to understand than it was before. The first instruction, MOV AX, 47104, tells the computer to copy the number 47104 into the location AX. The next instruction, MOV DS, AX, tells the computer to copy the number in AX into the location DS. The next instruction, MOV [3998], 36 tells the computer to put the number 36 into memory location 3998. Finally, INT 32 exits the programme by returning to the operating system.

Before we go on, I would like to explain just how this programme works. Inside the CPU are a number of locations, called registers, which can store a number. Some registers, such as AX, are general purpose, and don't do anything special. Other registers, such as DS, control the way the CPU works.

DS just happens to be a *segment register*, and is used to pick which area of memory the CPU can write to. In our programme, we put the number 47104 into DS, which tells the CPU to access the memory on the video card.

The next thing our programme does is to put the number 36 into location 3998 of the video card's memory. Since 36 is the code for the dollar sign, and 3998 is the memory location of the bottom right hand corner of the screen, a dollar sign shows up on the screen a few microseconds later. Finally, our programme tells the CPU to perform what is called an *interrupt*.

An interrupt is used to stop one programme and execute another in its place. In our case, we want interrupt 32, which ends our programme and goes back to MS-DOS, or whatever other programme was used to start our programme.

RUNNING THE PROGRAMME

Let's go ahead and run this programme. First, be sure to print these instructions out, since you will need to refer to them as we go on. Next, click on your start menu, and run the programme called MS-DOS Prompt. A black screen with white text should appear. We are now in MS-DOS, the way computers used to be 20 years ago. MS-DOS was before the days of the mouse, so you must type commands on the keyboard to make the computer do things.

The cursor should move down a line, and you should see the Debug prompt, which is a simple dash. We are now in a programme called *Debug*. Debug is a powerful utility that lets you directly access the registers and memory of your computer for various purposes. In our case, we want to enter our programme into memory and run it, so we'll use Debug's a command, for *assemble*.

Go ahead and type a100 now. The cursor will move down another line, and you will see something like 1073:0100. This is the memory location we are going to enter assembly language instructions at. The first number is the segment, and the second number is the memory location within the segment. Your Debug programme will probably pick a different segment for your programme than mine did, so don't worry if it's different. Another thing to note is that Debug only understands hexadecimal numbers, which are a sort of computer shorthand. Hexadecimal numbers sometimes contain letters as well as well as digits.

Let's go ahead and enter your programme now. Type each of the instructions below into Debug exactly as they appear, and press enter after each one. When you finish entering the last instruction, press enter twice to tell Debug that we are done entering instructions.

```
mov ax,B800
mov ds,ax
mov byte[0F9E],24
int 20
```

As you can see, I've converted all the numbers into hexadecimal, and have made a few other changes so Debug can understand what's going on. If you make a mistake while entering the above programme, press enter twice, type a100, and start entering instructions again at the beginning of the programme.

Once you have entered the programme, you can go ahead and run it. Simply type g for *go* and press enter when you are ready to start the programme. You should see a dollar sign in the lower right hand corner of your screen and the words Programme terminated normally. These words are put out by Debug to let you know that the programme ended normally.

HIGH LEVEL LANGUAGES

OVERVIEW

Very early in the development of computers attempts were made to make programming easier by reducing the amount of knowledge of the internal workings of the computer that was needed to write programmes. If programmes could be presented in a language that was more familiar to the person solving the problem, then fewer mistakes would be made. High-level programming languages allow the specification of a problem solution in terms closer to those used by human beings.

These languages were designed to make programming far easier, less error-prone and to remove the programmer from having to know the details of the internal structure of a particular computer. These high-level languages were much closer to human language. One of the first of these languages was Fortran II which was introduced in about 1958. In Fortran II our programme above would be written as:

C = A + B

which is obviously much more readable, quicker to write and less error-prone. As with assembly languages the computer does not understand these high-level languages directly and hence they have to be processed by passing them through a programme called a compiler which translates them into internal machine language before they can be executed.

Another advantage accrues from the use of high-level languages if some international body standardizes the languages. Then each manufacturer produces a compiler to compile programmes that conform to the standard into their own internal machine language. Then it should be easy to take a programme, which conforms to the standard, and implement it on many different computers merely by re-compiling it on the appropriate computer.

This great advantage of portability of programmes has been achieved for several high-level languages and it is now possible to move programmes from one computer to another without too much difficulty. Unfortunately many compiler writers add new features of their own which means that if a programmer uses these features then their programme becomes non-portable. It is well worth becoming familiar with the standard and writing programmes which obey it, so that your programmes are more likely to be portable.

As with assembly language human time is saved at the expense of the compilation time required to translate the programme to internal machine language. The compilation time used in the computer is trivial compared with the human time saved, typically seconds as compared with weeks.

Many high level languages have appeared since Fortran II (and many have also disappeared!), among the most widely used have been:

COBOL	Business applications
FORTRAN	Engineering and Scientific Applications
PASCAL	General use and as a teaching tool
C & C++	General Purpose - currently most popular
PROLOG	Artificial Intelligence
JAVA	General Purpose - gaining popularity rapidly

All these languages are available on a large variety of computers. High-level languages are those programming languages, which are customised and pretty convenient to use. These languages can be operated with several platforms. Some of the high-level languages have relevance even when not associated central processing unit.

CHARACTERISTICS OF HIGH-LEVEL LANGUAGES

In terms of technology, high-level languages are not better than the low-level versions. Rather the computing techniques used in high-level languages are simpler than those applied in low-level programming languages. The term high-level indicates greater degree of abstraction from the so-called computer languages. Unlike low-level programming languages, the high-level languages never come with opcodes. Among the other common features of high-level languages, object-oriented features, string handling schedules and modes for input or outputs of files are worth mentioning.

FUNCTIONS OF HIGH-LEVEL LANGUAGES

The main function of a high-level language is to simplify the use of programming systems to the users. The high-level languages break up the complicated chains of commands into simpler parts. For an efficient computer programming, the codes must be developed in low-level languages. However to make the best possible use of those codes, high-level languages are required.

Over the passage of time, the architectures of computers are becoming more complicated than before. Today's microprocessors require cutting-edge techniques to run the computer systems efficiently. Here comes the role of high-level languages. These programming languages are capable of designing cods that perfectly suit the requirements of modern computing.

DIFFERENT STAGES OF OPERATION

High-level languages operate through different models of programming. Interpreted and compiled are the two programming languages used in the intermediate steps. Intermediate representations and machine code generation are some other steps involved in the operation of high-level languages.

8

Network Communication

COMMUNICATION

In a mobile communication terminal for starting and simultaneously using a plurality of applications, one desired application starts fast to improve the operability when the number of started applications reaches a present limiting number of applications. An application start determining unit searches a list of started applications in response to the instruction of the start of application to obtain the number of started applications, and determines that the application cannot start when the number of started applications reaches a preset limiting number of applications.

An ending-application selecting unit selects, as an ending application to be ended, the application with the low priority from the start applications based on the preset priority of application when the application start determining unit determines that the application cannot start. An application ending unit performs the ending processing of the ending application selected by the ending-application selecting unit and deletes the selected ending application from the list of started applications.

A mobile communication terminal for starting and simultaneously using a plurality of applications, comprising: application start determining means which compares the number of started applications with a preset numerical value that is a maximum number of simultaneously used applications, determines that the application can start when the number of started applications is less than the numerical value, and determines that the application cannot start when the number of started applications reaches the numerical value; ending-priority list creating means which calculates values indicating the using situation of the started applications in response to the determination of the application start determining means that the application cannot start and creates a list of ending priority indicating the order of applications with low influence.

APPLICATIONS

In the case of ending the application; ending-application selecting means which selects the ending application based on the list of ending priority in response to the determination of the application start determining means that the application cannot start and clears the list of ending priority; application ending means which performs the ending processing of the ending application selected by the ending-application selecting means; application starting means which starts the application instructed by a user in response to the determination of the application start determining means that the application starts; and wherein the ending-priority list creating means collects data on evaluation items indicating the using situations including the total time displayed after starting the application, the number of switching times for display operation, and the last display time, obtains the order of started applications every evaluated item, multiplies the order by a weighting coefficient preset every evaluated item and every type of application, adds the multiplied result every application, calculates the values indicating the using situations, sorts the applications in order of the larger values, and creates the list of ending priority.

An application starting control method of a mobile communication terminal for starting and simultaneously using a plurality of applications, comprising the steps of: presetting a numerical value that is a maximum number of simultane-ously used applications; selecting, from started applications, an ending application to be ended based on a priority when the number of simultaneously used applications will exceed the numerical value; newly allowing to start an application after ending the selected ending application; and collecting data for the started applications, including a total time displayed after starting the application, the number of switching times for display operation, and the last display time, determining an order of the respective data for each of the started applications, multiplying each determined order by respective weighting coefficients for each of the started applications, adding the multiplied results for each of the started applications, and creating the priority by sorting the applications based on the added results.

MOBILE NETWORK

A mobile communication terminal for starting and simultaneously using a plurality of applications, comprising: application start determining means which compares the number of started applications with a preset numerical value that is a maximum number of simultaneously used applications, determines that the application can start when the number of started applications is less than the numerical value, and determines that the application cannot start when the number of started applications reaches the numerical value; selecting means which selects an ending application to be ended on the basis of low priority from the started applications, in response to the determination of the application start determining means that the application cannot start; application ending means which performs ending processing of the ending application selected by the ending application selecting means; application starting means which starts the application instructed by a user in response to the determination of the application start determining means that the application can start; and ending-priority list creating means for collecting data on evaluation items indicating the using situations including the total time displayed after starting the application, the number of switching times for display operation, and the last display time, obtaining the order of started applications every evaluated item, multiplying the order by a weighting coefficient preset every evaluated item and every type of application, adding the multiplied result every application, calculating the values indicating the using situations, sorting the applications in order of the larger values, and creating a priority list.

MEMORY

The present invention relates to a mobile communication terminal and an application starting control method thereof. More particularly, the present invention relates to a mobile communication terminal for starting and simultaneously using a plurality of applications and an application starting control method thereof. Recently, one type of mobile phones is sold to start a plurality of applications and simultaneously use a plurality of functions similarly to a personal computer or the like, under the improvement of CPU processing capacity. Such a mobile phone terminal enables a user to send an email while viewing a site screen on the Internet or to check the schedule by a scheduler while having a call.

However, the mobile phone terminal does not have a sufficient memory capacity or power capacity. Therefore, if many applications simultaneously start similarly to the personal computer, a malfunction is caused in the communication function or the started application operation becomes unstable. An unnecessary application must terminate without continuously staying resident in memory when the number of simultaneously-used applications reaches a predetermined limiting number.

Preferably, the unnecessary application automatically ends. As disclosed in the above-mentioned publication, the degree of importance is set to the application so as to use the application with the high degree of importance for a long time when the remaining amount of battery is reduced while a plurality of applications start, and the application with the low degree of importance ends when the remaining amount of battery reduces. However, when the number of applications to be started is over a predetermined number, the application to be ended does not automatically end.

DETAILS

It is an object of the present invention to provide a mobile communication terminal and an application starting control method thereof, for fast starting a desired application and improving the operability by automatically selecting and ending the application to be ended when the number of started applications reaches a predetermined limiting number upon starting the application. According to the present invention, there is provided an application starting control method of a mobile communication terminal for starting and simultane-ously using a plurality of applications, comprising the steps of presetting a limiting number of simultaneously used applications; selecting, from started applications, an ending application to be ended based on the priority when applications over a limiting number are going to be started; and newly allowing to start an application after ending the selected ending application.

The priority may be preset or may be determined based on a using situation of the started application. The selected ending application may be displayed on a screen in response to the selection of the ending application. In this case, the selected ending application is ended in response to the approval operation of a user.

According to the present invention, there is also provided a mobile communication terminal for starting and simultaneously using a plurality of applications, comprising application start determining means which compares the number of started applications with a preset limiting number of simultaneously used applications, determines that the application can start when the number of started applications is less than the limiting number, and determines that the application cannot start when the number of started applications reaches the limiting number; selecting means which selects an ending application to be ended on the basis of low priority from the started applications in response to the determination of the application start determining means that the application cannot start; application ending means which performs ending processing of the ending application selected by the ending application selecting means; and application starting means which starts the application instructed by a user in response to the determination of the application start determining means that the application can start.

NETWORK APPLICATIONS

The application starting means may start the application instructed by the user in response to the ending processing of the application ending means. The application start determin-ing means may determine whether or not the application starts in response to the instruction to start the application from the user.

The mobile communication terminal may have a list of started applications indicating the started applications. In this case, the application start determining means searches the list of started application to obtain the number of started applications. The application ending means deletes the selected ending application from the list of started applications. The application starting means starts the application determined as the start by the application start determining means and registers the started application to the list of started applications. The mobile communication terminal may further comprises means for receiving the approval of the user before the ending processing of the ending application in response to the selection of the ending application by the ending application selecting means.

According to the present invention, there is also provided a mobile communication terminal for starting and simultaneously using a plurality of applications, comprising application start determining means which compares the number of started applications with a preset limiting number of simultaneously used applications, determines that the application can start when the number of started applications is less than the limiting number, and determines that the application cannot start when the number of started applications reaches the limiting number; ending-priority list creating means which calculates values indicating the using situation of the started applications in response to the determination of the application start determining means that the application cannot start and creates a list of ending priority indicating the order of applications with low influence in the case of ending the application; ending-application selecting means which selects the ending application based on the list of ending priority in response to the determination of the application start determining means that the application cannot start and clears the list of ending priority; application ending means which performs the ending processing of the ending application selected by the ending-application selecting means; and application starting means which starts the application instructed by a user in response to the determination of the application start determining means that the application starts.

The ending-priority list creating means may collect data on evaluation items indicating the using situations including the total time displayed after starting the application, the number of switching times for display operation, and the last display time, place a number to each of started applications in the order of their magnitude every evaluated item, multiply the number by a weighting coefficient preset every evaluated item and every type of application, add the multiplied results every application, calculate the values indicating the using situations, sort the applications in order of the larger values, and create the list of ending priority.

The mobile communication terminal may have a list of started applications indicating the started application. In this case, the application start determining means searches the list of started applications and obtains the number of started applications; the application ending means deletes the selected ending application from the list of started applications, and the application starting means starts the application determined as the start by the application start determining means and registers the started application to the list of started applications. According to the present invention, the limiting number (maximum number) of applications for simultaneous use is set and when the start of a new application amounts to the number of applications over the limiting number, the application for ending is automatically determined and is ended in accordance with the priority from among the using applications. Thus, in case that the number of applications reaches the limiting number, the new application is started quickly and the operability upon starting the application is improved.

WIRELESS COMMUNICATIONS

Wireless communications is a rapidly growing segment of the communications industry, with the potential to provide high-speed high-quality information exchange between portable devices located anywhere in the world. Potential applications enabled by this technology include multimedia Internet-enabled cell phones, smart homes and appliances, automated highway systems, video teleconferencing and distance learning, and autonomous sensor networks, to name just a few. However, supporting these applications using wireless techniques poses a significant technical challenge.

This course will cover advanced topics in wireless communications for voice, data, and multimedia. We begin with a brief overview of current wireless systems and standards. We then characterize the wireless channel, including path loss for different environments, random log-normal shadowing due to signal attenuation, and the flat and frequency-selective properties of multipath fading. Next we examine the fundamental capacity limits of wireless channels and the characteristics of the capacity-achieving transmission strategies. These strategies are typically not practical. Thus, our next focus will be on practical digital modulation techniques and their performance under wireless channel impairments, including flat and frequency selective fading. The next part of the course is spent investigating techniques to improve the speed and performance of wireless links.

We will investigate the design and performance of adaptive modulation and diversity techniques to compensate for flat-fading. Three techniques to combat frequency-selective fading are then examined: adaptive equalization, multicarrier modulation, and spread spectrum. We will also study the multiple access capabilities of spread spectrum with multiuser detection. The course concludes with a brief overview of wireless networks, including multiple and random access techniques, WLANs, cellular system design, and ad-hoc network design.

Applications for these systems, including the evolution of cell phones and PDAs, smart homes and appliances, sensor networks, and automated highways and skyways, will also be discussed. Presenting comprehensive coverage of this fast moving field, Wireless Communications and Mobile Computing provides the R&D communities working in academia and the telecommunications and networking industries with a forum for sharing research and ideas. The convergence of wireless communications and mobile computing is bringing together two areas of immense growth and innovation. This is reflected throughout the journal by strongly focusing on new trends, developments, emerging technologies and new industrial standards. Under the guidance of an international editorial and advisory board drawn from academia and industry, this high quality, peer-reviewed journal, provides leading edge coverage of the opportunities and challenges driving the research and development of mobile communication systems.

All you need to stay ahead :

- High calibre survey papers
  Written by leading experts in the wireless and networking communities.
- Rapid publication times
  Due to electronic review and submission of original research papers
- Special Issues
  Addressing key topics of interest and managed by high profile editors
- An international forum for the sharing of research and ideas
  Key topics presented by leading individuals at the cutting edge of new technologies.

COMPUTER NETWORKS

In computer networks, bandwidth is often used as a synonym for data transfer rate - the amount of data that can be carried from one point to another in a given time period (usually a second). This kind of bandwidth is usually expressed in bits (of data) per second (bps). Occasionally, it's expressed as bytes per second (Bps). A modem that works at 57,600 bps hastwice the bandwidth of a modem that works at 28,800 bps. In general, a link with a high bandwidth is one that may be able to carry enough information to sustain the succession of images in a video presentation. It should be remembered that a real communications path usually consists of a succession of links, each with its own bandwidth. If one of these is much slower than the rest, it is said to be a bandwidth bottleneck.

In electronic communication, bandwidth is the width of the range (orband) of frequencies that an electronic signal uses on a given transmission medium. In this usage, bandwidth is expressed in terms of the difference between the highest-frequency signal component and the lowest-frequency signal component. Since the frequency of a signal is measured in hertz (the number of cycles of change per second), a given bandwidth is the difference in hertz between the highest frequency the signal uses and the lowest frequency it uses. A typical voice signal has a bandwidth of approximately three kilohertz (3 kHz); an analog television (TV) broadcast video signal has a bandwidth of six megahertz (6 MHz) -- some 2,000 times as wide as the voice signal.

BANDWIDTH MONITOR PRO

- Do you ever wonder how much bandwidth you are using?
- How fast you are downloading or uploading?
- Or if you're closing in on your monthly transfer limit?
- If so Bandwidth Monitor Pro is the utility for you!

Detailed Logging

Supports logging of all your network adapters at once

with separate statistics for each adapter. You can go back and check your daily, weekly, monthly, yearly or total transfer.

Always Control

With the small transfer graph placed in the system tray you always have control of your bandwidth usage.

Highly Customizable

Bandwidth Monitor Pro can be customized to display the information you want. You can also change the graph type and colours.

Advanced Alert System

- You can set up rules with various actions and conditions.
- Lets say that you have a monthly transfer limit of 30GB.
- You can then set up Bandwidth Monitor Pro to alert you when your approaching that limit.

MOBILE INTERNET WML

WML (Wireless Markup Language) is the new web language for making sites on mobile phones. Over the past few months new WAP (Wireless Applications Protocol) phones have become extremely popular and many large websites have created special 'mobile' versions of their site. Many people predict that, over the next few years, WAP sites will become even morepopular and e-commerce over mobile phones will be widely available.

USING WML

Although you might not have any plans immediately for creating a WAP version of your site, it is always a good idea to get involved in new technology. All you need to do is make a small site (even one page) which tells people a bit about your website. In the future you can develop the site further with things like e-mail and information for people to get directly off their phones.

The main sites which will benefit from WAP are ones providing a service like e-mail, live sports scores or a calendar service etc.

But there are many other uses. For example, a site giving music reviews could put their reviews on a WAP site. People could then read the reviews on their mobile phone while browsing through the CDs in a shop.

HAVING WAP PHONE

To create a WAP site you don't need a WAP enabled phone. You can get a WAP simulator for a PC. This is a piece of software which will give you a WAP phone on your desktop.

You can then type in the URLs of WAP sites and can view them on your PC. You can get a very good free WAP simulator from YourWAP

COMPARING SITES

WAP sites are not like standard web sites at all. As an example, you are looking at part of the Gowansnet web site. As you can see, sites written in WML are monochrome, very limited and there is very little screen space. Because of this you must be very careful when you are designing a WAP site as it is nothing like a web site.

BEGINNING WAP SITE

After reading the introduction you should understand about WAP sites, WML and what you can do with them so I will go straight into how to create a site. Note that you should really either have a WAP phone or a WAP simulator so that you can view your site and a knowledge of HTML is useful.

Finding A WML Host

Unfortunately WML cannot be run on all web hosts. For WML content to be run, a web host must make some changes to the configuration of their web server. If your host cannot do this for you, you can try WAPHosts.net. They can provide you with a server which will support WML.

Declaring A WML Document

Cards

Instead of having pages, WAP sites have cards. These are what is displayed on the screen at one time, just like a page. More than one card can be inserted in each WML document. To declare a card, insert the following:

```
<card id="index" title="My WAP Site"
newcontext="true">
```

This will make a card with the ID index (used for linking) and will display the text: My WAP Site at the top of the screen.

Closing Tags

Unlike with HTML, it is extremely important to close WML tags. If you do not, a page will certainly not work. You must close both the <card> and <wml> tags:

```
</card>
</wml>
```

ADDING TEXT

In the last part I showed you how to create the basic file which will contain your WAP site. In this part I am going to show you how to insert text and how to format it.

The <p> Tag

Just like in HTML the <p> tag is used to show where a paragraph begins and ends. Unlike HTML, though, all text on a WML page must be inside these tags. You are not allowed to nest these tags either. One important thing to remember about WML is that, unlike HTML where a page will still display even if there is bad code, a WAP phone will just reject a page if there is and code it doesn't understand.

As with HTML you use the tags as follows:

```
<p>
information
</p>
```

Aligning Text

Aligning text in WML is nearly exactly the same as in

HTML, except you can't use the centre tag. All aligning must be done using the following <p> tags:

Centre:

```
<p align="centre">
```

Right:

```
<p align="right">
```

The
 Tag

In WML (as mentioned earlier) all tags must be closed. This causes problems when using old HTML tags (like <Br>) which have no closing tag. To get around this, some tags have had a / put on the end e.g.

```
<Br />
```

This, like in HTML will make a line break.

Text

In WML there is actually no font tag (as you can only display text in the phone's default font in black). To show text all you need to do is put it in between the <p> and </p> tags. Here is an example of a full WML document:

```
<?xml version="1.0"?>
<!DOCTYPE wml PUBLIC "-//WAPFORUM//DTD WML 1.1/
/EN" "http://www.wapforum.org/DTD/wml_1.1.xml">
<wml>
<card id="index" title="My WAP Site"
newcontext="true">
<p align="centre">
Welcome to my new WAP site. You can view this on your mobile phone anywhere in the world!<Br /> It is amazing!
</p>
</card>
</wml>
```

HYPERLINKS & IMAGES

In part 3 I showed you how to create a basic WAP site with one page and some text. This week I will show you how you can make this better by adding extra parts, linking to them (and other sites) and how to add images to your site.

More Cards

As I explained in the second part of this tutorial, WAP sites have cards instead of pages. They are really the same as pages except they can all be written in one file. To add another card, all you need to do is put in another <card> tag with a different ID to the others. For example:

```
<card title="About Me" id="about">
  information
</card>
```

would be added below the first card but before the </wml> tag.

Linking

There are three ways to link to another WAP site, file or card. Just like in HTML these can either be the full path to a file or a relative link.

To link to a WAP site you use the following:

```
<a href="http://gowansnet.waphosts.net/">
  Gowansnet</a>
```

in your text. To link to another file on your site you would use:

```
<a href="links.wml">My Links</a>
```

and to link to another card in the same page you use:

```
<a href="#about">About Me</a>
```

For suppliers, the thought of a uniform operating environment was disconcerting. Consumer lock-in was woven tightly into the fabric of the industry. Individual consumers, particularly those with UNIX system experience, envisioned standardized environments, but had no way to pull the market in their direction. However, for one category of consumer -governments- the standardization of the UNIX system was both desirable and within reach.

Governments have clout and are the largest consumers of information technology products and services in the world. Driven by the need to improve commonality, both US and European governments endorsed a shift to the UNIX system. The Institute of Electrical and Electronic Engineers POSIX family of standards, along with standards from ISO, ANSI and others, led the way. Consortia such as the X/Open Company (merged with the Open Software Foundation in 1995 to form The Open Group) hammered out draft standards to accelerate the process. In 1994, the definitive specification of what constitutes a UNIX system was finalized through X/ Open Company's consensus process. The Single UNIX Specification was born-not from a theoretical, ivory tower approach, but by analyzing the applications that were in use in businesses across the world.

With the active support of government and commercial buyers alike, vendors began to converge on products that implement the Single UNIX Specification, and now all major vendors have products labeled UNIX 95, which indicates that the vendor guarantees that the product conforms to the Single UNIX Specification.

Vendors continue to add value to the UNIX system, particularly in areas of new technology, however that value will always be built upon a single, consensus standard. Meanwhile, the functionality of the UNIX system was established and the mid-life crisis was resolved. Suppliers today provide UNIX systems that are built upon a single, consensus standard. It is also important to remember that even when variance among UNIX systems was at its worst, IT professionals agreed that migration among UNIX system variants was far easier than migration among the proprietary alternatives.

TextProcessing and Word Processing

Almost every computer user needs a method of preparing documents. In the world of personal computers, word processing is the norm: editing and manipulating text in a ``What-You-See-Is-What-You-Get" (WYSIWYG) environment and producing printed copies of the text, complete with graphics, tables, and ornamentation.

Commercial word processors from Corel, Applix, and Star Division are available in the UNIX world, but text processing, which is quite different conceptually, is more common. In text processing systems, text is entered in a page-description language, which describes how the text should be formatted. Rather than enter text within a special word processing environment, you can modify text with any editor, like vi or emacs. Once you finish entering the source text (in the typesetting language), a separate programme converts the source to a format suitable for printing. This is somewhat analogous to programming in a language like C, and ``compiling'' the document into printable form.

Many text processing systems are available for Linux. One is groff, the GNU version of the classic troff text formatter originally developed by Bell Labs and still used on many UNIX systems worldwide. Another modern text processing system is TeX, developed by Donald Knuth of computer science fame. Dialects of TeX, like LaTeX, are also available.

Text processors like TeX and groff differ mostly in the syntax of their formatting languages. The choice of one formatting system over another is based upon what utilities are available to satisfy your needs, as well as personal taste.

Many people consider groff's formatting language to be a bit obscure and use find TeX more readable. However, groff produces ASCII output which can be viewed on a terminal more easily, while TeX is intended primarily for output to a printing device. Various add-on programmes are required to produce ASCII output from TeX formatted documents, or convert TeX input to groff format.

Another programme is texinfo, an extension to TeX which is used for software documentation developed by the Free Software Foundation. texinfo can produce printed output, or an online-browsable hypertext ``Info'' document from a single source file. Info files are the main format of documentation used in GNU software like emacs. Text processors are used widely in the computing community for producing papers, theses, magazine articles, and books. (This book is produced using LaTeX.) The ability to process source language as a text file opens the door to many extensions of the text processor itself. Because a source document is not stored in an obscure format that only one word processor can read, programmers can write parsers and translators for the formatting language, and thus extend the system. What does a formatting language look like? In general, a formatted source file consists mostly of the text itself, with control codes to produce effects like font and margin changes, and list formatting.

Programming Languages and Utilities

Linux provides a complete UNIX programming environment which includes all of the standard libraries, programming tools, compilers, and debuggers which you would expect of other UNIX systems.

Standards like POSIX.1 are supported, which allows software written for Linux to be easily ported to other systems. Professional UNIX programmers and system administrators use Linux to develop software at home, then transfer the software to UNIX systems at work.

This not only saves a great deal of time and money, but also lets you work in the comfort of your own home. (One of the authors uses his system to develop and test X Window System applications at home, which can be directly compiled on workstations elsewhere.) Computer Science students learn UNIX programming and explore other aspects of the system, like kernel architecture.

With Linux, you have access to the complete set of libraries and programming utilities and the complete kernel and library source code. Within the UNIX software world, systems and applications are often programmed in C or C++. The standard C and C++ compiler for Linux is GNU gcc, which is an advanced, modern compiler that supports C++, including AT&T 3.0 features, as well as Objective-C, another object-oriented dialect of C. Besides C and C++, other compiled and interpreted programming languages have been ported to Linux, like Smalltalk, FORTRAN, Java, Pascal, LISP, Scheme, and Ada (if you're masochistic enough to programme in Ada, we aren't going to stop you).

In addition, various assemblers for writing protected-mode 80386 code are available, as are UNIX hacking favorites like Perl (the script language to end all script languages) and Tcl/Tk (a shell-like command processing system which has support for developing simple X Window System applications). The advanced gdb debugger can step through a programme one line of source code at a time, or examine a core dump to find the cause of a crash.

The gprof profiling utility provides performance statistics for your programme, telling you where your programme spends most of its execution time. As mentioned above, the emacs text editor provides interactive editing and compilation environments for various programming languages. Other tools include GNU make and imake, which manage compilation of large applications, and RCS, a system for source code locking and revision control.

Finally, Linux supports dynamically linked, shared libraries (DLLs), which result in much smaller binaries. The common subroutine code is linked at run-time. These DLLs let you override function definitions with your own code. For example, if you wish to write your own version of the malloc() library routine, the linker will use your new routine instead of the one in the libraries.

X Window System

The X Window System, or simply X, is a standard graphical user interface (GUI) for UNIX machines and is a powerful environment which supports many applications. Using the X Window System, you can have multiple terminal windows on the screen at once, each having a different login session. A pointing device like a mouse is often used with X, although it isn't required. Many X-specific applications have been written, including games, graphics and programming utilities, and documentation tools. Linux and X make your system a bona fide workstation. With TCP/IP networking, your Linux machine can display X applications running on other machines.

The X Window System was originally developed at the Massachusetts Institute of Technology and is freely distributable. Many commercial vendors have distributed proprietary enhancements to the original X Window System as well. The version of X for Linux is XFree86, a port of X11R6 which is freely distributable. XFree86 supports a wide range of video hardware, including VGA, Super VGA, and accelerated video adaptors. XFree86 is a complete distribution of the X Windows System software, and contains the X server itself, many applications and utilities, programming libraries, and documents.

Standard X applications include xterm, a terminal emulator used for most text-based applications within a window, xdm, which handles logins, xclock, a simple clock display, xman, a X-based manual page reader, and xmore. The many X applications available for Linux are too numerous to mention here, but their number includes spreadsheets, word processors, graphics programmes, and web browsers like the Netscape Navigator. Many other applications are available separately. Theoretically, any application written for X should compile cleanly under Linux.

The interface of the X Window System is controlled largely by the window manager. This user-friendly programme is in charge of the placement of windows, the user interface for resizing and moving them, changing windows to icons, and the appearance of window frames, among other tasks. XFree86 includes twm, the classic MIT window manager, and advanced window managers like the Open Look Virtual Window Manager (olvwm) are available. Popular among Linux users is fvwm--a small window manager that requires less than half the memory of twm.

It provides a 3-dimensional appearance for windows and a virtual desktop. The user moves the mouse to the edge of the screen, and the desktop shifts as though the display were much larger than it really is. fvwm is greatly customizable and allows access to functions from the keyboard as well as mouse. Many Linux distributions use fvwm as the standard window manager. A version of fvwm called fvwm95-2 offers Microsoft Windows 95-like look and feel.

The XFree86 distribution includes programming libraries for wily programmers who wish to develop X applications. Widget sets like Athena, Open Look, and Xaw3D are supported. All of the standard fonts, bitmaps, manual pages, and documentation are included. PEX (a programming interface for 3-dimensional graphics) is also supported.

Many X application programmers use the proprietary Motif widget set for development. Several vendors sell single and multiple user licenses for binary versions of Motif. Because Motif itself is relatively expensive, not many Linux users own it. However, binaries statically linked with Motif routines can be freely distributed. If you write a programme using Motif, you may provide a binary so users without the Motif libraries can use the programme.

A major caveat to using the X Window System is its hardware requirements. A 80386-based CPU with 4 megabytes of RAM is capable of running X, but 16 megabytes or more of physical RAM is needed for comfortable use. A faster processor is nice to have as well, but having enough physical RAM is much more important. In addition, to achieve really slick video performance, we recommend getting an accelerated video card, like a VESA Local Bus (VLB) S3 chipset card. Performance ratings in excess of 300,000 xstones have been achieved with Linux and XFree86. Using adequate hardware, you'll find that running X and Linux is as fast, or faster, than running X on other UNIX workstations.

Networking

Would you like to communicate with the world? Linux supports two primary UNIX networking protocols: TCP/IP and UUCP. TCP/IP (Transmission Control Protocol/Internet Protocol) is the networking paradigm which allows systems all over the world to communicate on a single network, the Internet. With Linux, TCP/IP, and a connection to the Internet, you can communicate with users and machines via electronic mail, Usenet news, and FTP file transfer.

Most TCP/IP networks use Ethernet as the physical network transport. Linux supports many popular Ethernet cards and interfaces for personal computers, including pocket and PCMCIA Ethernet adaptors.

However, because not everyone has an Ethernet connection at home, Linux also supports SLIP (Serial Line

Internet Protocol) and PPP (Point-to-Point Protocol), which provide Internet access via modem. Many businesses and universities provide SLIP and PPP servers. In fact, if your Linux system has an Ethernet connection to the Internet and a modem, your system can become a SLIP or PPP server for other hosts.

NFS (Network File System) lets your system seamlessly share file systems with other machines on the network. FTP (File Transfer Protocol) lets you transfer files with other machines. sendmail sends and receives electronic mail via the SMTP protocol; C-News and INN are NNTP based new systems; and telnet,rlogin, and rsh let you log in and execute commands on other machines on the network. finger lets you get information about other Internet users.

The full range of mail and news readers is available for Linux, including elm, pine, rn, nn, and tin. Whatever your preference, you can configure a Linux system to send and receive electronic mail and news from all over the world. The system provides a standard UNIX socket programming interface.

Virtually any programme that uses TCP/IP can be ported to Linux. The Linux X server also supports TCP/IP, and applications running on other systems may use the display of your local system.

UUCP (UNIX-to-UNIX Copy) is an older mechanism to transfer files, electronic mail, and electronic news between UNIX machines. Historically, UUCP machines are connected over telephone lines via modem, but UUCP is able to transfer data over a TCP/IP network as well. If you do not have access to a TCP/IP network or a SLIP or PPP server, you can configure your system to send and receive files and electronic mail using UUCP.

Several conventions have sprung up around the development effort. Anyone who wishes to have their code included in the ``official'' kernel, mails it to Linus Torvalds. He will test and include the code in the kernel as long as it doesn't break things or go against the overall design of the system. The system itself is designed using an open-ended, feature-minded approach. The number of new features and critical changes to the system has recently diminished, and the general rule is that a new version of the kernel will be released every few weeks. Of course, this is a rough figure. New release criteria include the number of bugs to be fixed, feedback from users testing pre-release versions of the code, and the amount of sleep Linus Torvalds has had this week.

Suffice it to say that not every bug is fixed, nor is every problem ironed out between releases. As long as the revision appears to be free of critical or recurring bugs, it is considered to be stable, and the new version is released. The thrust behind Linux development is not to release perfect, bug-free code: it is to develop a free UNIX implementation. Linux is for the developers, more than anyone else.

Anyone who has a new feature or software application generally makes it available in an alpha version--that is, a test version, for those brave users who want to hash out problems in the initial code. Because the Linux community is largely based on the Internet, alpha software is usually uploaded to one or more Linux FTP sites and a message is posted to one of the Linux Usenet newsgroups about how to obtain and test the code. Users who download and test alpha software can then mail results, bug fixes, and questions to the author. After the initial bugs have been fixed, the code enters a beta test stage, in which it is usually considered stable but not complete. It works, but not all of the features may be present. The software may also go directly to a final stage, in which the software is considered complete and usable.

Keep in mind that these are only conventions--not rules. Some developers may feel so confident of their software that they decide it isn't necessary to release alpha or test versions. It is always up to the developer to make these decisions. You might be amazed at how such an unstructured system of volunteers who programme and debug a complete UNIX system gets anything done at all. As it turns out, this is one of the most efficient and motivated development efforts ever employed. The entire Linux kernel is written from scratch, without code from proprietary sources. It takes a huge amount of work to port all the free software under the sun to Linux. Libraries are written and ported, file systems are developed, and hardware drivers are written for many popular devices--all due to the work of volunteers.

Linux software is generally released as a distribution, a set of prepackaged software which comprises an entire system. It would be difficult for most users to build a complete system from the ground up, starting with the kernel, adding utilities, and installing all of the necessary software by hand. Instead, many software distributions are available which include everything necessary to install and run a complete system. There is no single, standard distribution--there are many, and each has its own advantages and disadvantages. We describe installation of the various Linux distributions starting on.

Of course, you may copy Linux from a friend who already has the software, or share the purchase cost with someone else. If you plan to install Linux on a large number of machines, you need only purchase a single copy of the software--Linux is not distributed with a ``single machine'' license.

The value of commercial UNIX implementations should not be demeaned. In addition to the price of the software itself, one often pays for documentation, support, and quality assurance. These are very important factors for large institutions, but personal computer users may not require these benefits. In any case, many businesses and universities have found that running Linux in a lab of inexpensive personal computers is preferable to running a commercial version of UNIX in a lab of workstations.

Linux can provide workstation functionality on a personal computer at a fraction of the cost. Linux systems have travelled the high seas of the North Pacific, and manage telecommuni-cations and data analysis for an oceanographic research vessel. Linux systems are used at research stations in Antarctica. Several hospitals maintain patient records on Linux systems. Other free or inexpensive implementations of UNIX are available for the 80386 and 80486.

One of the best known is 386BSD, an implementation of BSD UNIX for the 80386. The 386BSD package is comparable to Linux in many ways, but which one is better depends on your needs and expectations. The only strong distinction we can make is that Linux is developed openly, and any volunteer can aid in the development process, while 386BSD is developed by a closed team of programmers. Because of this, serious philosophical and design differences exist between the two projects. The goal of Linux is to develop a complete UNIX system from scratch (and have a lot of fun in the process), and the goal of 386BSD is in part to modify the existing BSD code for use on the 80386.

NetBSD is another port of the BSD NET/2 distribution to several machines, including the 80386. NetBSD has a slightly more open development structure, and is comparable to 386BSD in many respects.

Another project of note is HURD, an effort by the Free Software Foundation to develop and distribute a free version of UNIX for many platforms. Contact the Free Software Foundation (the address is given in Appendix C) for more information about this project. At the time of this writing, HURD is still under development.

NETWORK TOOLS

VeriCenter remotely manages your network infrastructure, including routers, hubs, and switches, for the highest reliability and optimized performance. When a problem is detected and isolated, VeriCenter takes the steps necessary to coordinate with hardware vendors and carrier partners for problem resolution. At all times, you're able to access critical information about your network through our secure Web-based Customer Portal. Our services are designed to provide you with complete management of critical network devices within your environment, using the tools and expertise of our Network Operations Centre (NOC).

Every productive data network is made up of two intergral parts - infrastructure (communications environment) and active elements, which utilise the communications environment. The infrastructure can be made up of a structured cabling system based on melicke or optical lines, wireless transfer system etc. The quality and performance of the infrastructure directly affects the resulting attributes and output of the data network.

With the rapid development of Internet applications and technology, more and more emphasis is being put on securing access to data networks and on protection of the actual data with systems against misuse or attack. There is an evident trend of integrating various security functions into basic network elements, such as switches, routers etc.

The convergence trend for data and telephony into one communications infrastructure has brought the need to secure the necessary quality of service (QoS) for operations sensitive to the quality of the data network (IP telephony, video-conferencing). A modern data network is capable of working with several classes of operations and each of these classes is capable of securing the necessary quality of service. Since it was established, GiTy has been oriented to the most up-to-date technologies, which guarantee the maximum possible output for data networks and their long technological lifetime. Key components of data networks developed by us are products from the foremost technological manufacturers, such as Siemon, Cisco Systems, Enterasys Network, 3COM, Allied Telesyn and Crossbeam.

Data networks developed by us provide users with high performance, the maximum level of security and the tools needed for management of the quality of services for individual applications.

One way of conserving this network traffic is to slice the network up into smaller segments. These segments are connected to a bridge. Bridges are smarter than hubs and repeaters. They also use software to help get the job done. Bridges are able to read MAC addresses, which are also known as hardware addresses that are burned onto the NIC inside every computer on the network, of each data packet the is circulated on the network segments connected on the bridge. It is by learning which MAC addresses are live on the network that the bridge is able to control traffic that is local to a particular segment and keep it from spreading to other network segments that are being serviced by another bridge. A bridge device filters data traffic at a network boundary. Bridges reduce the amount of traffic on a LAN by dividing it into two segments. Bridges operate at the data link layer (Layer 2) of the OSI model. Bridges inspect incoming traffic and decide whether to forward or discard it. An Ethernet bridge, for example, inspects each incoming Ethernet frame - including the source and destination MAC addresses, and sometimes the frame size - in making individual forwarding decisions.

Bridges serve a similar function as switches, that also operate at Layer. Traditional bridges, though, support one network boundary, whereas switches usually offer four or more hardware ports. Switches are sometimes called "multi-port bridges" for this reason. Computer networks serve the purpose of connecting many different computers or terminals to each other, host computers, printers, file servers etc. so that expensive computing assets, programmes, files and other data may be shared among many users. A large network may typically contain one or more gateways, routers and bridges operating in conjunction with one or more network segments.

A segment is section of a network connected to a group of machines which may communicate with each other via repeater operations without having to traverse a bridge or router. Bridges and routers are useful in that they allow connections of multiple segments such that more computers may communicate with each other than would otherwise be possible given the limited bandwidth of the media.

Bibliography

Agrawal, C.: *Library Literature,* New York: Guilford, 1998.

Andrea, M.: *An Empirical Investigation of Internet Privacy: Customer,* Athens: U of Georgia Press, 2005.

Arthur, V.: *Isaac Newton and the Laws of Motion,* New York: Routledge Press, 1996.

Burton, S.: *Encyclopedia of Business and Finance,* Cambridge, MA: Harvard University Press, 1996.

Elizabeth, B.: *The Challenge of Internet Literacy*: The Instruction-Web Convergence, New York: Routledge Press, 1996.

Elizabeth, W.: *Literature and the Internet: A Guide for Students, Teachers,* Athens: U of Georgia Press, 2005.

George, H.: *Computer Sciences,* London: Blackwell Scientific Publications, 1994.

Gianopoulos, B.: *Managing Information,* Columbia, NY: Univ. Press, 1991.

Henderson, H.: *Internet Predators,* New York: Oxford University Press, 1986,

Jacobson, *K.: Internet and Wireless Privacy: A Legal Guide to Global Business,* New York: Guilford, 1998.

John, M.: *Animal Rights: A Subject Guide, Internet Companion,* London: Prentice Hall, 2001.

Lyn, M.: *Library Literature & Information Science,* US: Yourdon Press, 2005.

Mougayar, W.: *Economic Review,* UK: Addison-Wesley Prees 1993.

Patrick, M.: *Multimedia and the Web from A to Z,* New York: Addison Wesley Press, 2003.

Peter, G.: *The Business Internet and Intranets: A Manager's Guide,* New York: John Wiley & Sons Publication, 2001.

Rawson, K.: *Basic Ship Theory,* NY: Routledge Press, 1998.

Roger, R.: *Online Information,* Lexington, KY: University Press of Kentucky, 1996.

Thomas, W.: *Record Label Marketing,* New York: Oxford University Press, 1989,

Tupper, M.: *Inventing the Internet,* New York: Wiley, 1999.

Warschauer, M.: *Virtual Connections: Online Activities & Projects for Networking,* Tucson: University of Arizona Press, 1999.

Wilburta, Q.: *The Environment Encyclopedia and Directory,* Boston: South End Press, 1993.

Index

F

I

M

N

O

S

T

V

W